**WITHDRAWN**
University Libraries
University of Memphis

# The American Journalists

# FREMONT OLDER

Evelyn Wells

ARNO
&
The New York Times

Collection Created and Selected
by Charles Gregg of Gregg Press

Reprint edition 1970 by Arno Press Inc.

Reprinted by permission of Hawthorne Books, Inc.

LC# 70-125722
ISBN 0-405-01705-7

*The American Journalists*
ISBN for complete set: 0-405-01650-6

Manufactured in the United States of America

PN
4874
O6
W4
1970

# FREMONT OLDER

FREMONT OLDER
His last photograph.

# FREMONT OLDER

*By* EVELYN WELLS

D. APPLETON-CENTURY COMPANY
INCORPORATED
NEW YORK      1936      LONDON

COPYRIGHT, 1936, BY
D. APPLETON–CENTURY COMPANY, INC.

*All rights reserved. This book, or parts thereof, must not be reproduced in any form without permission of the publisher.*

PRINTED IN THE UNITED STATES OF AMERICA

TO
CORA BAGGERLY OLDER
HIS WIFE AND DEAREST FRIEND

# FOREWORD

FREMONT OLDER valued truth above all things. As an editor he tried daily to achieve it. As a man he lived honestly, facing himself, the many stormy and inexplicable sides of him, with a frankness which was often puzzled and sometimes despairing. There was not a moment of his life he would have wanted glossed over. So if at times this book appears harsh, it is not with my harshness. I have tried to write his life my editor's way.

There were many Fremont Olders. It was not easy for one person to know the many personalities that made up the West's fighting editor.

The Fremont Older I knew gave me my first newspaper assignment. What I know of writing and newspaper work he taught me. For the last sixteen years of his life we were in almost daily communication. During six of these years, as a member of his household, I knew him too as the head of the family on his beloved hearth.

Commuting together from the office during these years, we talked. More and more he liked telling of his strange and lonely boyhood. Many of the conversations in this book are from memory. Others are taken from Fremont Older's book, *My Own Story*, with the gracious permission of the Macmillan Company.

As one of the eager group surrounding Fremont Older in his office, I rejoiced in his victories and hated his enemies. One could not work with the editor and remain impersonal. It is strange now to stand apart, to view him not as friend and chief, but as a life that was lived, and try to evaluate its once tremendous power.

His friends always held that Older was greater as a human being than as an editor. I have no need to name these friends. Someone has said that their passionate loyalty to Older and to one another was equivalent to a blood relationship. Sufficient to say they are the true authors of this book, having lived it with Fremont Older.

EVELYN WELLS

# CONTENTS

| | | PAGE |
|---|---|---|
| FOREWORD | | vii |
| ILLUSTRATIONS | | xi |

| CHAPTER | | |
|---|---|---|
| I. | THE RALLY IN THE CLEARING | 1 |
| II. | A SQUIRREL DIES—AND LINCOLN | 15 |
| III. | PRINTER'S DEVIL | 31 |
| IV. | TRAMP PRINTER | 49 |
| V. | THE REPORTER | 65 |
| VI. | MANAGING EDITOR | 84 |
| VII. | OLDER THE SENSATIONALIST | 101 |
| VIII. | TASTE OF POWER | 114 |
| IX. | THE POLITICIAN | 123 |
| X. | "AN ENEMY OF THE PEOPLE" | 133 |
| XI. | THE GRAFT-HUNTERS | 146 |
| XII. | BLACK FRIDAY | 159 |
| XIII. | THE DYNAMITERS | 168 |
| XIV. | THE KIDNAPPING | 182 |
| XV. | THE TIGER | 199 |
| XVI. | THE EDITOR IN HIS OFFICE | 215 |
| XVII. | CAMPAIGN FOR JOHNSON | 228 |
| XVIII. | PRISON REFORM | 240 |
| XIX. | THE EDITOR AND THE LOST LADIES | 256 |
| XX. | PRISONERS | 271 |
| XXI. | MOONEY | 289 |
| XXII. | A NEWSPAPER TRAGEDY | 310 |

## CONTENTS

| CHAPTER | | PAGE |
|---|---|---|
| XXIII. | MOONEY AGAIN | 321 |
| XXIV. | THE PESSIMIST | 337 |
| XXV. | THE EDITOR WRITES | 353 |
| XXVI. | THE DEPRESSION | 366 |
| XXVII. | "THIRTY" | 382 |
| INDEX | | 399 |

# ILLUSTRATIONS

| | |
|---|---:|
| FREMONT OLDER | *Frontispiece* |
| | FACING PAGE |
| SQUIRE LEWIS AUGUR | 46 |
| CELIA AUGUR OLDER | 46 |
| THE REPORTER | 86 |
| CORA BAGGERLY OLDER | 86 |
| THE GRAFT-HUNTERS | 154 |
| THE FIGHTING EDITOR | 208 |
| OLDER FRONT PAGES | 242 |
| THE ADOBE STUDY AT "WOODHILLS" | 284 |
| THE EDITOR AT HIS DESK | 354 |

# FREMONT OLDER

## Chapter I

### THE RALLY IN THE CLEARING

B EHIND Fremont Older's head the wall plaster was battered. The "greatest editor in the West" did that when angry, tossing his large head back like a bull about to charge. In such moments he roared until the cubs in the local room quaked.

But his own reporters gloated. They knew some big story was fermenting in Older's dingy little front office. Something tremendous, like the graft prosecution or the prostitution crusades or the fight to free Mooney. Something to split San Francisco into two camps and turn the mobs of misrule—and the stuffed shirts—once more against Fremont Older.

The man who owned the paper frowned at that dingy office. He would have liked to see his impressive managing editor surrounded by as impressive mahogany. But toward his office, as toward many other things, Older was stubborn.

Older himself was always splendidly groomed, but his small, shabby room was flooded with proofs, copy, marked newspapers, and unfiled letters. His battle-scarred desk was rimmed anew each day with the butts of twenty or more Havana cigars. He read every line in every edition of the paper, carpeting the floor with the discarded sheets. And he preferred a small office because he wanted the men he talked with close to him, to feel the magnetism of his flashing dark eyes and sense his indomitable power. Few men talked back to Older.

He had a way of gently twisting his fine, long hands as he talked as if wringing all the juice out of his words. He talked in headlines.

His enemies said Older hypnotized men. He had a way of thundering to a reporter, "Get Pete Blank down here!"

Pete Blank might hold high political office. But, summoned by the quavering voice of an Older aide, the Pete Blanks invariably appeared, often with worried looks, in that unspeakably unkempt office.

Once Older ordered a prisoner brought to his office from the jail.

"Strike off his irons!" he ordered the guard.

He could not talk freely to a man wearing handcuffs. The man was unshackled, the guard sent outside, and the prisoner sat and talked with Older for an hour by an open window with never a thought of attempting to run for freedom.

Politicians, financiers, people in trouble, flowed steadily through Older's office. He made mayors and governors for California. He hobnobbed with Presidents. He knew the riffraff, too, of a state that was being run by riffraff.

These he fought with headlines of a violence never seen before in the West. They fought back with lies, with bullets and dynamite. For years he walked in danger of death.

He was keenly aware of this danger.

"God, if only they make a complete job of it—not maim me!" he muttered once, striding down Montgomery Street with a friend ahead and behind to guard him.

A well-known gunman was stationed on the opposite sidewalk. Friends from the underworld had acted as "tip-off." On such occasions Older sent word to Jack Black, the ex-burglar he had rescued from prison. Mobsters fell back

## THE RALLY IN THE CLEARING

before that ingenuous countenance, for Jack was dreaded and respected in the San Francisco tenderloin.

Once a gunman hired by political bosses came up one elevator as Older slipped down the other. Another time he was trapped in his own office by a man with a gun.

"Sit down, let's talk this over!" he boomed.

At the end of an hour Older and the gunman were smoking cigars and exchanging experiences in living. And again, when Older was kidnapped in the street in broad daylight, he talked the gangsters hired to kill him out of murder.

This was Older the fighter, the Western editor the West knew. But he had other sides as dramatic and as strange.

His tenderness was magnificent. He poured over thousands his warmly beautiful smile, his benign yet salty guidance, the very salary he earned. Every day he gave all of himself to the immediate need for dramatic living.

For fifty years Fremont Older was a mystery to the West that dreaded and idolized him. Handsome, with the bearing of a conqueror, six feet two inches tall, this warrior-editor was to evolve from a little boy born in a log cabin who wept in a Wisconsin clearing one autumn night, shortly before the Civil War.

The child Fremont Older was four. Tall for his years, his head and joints were large, and the long bones of legs and arms appeared too thin in the pantalooned suit of homespun. But chest and shoulders were held sturdily.

Only his hands were alien—flexible and delicately fingered. From elsewhere out of this pioneer scene and time they had come down to Fremont Older.

The boy was watching a maple bonfire lighting the forest and sky before his grandfather's two-story frame farm-house. This house was superior to most of the log-cabin homes in Freedom Township.

Superior too was the boy's grandfather, Squire Lewis Augur, a bearded pioneer standing before the fire with three younger giants who were Fremont's father and uncles, surrounded by a hundred frontiersmen like themselves.

All the men held flaming torches. Over their homespun garments they wore black oilskin capes and caps. The firelight running in hot streams over the shining cloth sent a sharp, exciting odor to the eager nostrils of the boy.

These men were Wide-Awakes, rallying for Abraham Lincoln. Every farmer and woodsman in Freedom Township had marched over the nearly impassable forest roads this night to Squire Augur's farm.

Five months before, in the spring of 1860, Lincoln, a frontiersman like themselves, had been nominated for President. He was pledged to preserve the Union. Already slave states were pulling away from the North. Squire Augur had called this rally to aid Lincoln.

He stood with the hot light beating on face and beard while around him deep-chested pioneers chanted the Wide-Awakes' anthem:

*Old Abe Lincoln came out of the wilderness,*
*Down in Illinois—*

The flames heightened. There sprang into existence a cleared space that was the farm set with sheds and barns and apple-trees, but around it, mysterious and unredeemed, circled the black forests of north Wisconsin.

The boy saw the Squire's arm lift slowly. His grandfather's voice rose as he had heard it many times in prayer.

"Men of Freedom Township," the old man began in a voice like rumbling thunder. "We're more than neighbors. We're Wide-Awakes! We're Northerners! We're brothers, rallying for Abraham Lincoln.

## THE RALLY IN THE CLEARING

"Oh, it's a rough road Honest Abe has been walking since they nominated him last May in Chicago. He gave us his pledge to preserve the Union, and for those almighty words the godless are deserting him. The Southerners are talking of setting up their own Confederacy founded on the black curse of slavery!"

The crowd murmured, like responses in prayer-meeting. Rough pioneer faces were fixed reverently on the patriarch. Squire Augur was their judge, the wealthiest farmer and the Nestor of Freedom Township. He settled their family troubles and business disputes. He pulled their aching teeth. He married them.

Squire Augur had been one of the first Abolitionists in Wisconsin. For twenty-five years he had reviled slavery. As he talked, his scythe-like features locked in the expression of a fanatic.

Now his gray face lifted with passion. Words poured from him. Clearly as in a vision the boy Fremont saw, painted in words by this pioneer Isaiah, great slave-ships from Africa, their stench poisoning the ocean air, carrying human cargo into the America both Older and Augur men had suffered to make free. He saw five million men and women and children upon auction-blocks, shamed and stared upon, bidden for and sold. He heard of cruelties he could not understand, of unbearable humiliations.

The boy's cheeks dripped hot tears. All around him men were weeping. His father, the lean and bearded Emory Older, wept unashamed. To this youthful pioneer Fremont Older would owe a serious nature which was almost morose, but there was French blood and laughter also in the veins of the little boy sobbing in the firelight.

"Only one man can save our Union!" cried the old Squire.

The flames crackled. Squire Augur's spare form quivered and his wet forehead shone.

"Vote for Lincoln!" he trumpeted to the surrounding forests.

All Fremont Older's life he would be able to close his eyes and see the pioneers in their shining capes and scent the hot oilcloth. For more than seventy years he would be shaken by that almost unbearable emotion which was hatred of injustice.

He was to write of this long after:

"That meeting held in the night in the wild forest and under the stars is where my memory of life begins."

On both sides he was descended from fighters. Both Older and Augur men were pioneers, moving westward with the frontier and taking part in any battles that came their way.

The Augurs had gone to England from France hundreds of years before. The boy's grandfather, Squire Augur, settled in Wisconsin in 1836. After twenty years of almost daily toil he had cleared forty acres of forest land.

The first Older to come to America was one Thomas Older, who on a foggy night in 1749 was driving his horse and cart across London Bridge. A "press-gang" recruiting soldiers for the king kidnapped Thomas and rushed him aboard a ship bound for the Americas.

In New York State Thomas fought Indians and was captured by the French, escaped, married, settled down, and returned to battle again in the War of the Revolution.

Thomas Older fought in two wars with George Washington; he helped create a new republic; he died peacefully at the age of seventy-seven and was buried in Middletown, New York.

His son William moved on to new frontiers. In 1817 he left eastern New York with his family and moved to Farmersville, Cattaragus County, in western New York. This part of the state was still wild and a hunting- and fishing-ground for Indians. The Olders suffered depredation and fear of death from the tribes.

But William Older had his way with the wilderness. He planted crops and raised fine fruits. He succeeded in cultivating a seedless apple. He fathered sixteen children and died at the age of seventy-eight.

His sixteenth child was Emory, father of Fremont Older. In 1837, when Emory was twelve, his family moved behind ox-teams into the wilds of Wisconsin. The growing Emory found work in a sawmill on Green Bay that was owned by Squire Augur. He met and loved Celia, daughter of the Squire.

When these two married, Augur gave them eighty of his one hundred and sixty acres in Freedom Township, and Emory left the mill to farm with the Augur men.

In a cabin in this clearing, built of logs felled and hewn by his father, on August 30, 1856, the boy Fremont Older was born. Another son, Herbert, had been born to Emory and Celia two years before.

In the year Fremont Older was born, General Fremont of California was Presidential candidate of the Republican Party, created that same year. "Fremont the Pathfinder," he was called, having been among the first to explore little-known California and the first to claim it for the United States. The men of the clan in the clearing were ardent Free-Soilers and wanted the baby named for the Pathfinder, John Charles Fremont Older.

But Celia the pale, plump young mother, spoke from the hand-hewn bed where she lay under patchwork, in the single room smelling of burning pine-knots, resin starting from log walls, and the indefinable scent of new human life. Celia's eyes were black and mischievous, and her dark curls fell to her shoulders. Despite the sternness of her mother, Maria Augur, and her young husband Emory, Celia remained defiantly, charmingly gay, and from her

Fremont Older would inherit a love for teasing and for laughter.

"It's not fair to load down a child with so many names," she protested.

"Fremont, then," said the strapping six-foot father. "Fremont Older!"

They liked the sound of that name. It contained promises. The child seemed born in the very path of destiny. Or was it destruction?

Gigantic forces of hatred and evil and good were stirring, North and South, when this long-boned pioneer babe was born.

In the March following the rally, word reached the isolated farm that Abraham Lincoln had been inaugurated President of the United States. The four-year-old Fremont knew this as he was to know many things, not absorbing them fully at the time, knowing later they had been part of his growing body and thoughts. He only knew that March brought sap to the toes of a boy itching to be free of bulky home-made moccasins, and sap to the hearts of the sugar-maples around the clearing.

The sun was over Wisconsin, but snow still lay on the ground, when Fremont carried a bundle of goose-quills after his father, who bore heavy wooden buckets into the forest. Emory tapped the likeliest maples and set the slow cold sap dripping through the quills. When the buckets were full, Emory sent word through the township of a "sugarin' bee."

Families arrived early behind trudging oxen. The sap was boiled in great iron kettles over open fires. Everyone had his own shining brown puddle of sweet wax on a patch of clean snow. After the bee was over, enough maple sugar was stored in Squire Augur's cellar to last the family in the clearing a year. The remainder was carried by ox-cart over

## THE RALLY IN THE CLEARING

the nearly impassable eight miles to Appleton, where it was traded at the village store for the few necessities and luxuries the farm could not provide. Squire Augur was rated the wealthiest farmer in Freedom, but, like all the other pioneers, he had no money. Maple sugar was their equivalent for cash.

Fremont made his first journey to Appleton in the jolting cart.

Later he would experience the excitement of logging bees, shearing bees, wool-carding, knitting, sewing, and quilting bees. Labor, food, and friendship were shared by the pioneers.

That spring Emory Older killed two lambs and carried portions to all the neighbors. That was the law of the frontier. Its way was generous. It would remain—to his detriment, perhaps—Fremont Older's way.

The boy remembered, of this spring of '61, fragrant wild strawberries, hazelnuts in furry coats, bees in warming air, willow whistles, and white dogwood coming shyly to the edge of the clearing. He was forbidden to wander beyond the cleared space that was their universe.

But at times Fremont sat on the stoop outside the Older cabin, his dark eyes narrow and still. Beyond these surrounding forests lay what world?

That summer he helped with the endless chores of the farm. In the smoke-house he reached through the smolder of the ever-burning hickory fire for slabs of pork-fat and bacon. He carried a tallow dip down earthen steps to the cellar under his grandparents' farm-house and in that clammy place selected the best of last year's potatoes, turnips, pumpkins, and apples. By the flickering light he gloated over long bins and shelves of farm provender—jars of jellies, jams, and preserves and crocks of maple syrup and honey. Through the long winter months hives of wild bees captured by Squire Augur would drowse in the cellar.

There would remain with Fremont Older a love for plenitude and richness of living, but it must be for all.

Fremont helped plant seed corn, later to grow so tall he could hide in its leafy rows. On aching knees he rooted out the tender pigweed. He carried swill to the appreciative pigs and flung hay to the cows. Later he gathered elderberries and blackberries for pies and wild grapes for jelly.

It was as unthinkable to protest against work as to complain of the food set before you or to interrupt your elders at table.

That summer Emily Kimball Harley of New York City, sister of Fremont's grandmother, Maria Kimball Augur, wrote of making the long trip to Wisconsin with her little sons. Mrs. Augur wrote back eagerly. She could not but add a postscript. She was a woman of great pride.

"Augur is pretty well known in Appleton and you need not fear any difficulty in finding us."

Fremont drove to Appleton with his grandfather to meet the city cousins. He was glad they took the horses and farm wagon instead of the ox-team. Squire Augur drove horses instead of oxen, just as he had a frame house instead of the usual log cabin.

Factories were rising in Appleton along the wide and beautiful Fox River. Millstones were grinding corn and wheat to velvet smoothness. Sawmills were beginning to run night and day. The maws of these mills would widen to consume the great forests of Wisconsin.

The city cousins awed and impressed the wide-eyed Fremont. One of these little boys, Henry Farley, would become the brilliant engineer who defied the monopoly attempted by Standard Oil. As president of the Pennsylvania Transportation Company, he built a pipe-line through that state and proved himself of the breed of fighters and crusaders, as is described in Ida Tarbell's history of Standard Oil.

Jolting out of Appleton on a rough plank across the

wagon-bed that served as seat, Fremont pointed out to his cousins the modest stone building that was Lawrence College.

"There, I guess you haven't anything in New York as big as that!" he boasted . . . and all his life would chuckle, remembering.

But at supper in the farm-house they had him awed. They cut their chicken from the bone and did not drink from their saucers. As for the stylish Aunt Emily, she had seen the visiting Prince of Wales in all his splendor on Broadway and had actually been introduced to Horace Greeley!

The Harleys' way of eating and speaking was Fremont's first glimpse of life off the frontier. Long after that summer he would remember with a puzzled wistfulness the ways and manners of the city cousins.

Winter shut the clan into the farm-houses in the clearing, but Greeley's *Tribune* brought them the tremendous news of the world. The New York editor was nearly as respected an authority on the farm as the Bible that grandmother Augur read to them every night before family prayers. Squire Augur read every line of the *Tribune,* even the advertisements, by taper-light. As he read Greeley's diatribes against slavery, his voice grew louder and more threatening.

Fremont, not permitted to interrupt, listened enthralled to the trumpeted words. Sometimes the faces of the women whitened as the grandfather read. Sometimes the hands of the young men, Emory Older and the Squire's sons Allan and Duane, fell from the shoes or harness they were making, and their jaws grew tight with resolution.

Whatever took place North or South, whether hail or snow fell on the lonely farm, the work must go on. Even the evenings were spent in almost incessant labor. The women spun and wove, knitted and patched, dipped candles made of their own sheep-tallow, and boiled and tasted soap, their finger-tips dipped quickly into the vile-smelling pot and as quickly licked. The men made harness for horses and oxen or the home-made shoes that protected their own feet from the virgin soil.

In the summer all would wear moccasins fashioned by the cobbler in Appleton from deer-hide the men stretched and now cut in the kitchen.

Even the two little boys, their thin legs wrapped around wooden buckets, shelled seed corn and cut the eyes from potatoes for seed.

In April the *Tribune* brought shattering news to the farm.

"The rebels have fired on Fort Sumter!" the Squire read. "They have dared assault the Flag!"

Not one of that peaceful group realized that with the firing of Southern guns in Charleston harbor the Civil War had begun. Destruction might threaten the Union, but there was plowing and seeding to be done on the farm. The men sowed wheat in newly broken fields, but as they followed harrow and plow, their lips moved in prayer as they asked God what He required of them.

That spring Emory Older cleared more land. The child Fremont heard the sound of his father's ax ringing in the forest and the crash of great trees falling. Foot by foot the pioneers were claiming their realm in the wilderness.

Then in July came the news, too terrible to be grasped at first, of Bull Run. The Union forces were scattered. Desolation fell over the North.

If they could but capture Richmond—nest of the Copperheads! All the North was saying that. Then the Augur boys and Emory Older gave one another long, intense looks of consecration and knew what they must do. Of no avail the sobbing of their women. Of no avail the prayers. The young men had prayers of their own—for freedom, for the

## THE RALLY IN THE CLEARING

Union everlasting, for the deliverance of the slaves. They were like prophets exalted.

"Remember Bull Run!" was their answer, as their fathers had said, "Remember Valley Forge!" And they told of the preacher in Illinois who heard of Bull Run and cried to his flock, "Brethern, it's time to adjourn this meeting and go home and drill!"

Now sad family councils were held each evening in farm-house or log cabin. The elders talked in low voices so the children could not hear. Dimly and with terror Fremont knew that the gaunt man Lincoln was crying for aid in Washington and a call had gone out over the wires for seventy-five thousand men. Dimly, that men were dying horribly on fields a few months before beautiful with spring. Dimly, that two mothers and a father were trying to justify their opposition to three stalwart young settlers determined to offer their lives to Lincoln. Squire Augur would have died to free the slaves, but he quailed before the sacrifice of his sons.

"To defend, protect, and preserve the Union," Lincoln had promised.

Young and powerful and passionately believing, these men were with Lincoln.

One morning that same July, Emory Older led Fremont past the wheat-fields to the little log school-house that stood on their land near the forest. Fremont was not yet five years old.

"Here is a little shaver for you," Emory told the school-master.

Little girls and boys in homespun sat at log desks on either side of the small room. They whispered their studies aloud as they stared over grimy slates. The master looked fierce and terrible.

Fremont burst into tears. He clung to his father's legs.

But protection and tenderness walked away, leaving him in that alien room. The master handed him a word primer. The boy gulped and read it glibly. He had taught himself to read.

That night, he would always remember, there was long talk in the Older cabin. Fremont lay in the truckle-bed beside his brother Herbert and heard his grandfather and grandmother, his mother and uncles and father, all brokenly weeping. Then they were on their knees, praying.

"The die is cast!" his grandmother sobbed as she rose.

The next morning his mother's eyes were swollen.

"Your father has gone to the war," she told her little sons. "He kissed you goodby while you slept."

They crowded to her knees, asking many questions. The indignation and passion of the Civil War was in her answers. But Fremont could fix none of it in his mind. He wandered out into the sunshine and sat on the stoop before the kitchen door.

The forests looked nearer and menacing though they were beginning to be touched with gold. Winter was coming on, and with it war seemed closer and more terrifying. Against the cold sky wild geese cried their way southward. A belated meadowlark called thrillingly from an apple-tree, but even its song seemed poignant.

Seventy years later the editor Fremont Older would vividly recall that little boy that had been himself, sitting oppressed by his first knowledge of loneliness in the Wisconsin sunshine. So real the child would seem to him that at times, he said, he felt he could almost reach out his hand and touch that tousled, dreaming head, in pity for all that was to come.

## Chapter II

### A SQUIRREL DIES—AND LINCOLN

SHORTLY after Emory Older left the clearing, Fremont's Augur uncles, Allan and Duane, followed to the battlefields. Winter came on like an enemy. Fremont at five began his struggle against the Wisconsin elements. It was the child's duty to see that the fireplaces of both farm-houses were fed.

Through many winters and summers, in snow and blazing sun, Fremont Older would chop and split and stack logs for the devouring fires. His arms would harden and lengthen, his chest deepen, to woodsman's stature. One shoulder would remain permanently higher from the swing of his ax, annoying, in later years, his fashionable tailors.

Squire Augur at sixty years was left alone to work the farm. He was racked with dyspepsia and with anxiety for his soldier sons. There were no men to be hired even had there been money to hire them. From every farm in Freedom the men were gone.

The wheat his sons had planted grew to a golden lake. That fall, alone, the bearded patriarch completed the almost impossible task of cutting it. It lay parching in the sun awaiting the garnering.

One morning Squire Augur came to his kitchen door and saw clouds rolling over the green rim of forest. Rain was in their blackness, and the ruin of his harvest.

The Squire cursed. Shaking his gnarled old fist at that glowering sky, he gave his true opinion of an omniscient injustice. There was something sublime in the awfulness of his attack. Fremont, who spent much of his time with his grandparents, listened gravely. But his tiny grandmother rushed to the Squire, her plump form bristling.

"How dare you!" she screamed. "How dare you curse God!"

At noon, when the Squire returned from the fields for his too heavy noon meal, she did not speak to her husband. That night at family worship she prayed for his sin-stained soul. Fremont, on his knees by a split-hickory chair, admired the grandmother who dared so shrilly and intimately petition God.

But his greater pride was in his grandfather, who had dared to question the doings of the Almighty.

The God of Maria Augur was one of wrath. Once Fremont fled screaming from the farm-house parlor when a visiting preacher gave a too realistic picture of His capacity for meting out punishment. Thoughts of that God often oppressed the boy during the long nights when, secure in his truckle-bed, he heard the wolves howling in the wilderness surrounding the patch of farm.

Around the clearing the woods were deep and green. Sometimes Squire Augur took the boy hunting in the forest. He was a master shot—out of economy's sake, he told Fremont, for during the war years powder and shot were too expensive to be wasted. Whenever he took aim at a deer, the small boy put his hands over his eyes.

"Oh Lord, this time," he would pray frantically, "please let him miss!"

The frontier was callous toward the creatures of forest or farm. The boy could not be. Sometimes Squire Augur frowned at the sensitive qualities of the childish face with its high cheek-bones and dark, alert eyes which reflected all moods. His grandson was strong and of his own gigantic breed, but with an incomprehensible gentleness which baffled the old Squire.

The war years went by sorrowfully in the clearing. The women kept their courage alive by humming the "Battle Hymn of the Republic" as they tried to aid the Squire in carrying on the farm.

"Money had apparently entirely disappeared," Older wrote of this period long after. "No one around us seemed to have any, although my grandfather managed to keep his subscription paid up for Greeley's weekly New York *Tribune*. Out of it he kept track of the war, reading every line in each issue, including the advertisements. The *Tribune* was his Bible.

"But while no one had any money in those war days, no one went hungry. There was an interchange of food. When a steer was killed, each neighbor received a part of it. If we ran out of hay, a neighbor who had hay would supply us. It was so with everything.

"When the minister had preached his hell-fire sermon in our parlor and was ready to go, he was given his dinner and a peck of oats for his horse. That was his pay."

The first of their soldiers to return to the clearing was Duane. The Squire carried into the farm-house the living frame of his giant son. Duane had contracted dysentery, that incurable scourge of the Civil War.

One week after his home-coming, Duane died.

Soon after, in the summer of 1862, Fremont's father was brought home. And Emory Older looked as had Duane.

"But I'm not going to die!" he promised his two little sons.

Emory had been quartered in northern Arkansas with the First Wisconsin Cavalry when they were surrounded at night by men in gray. The Confederates marched the Northerners in their stocking-feet one hundred miles to the prison in Little Rock. Emory and many others fell ill and were exchanged for Southern prisoners.

But whatever Emory told of the war, the old Squire heard doubtfully.

"I don't believe that," he would interrupt stubbornly. "It wasn't that way in Greeley's *Tribune.*"

The printed word of the *Tribune* was final in the clearing.

Emory Older was a patient and gentle invalid. For a while he was strong enough to sit by a window, his shoulder-blades cutting through his coat of Union blue. The soft-voiced woodsman was dying.

The Union, too, seemed perishing with Emory Older. Winter closed in its darkling, cruel beauty over Wisconsin. The boy Fremont would later recall his grandfather's sonorous voice reading to them Lincoln's speech delivered on the battle-field of Gettysburg. He would recall that December of 1863 when Sherman began his march to the sea. He heard of twenty-four hundred battles fought and trembled at the bloody names of Shiloh and Vicksburg, Lookout Mountain and Chattanooga.

"I shall not see another winter," Emory Older told him the summer after his return.

A few weeks later Fremont's father was dead. The family rode to the Freedom cemetery in a rented "four-seater." Fremont sat by the driver.

All the way the driver bragged about his horses and their fine new harness.

The little boy sniffed the odor of new leather. It lodged in his memory with that of the hot oil-cloth capes at the Lincoln rally. All Fremont Older's life the scent of leather would bring back a memory of his mother sobbing over an open grave.

But Emory Older lived on in his son's thoughts, having died for three magic words: "The Republic Forever."

## A SQUIRREL DIES—AND LINCOLN

And from his army uniforms his desperately poor widow made coats and trousers for her little boys, and it was in a cut-down suit of Union blue and a soldier's cap that Fremont Older set off, late that summer, to the Appleton grammar-school.

The Squire's last son, Allan, died on April 9, 1865, one hour before the Civil War ended with Lee's surrender. Allan was buried on the battle-field. Fremont Older had lost his father and six uncles, all over six feet tall and one six feet six, in the war that freed the slaves.

"All our men were dead," wrote Older of this harrowing time.

"Conditions grew worse after the Civil War ended. The country was drained of its man power and the common necessities of life. My grandfather faced his new responsibilities bravely. Now, on the threshold of old age, his health undermined and his heart sad, he had us all on his hands—my grandmother, two widows, and four children.

"The work was too hard for my grandfather, and when he was on the verge of a breakdown, he sold the farm for $2,800. His sheep, cattle, horses, and farm tools brought him an additional $700.

"In those days $3,500 was a small fortune. With it my grandfather bought a home in Omro, a small town on the Fox River. There was a good-sized vegetable-garden surrounding the house, but that was all. No income whatever, and eight people to feed."

Fremont's mother had bought a tiny house in Appleton after his father died. The Squire moved them in the farm wagon. It took the oxen two days to make the eight-mile trip over the rutted road to the village on the Fox.

On the last trip Celia and the two little boys rode on the wagon atop their household furnishings. As they jolted into the dark forest, Fremont looked back across the clearing and saw the morning sun striking ruddily on the small windows of the log cabin where he had been born. He heard the clangor of an ax in the woods and realized that as far back as he could remember he had heard the sound of his grandfather's and father's axes reclaiming their land from living forests. He felt a wild passion for the land they were deserting.

"Someday," he thought fiercely, "I'll come back."

He would return to wilderness many times during his adventurous lifetime. He would go back to forests after fighting and turmoil and find himself suddenly at peace.

Late in the summer of 1865, before Fremont Older was nine, he became janitor of the frame school-house in Appleton.

For twenty-five cents a week he arrived early, built fires in the two rooms, swept the floors, and shoveled snow from the yard. This monthly dollar and the eight dollars widow's pension Celia Older received from the Government was all she had with which to feed and clothe herself and her two sons.

Most of the other school children were left as badly off by the war. Fremont, wearing to school his father's cut-down blue army suit and peaked Union cap, was no more poorly dressed than many.

But even in that era of fierce democracy boys were cruel. A mob backed the little janitor against the fence and jeered.

"Yah! He's so poor his mother has to make pants of his father's uniform!"

Fremont rushed home to his mother and tearfully begged not to be sent back to school. But Celia knew that the days of her son's schooling were numbered. She forced him to return the next day.

The boy hated and would always hate fighting. At six he had learned that he could lick his brother Herbert, two years older, but he had never abused that power. Yet now

## A SQUIRREL DIES—AND LINCOLN

he returned to school with his small face squared with a purpose as great as that responsible for the Civil War.

"I had discovered the cause of my humiliation," Older said of this. "It was the War—the just and righteous War for which the men of my family had died! The War was responsible for my poverty. Now it was my turn to fight in defense of that poverty."

This was Fremont Older's first crusade.

An odd little fellow in baggy army pants and peaked cap, he backed against the school fence and awaited his enemies.

That morning the Appleton school yard was a shambles. The boy who had swung an ax since he was five gave himself over to a fury of traffic in bloodied noses and bruised eyes. After that Fremont wore his cut-down uniform like a conqueror.

He would remember, this same year, the assassination of President Lincoln, when his family gathered to weep and pray as for another son.

He remembered, too, the death of a forest squirrel.

He was standing with other boys on the bank of the Fox. A tiny creature was fighting its way through the deep water. A red tree squirrel was swimming for its life.

"He's giving out," gloated one of the boys.

Fremont thought the boy spoke harshly. In his heart he urged the little animal to keep trying. It fought through the last thin inches of water and fell exhausted and panting at their feet.

The boy who had spoken brought a stick down on the squirrel's head. He beat it to death.

Fremont shrieked. He ran home, to his own room, where he lay sobbing. His mother hurried to him.

"Oh, mother!" he cried wildly. "He trusted us! He trusted us!"

She wrung the story from the tortured child. She

laughed. And he felt toward his mother as once years before in the clearing, when he, a tiny boy, had trustingly gathered for her a great armful of starry mayweed, thinking it beautiful.

"Silly!" she had laughed, tossing the offering into the woodbox. "They are only weeds."

Through his long lifetime Fremont Older would feel toward many men and women as he had felt toward the squirrel.

The month Abraham Lincoln died the boy Fremont went to work in a rake factory in Appleton. He was the youngest and strongest of the children and the first to help support the family. Ten hours a day he worked, six days a week, in a dusty loft, polishing wooden handles with sandpaper. It was a man's job but without a man's pay. He worked for five dollars a month.

In his rare free hours he learned to swim, when some larger boys tossed him into the Fox, shouting, "sink or swim."

That winter he was nine he worked on Saturdays in a shingle factory, and all his life he bore a ragged white scar from a saw on his amazingly delicate hand. Sawmills were running now night and day on the Fox River. The massacre of the vast Wisconsin forests had begun.

He worked after school every day and on Saturdays, but that was not enough. Celia Older could not support both her sons. She studied them with black eyes filled with despair. Fremont was the younger, but sturdy and straight, while Herbert had never been strong.

"Fremont, I can't keep you any longer," she was forced to tell him.

Sorrowfully he packed his few possessions to take with him to his grandparents at Omro. Fremont loved his mother dearly. A large and powerful lad of nine who had worked hard half his life, he wept like any child at leaving her. But once in Omro with the Squire and Maria Augur, he brightened at seeing his friend the Fox again.

For Omro as well as Appleton snuggled against the river, before it met the Wolf a few miles away. Omro was ten miles west of Oshkosh, farther from Lake Winnebago than Appleton.

The Squire's new home was of a stiffly formal type of pioneer architecture, but it smelled deliciously of newly cut pine. A good sized vegetable-patch surrounded it. The Squire had no income, and all their living must be wrung from this patch of land.

The place seemed poor to Fremont as he recalled the rich harvests and well-stocked cellar of the farm. Even his grandparents seemed meager and older.

But war and poverty and the death of her sons had not softened his grandmother. Maria Augur still bowed to a righteous Lord of Anger who attended personally to all the affairs of earth. Right away, in her clean-smelling new house, Fremont got into his first difficulties with God.

Omro was a quiet, God-fearing village. In the red-brick school-house Fremont attended, which even in this year of 1866 was very old, there were sharp lines of religious caste. The few Catholic children played by themselves. The Methodists did not play with the Baptists. Maria Augur, a pillar of the Presbyterian church, saw to it that her grandson played with that group and attended preaching and Sunday-school three times every Sunday.

"Sunday was a terrible day in this little town," Older groaned in retrospect years later. "We children were scrubbed early in the morning and stuck into our Sunday clothes, and warned not to leave the house until it was time to go to church. The service lasted at least two hours, and then there was another hour of Sunday-school. Then home to dinner at one o'clock. There were prayers and

Bible readings in the afternoon, and church again in the evening."

At Sunday-school Fremont heard of the boy David who slew the giant Goliath with a sling-shot.

"I don't believe it," Fremont announced at the dinner-table.

For doubting the Bible his grandmother sent him to bed, with promise of food and forgiveness should he recant. All day he lay there, his small and stubborn chin, so like his grandmother's, thrust over the patchwork. At school time the next morning Maria Augur, who never before had been thwarted by any of her clan, was forced to give way.

For days Fremont was oppressed by a sneaking expectancy of being struck by lightning. Almost defiantly he awaited divine punishment. But no sign come from on high.

He found other food for his rebellion. There lived in quiet Omro a man outside the moral pale, the lawyer John B. Felker from Milwaukee.

"He reads Tom Paine!" Fremont's grandmother said of Felker in awful tones.

And she told her grandson of the freethinker Paine, who had, she said, denied God and suffered agonies of remorse on his death-bed.

Felker lived in a handsome white house with pillars near the modest Augur home. Fremont, barefooted and fascinated, hung around the gates of the sinner . . . until one day he entered the garden, pattered through the house on his dusty feet, and came out on a wide porch where Felker sat reading. He stood staring in an agony of curiosity.

"Are you reading Tom Paine?" he demanded.

Felker started, and smiled at the staring, black-eyed lad.

"My grandmother says you'll go to hell for reading Paine," pursued Fremont. "She says Paine's there already!"

Felker started to laugh. Then, simply and with great

kindliness, he pulled the barefooted boy to his side and talked. He gently drew a picture of Paine as a good man who had tried to free people from the fear of a merciless God.

The dark-eyed boy was listening avidly. Something in the words fitted the strange rebellion in Fremont's thoughts.

Felker drove Fremont home later in his buggy. As they stopped at the picket gate, the boy's heart pounded. Maria Augur in a huge sunbonnet was weeding among the sunflowers. She straightened her plump but agile body, and her square features locked in an awful calm.

She met Fremont in the garden path, her stained hands on her checkered hips.

"You rode with that . . . that disciple of the Devil! Fremont, you're headed straight for perdition!"

The boy did not hear her tirade. His head ached with emotion. He had met a man who spoke thoughts he could understand, who had talked to him as to another man. He had made his first friend.

A half-century later Fremont Older sat with his close friend Clarence Darrow on the porch of the Older home overlooking the Santa Clara Valley. Older recalled this episode.

"Why, I knew Felker well!" Darrow interrupted. "He was a liberal, a fine attorney and a splendid man."

The man Felker set his mark on the bewildered country boy. Unwittingly he helped set free that eager and hungry young mind.

Another "disciple of the Devil" of Omro held the attention of Fremont. This was the owner of the single saloon, patronized by the mill hands.

"This terrible man fascinated me," wrote Older.

"He was Omro's personal and private devil. I never tired of watching him walk up and down in front of his saloon with a big black cigar in his mouth, tipped upward to a rakish angle, and his hat pulled down over one eye. He seemed to be utterly oblivious of the hatred the town felt for him. No one but the 'doomed' ever spoke to him or entered his place.

"For the preachers he was a choice morsel. How they rolled his name around in their mouths as they warned the congregations to beware of this follower of the devil! Even his wife and children were ostracized.

"When my grandmother learned that her washerwoman was also doing the saloon man's laundry, the woman was told to choose between the two. She chose to wash for the lost one because the pay was better.

"Secretly, I considered the saloonkeeper the most interesting man in Omro."

Was it coincidence that years later the fighting editor Fremont Older would wear a mustache, carry his cigar at a rakish angle, and wear his hat down over his eyes?

His rebellion against a merciless religion was secret. His grandmother often said there was no better boy. He obeyed his elders, not because he was by nature docile, but because his training had been practical and stern.

There was little in his life that was amusing. His naughtiest prank was swimming in the Fox oftener than was permitted. But glimpses came to him of the world beyond Omro, unbearably thrilling.

A tent show produced *Uncle Tom's Cabin* and *Ten Nights in a Bar-Room*. He had no money, but he ran errands for the troupe, and later in that lamplight-haloed canvas world he lost himself utterly. When he groped his way from the tent, he was blind with emotion. For weeks he "mooned" around the house, lost in the world of make-believe.

Again large posters splashed the board fences. "See the Horseless Carriage at Dan Rice's Circus." They bore the woodcut of a buckboard mounted with a steam-engine.

The boy was determined to see that. He carried thirty buckets of water to the elephants and was rewarded with a glimpse of an ancestor of the automobile, burning cord wood under its boiler, as it snorted its way around the sawdust ring.

Once before, in Appleton, he had attended a circus. "Older's Traveling Circus," owned by a cousin of his dead father, had come to the village, and the Older boys had experienced the supreme glory of being passed in free.

Maria Augur's lips drew down at Fremont's account of the horseless carriage. Such a contraption was certainly against the laws of Providence. But Squire Augur was interested. There had grown a friendly understanding between the fine old giant and the fatherless boy.

That Christmas he drew Fremont aside.

"Here's a present for you," he whispered sheepishly. "But keep it hid from your grandma!"

Maria Augur permitted only the Bible, other religious books, and Greeley's *Tribune* in her house. In the barn Fremont unwrapped his present. There lay two books concerning the amazing adventures of a young man who had fought Indians, shot buffalo, and hunted gold in the Far West.

They introduced Fremont to adventure. He memorized them, word for word. Later another boy loaned him the works of J. Fenimore Cooper.

He began living in romantic dreams. As bones and muscles grew, his thoughts grew longer, reaching far off into western places.

The grandparents grew steadily poorer. When harvest-time came that fall, Squire Augur drove Fremont in his buggy over the roads around Omro, offering the boy to every farmer they met.

"Being ten years old and strong for my age, I was snapped

up as a bargain," Older wrote of this adventure. "I milked ten cows the first evening and went to bed. My new master called me at four in the morning and told me to jump up quickly and milk the cows. He then went back to bed and slept another hour.

"After milking, feeding the cows, and churning, I had breakfast. Then the real day's work began. It was haying time and my job was to 'mow the hay away' in the barn as my master pitched it in to me. The weather was boiling hot, and even hotter than that in the haymow. The only time I could breathe freely was when the farmer would toss in a big bunch of hay. It created a momentary breeze, which saved me from suffocation. At six o'clock we went to the house, the farmer to rest for an hour, while I milked the cows!"

He picked potato-bugs in the broiling sun. He hoed. He milked ten cows morning and evening and slept on a straw pallet in a sweltering loft. He drove the reaper. He was always weary, always hungry, but unrebellious. His mind was fixed on the season's end when he could proudly carry home his pay.

He was given ten dollars for that three weeks. Choking with disappointment, he accepted the money. He gave it to his grandfather without a word.

That autumn his hopes of continuing his scanty schooling grew faint. He had worked to the limit of his strength and opportunities. He had run a saw in a shingle-mill on Saturdays and split wood after school. He had spent every day of vacation at one or another poorly paid task. But as he grew in strength, his grandparents were failing. Life was a matter now not of learning but of food.

Then, over at Appleton, Celia Older pushed her eager way into the foreground of events. No one had ever thought pretty little Celia capable of making money. But in the very midst of the after-war depression the plump young woman with dark curls to her shoulders and the shyly gay, touching smile walked from door to door peddling books—*The Life of Horace Greeley*, *The Life of Schuyler Colfax*, and *Men of Our Times*.

She sent copies of the three books to Fremont. The boy pored over them. His grandfather read the Greeley book aloud at evening. To Fremont Older the life story of Horace Greeley, who tramped into New York with all his possessions on his back, who became a printer and finally the greatest of American editors, was no less romantic than the life of the Indian-fighter hidden away in the barn loft. Ambition and hero-worship smote the boy together.

He wanted to be an editor, like Horace Greeley. He wanted to go West, to adventure, like the Indian-fighter.

From his strange assortment of heroes he wove visions. He was to become, in a way, like them all.

Celia Older's book canvassing brought in money beyond her wildest hopes. A gay letter came, the cheerfulest Fremont would ever receive from her. With her earnings she was determined to send her two sons to Ripon College, twenty miles from Omro.

Fremont and his brother Herbert entered this school in September, 1868, a few days after Fremont's twelfth birthday.

It was a Presbyterian college. Nearly the entire faculty were ordained ministers. Fremont twisted his alert thoughts around Latin verbs and other recondite and academic subjects. He attended church twice every Sunday. His long wood-chopping arm won him the position of pitcher on the college baseball-team.

One month after the boys entered Ripon, Celia Older's book sales dwindled to nothing. Word came that the boys must leave the school. Herbert returned obediently to Appleton. But Fremont refused to leave Ripon. He would work his way through college, he wrote his mother.

Without any help he managed to remain in the school a year. It was the most contented year of his life. His grades were good, yet he had little time for study outside of school hours. Until nine every evening the sound of his saw could be heard on the campus as he toiled over the woodpiles of the professors or wealthier students.

He found time for his first love. Pretty Fanny Thomas was his first romance, and her folks were "well-fixed." Fremont walked home with her one day from school. Embarrassed, he did not utter a word the whole way. Suddenly he had remembered that his heavy shoes were "foxed"—patched by his grandfather. Fanny's daintiness confounded him.

After that he hid his clumsy shoes under his desk and was content to dream of Fanny. Years later, during lonely years of wandering, he wrote her sentimental letters and was not hurt when she answered none of them. He was content to have someone to write to and dream about who was beautiful and rich and untroubled by the problems that oppressed his own youth.

In May, Fremont closed the year with good marks. It was his last in any school. Back in his grandfather's house at Omro his mother told him he would have to learn a trade.

Celia Older was still very young and pretty and had plans of her own, but Fremont knew nothing of these.

"Choose any trade you like," she said.

Fremont's dark eyes blazed.

"I want to be a printer!" he said eagerly. "Horace Greeley began as a printer!"

## Chapter III

### PRINTER'S DEVIL

ON THE WALL of the composing-room of the *Courant* of Berlin, Wisconsin, is carved his name: FREMONT OLDER.

He carved it there when he was barely thirteen and had begun work on the newspaper for fifty cents a week and board.

In this September of 1869, while North and South struggled in the pangs of reconstruction, Fremont Older worked as printer's devil.

"Doing all the dirty work of the *Courant* office was my job," Older wrote of his apprenticeship. "Washing the ink rollers on the big press, and the small job-work press; sweeping the floors, cleaning the windows; and in the winter months splitting the wood and carrying it in my arms up a long flight of stairs; running errands, delivering the weekly edition of the paper to two hundred homes, sometimes wading through two feet of snow.

"When all that work was out of the way I was allowed to practise setting type, or running the job press, learning to be a printer."

Handling the type with long, sensitive fingers, he dreamed. Like his hero Horace Greeley he was beginning as a printer. Soon, when he was well started on his career, his mother and brother Herbert would come to live with him in Berlin, and someday he would be a famous editor like Greeley.

He planned this, carving his name hopefully on the *Courant* wall.

That carved name is framed today. Under it is the story of the printer's devil who became one of America's great editors.

But his dreams crashed. Celia Older wrote her son that she was marrying a man named Sherwood and moving to California.

The shock of this sickened him. Yet he knew that his mother was entitled to happiness. She had experienced the war years, widowhood, poverty. She had provided for her two sons as best she knew by apprenticing them to printers.

And Celia was only thirty-two, pretty, charmingly gay.

But he was little more than a child. He felt the heartbreak of desertion. He spent long hours of jealous brooding, hating the unknown man his mother had married.

Celia's face was round and piquant, a little pathetic in her effort to look always glad. Her dark curls had tumbled over his face when she bent to kiss him good night. These things the boy Fremont remembered, growing more listless, slackening in his work.

He wrote long letters to her when she left with her new husband for California, letters unboyish in their tragic intensity. In return she wrote praying him to work hard, to save his money and join her in the far-off West. More than ever the word California cried out to him.

Editor Terry who owned the *Courant* had children of his own. He was touched by the white features and listless air of his printer's devil. He took the lad home to live with his own large family, and Fremont slept with the youngest boy. Every night the oldest Terry daughter came in to kiss both boys good night.

It was Fremont's first experience of a wholesome and jolly family life. His childhood had been oppressed by his grandmother's fire-and-brimstone God and the adage, "Speak when spoken to." Meals had been eaten in silence in his grandmother's home. Prayer was a form of spiritual wrestling, and God a jealous watchman.

There were no spiritual wrestlings among the Terrys. The God who heard their family prayers listened in love and understanding. The children chattered gleefully at table. There was much laughing and friendly taunting and lifting of voices at evening around a wheezy organ.

After a few weeks Fremont found that he could smile again. After a few more he realized that he was very happy. Sorrow held a piercing quality for his volatile soul, as did happiness, so that all his life he would wince or warm to memories.

Again, with devastating force, as he was to do everything, he fell in love. Strolling players brought *Fanchon the Cricket* and *The Sea of Ice* to Berlin. As a newspaper employee Fremont received passes.

The plays, it seemed to the boy, represented life as it should and must be—the good man vindicated, the villain invariably punished.

"Strangely enough," Older said later, "I would believe this nearly fifty years."

Amelia Watts, the leading lady, left him madly enamoured.

"It was not a selfish love," he explained. "I didn't want her for myself. I wanted Amelia to marry the leading man, Edwin Clifford."

By bribing the bellboy at the primitive hotel he met Amelia, the object of his dreams, face to face in the lobby.

"What a shock!" related Older. "Her face, without the stage make-up, was pale, haggard, and, worse still, heavily pitted with the scars of smallpox. I was stunned, and momentarily the beautiful girl that had come so suddenly into my life had as suddenly died.

"With a heavy heart I returned to the office and to the

stark reality of life as it is. But gradually the lovely 'Fanchon' came to life again. That night I saw her in the same character, with Edwin Clifford, the passionate lover, overcoming all obstacles and the curtain dropping with 'Fanchon' in his arms. I went happily to bed. My Goddess of Love was back on her pedestal.

"The next day while delivering my papers I saw my hero in the lobby of the hotel, staggering drunk. He lurched over toward me with: 'Sonny, gimme a paper.' Trembling I handed him one, but resolutely refused the dime he handed me.

"Take money from my hero? I'd rather starve!"

After the troupe left, life seemed dull in Berlin. Fremont spent his spare time on the wharf beside the Fox. Every day the side-wheel steamer *Berlin City* puffed up the river from Oshkosh. The boy watched its arrival and departure wistfully. Above all living creatures he envied the cabin-boy, who every day sailed past Omro, where Fremont's grandparents lived, and the shores of Lake Winnebago, and the dreamed-about city of Oshkosh.

One day the cabin-boy of the *Berlin City* told Fremont he was leaving the boat. Fremont might have his job.

The printer boy was standing on the wharf watching the unloading. He forgot Horace Greeley, Editor Terry, the *Courant,* and all his editorial dreams. He walked directly up the gangplank and sailed away down the Fox toward Oshkosh.

He would relive this mad moment many years. It made of him a wanderer.

He saw the kindly Terrys once more, when on his return trip he called for his trunk. Motherly Mrs. Terry sat on the plain little leather box and wept.

"I can't let you go, Fremont," she protested. "You're a poor, motherless boy . . . and there is gambling and drinking aboard those boats."

# PRINTER'S DEVIL

Fremont wept with her. He knew she was right. In the few hours he had grown utterly sick of life as a cabin-boy. He had scrubbed staterooms and decks, waited on table, washed dishes in a hot galley, taken orders from a large black cook. He had seen nothing of Omro or Oshkosh. Every hour horror of the thing he had done was growing.

Pride kept him from admitting this to Mrs. Terry. He shouldered his little trunk, but as he carried it to the waiting boat, his eyes swam with tears.

"The Terrys had won," he wrote later, "although they didn't know it for many years.

"I was ashamed to return to the *Courant* office and face the taunts and sneers of my boy companions, who would consider me a cry-baby and a fool to give up such a glorious job as cabin-boy of the *Berlin City*.

"But that evening I gave the steward notice to get a boy in my place. Within two weeks I left the boat."

Fremont had saved enough money to cross Wisconsin by train, to the Mississippi. He found work as a roustabout on a packet plying the mighty river. Behind his troubled wanderings was a tremendous longing.

Borne along the dark river at evening, he looked tragically westward into the setting sun.

"Out there is California," he thought. "Out there is my mother. Somehow, I'm going to her."

He wrote to her every week.

Life on the river led nowhere, he discovered before long. His conscience tormented him, and he knew he must return to his trade. But he could not bring himself to return to the *Courant*. He worked his way to Hudson, Wisconsin, on the St. Croix River, where his brother Herbert was printer's devil on the *Democrat*. Fremont was still a child, but a resourceful child.

He arrived at the *Democrat* office without a penny. His one suit was ragged from his work as a roustabout. He dreaded presenting himself in that condition before his older brother. But he remembered Greeley, who had arrived in New York with a pack on his back. He squared his shoulders and walked into the office of the country paper.

He was permitted to work with Herbert at two dollars a week.

To his surprise, Herbert was developing into a fine typesetter. Fremont's pride kindled and kept him earnestly at work for several months. At the end of that time he was a fairly good printer. But he had made up his mind never to be a first-rate printer.

"Because then I'll always be a printer," he argued to himself. "And I don't want to be a printer. I want to be an editor."

Horace Greeley was shining in his thoughts again. But the two-dollar-a-week wage humiliated him. Also, Herbert, who was weaker and less alert, was permitted to set up stories, while to Fremont was relegated the harder work of washing the press. Every night the boys worked until midnight.

And, besides, something had happened to Fremont during his weeks of wandering on the rivers. Dreaming over the press, he recalled nocturnal forests, magic gleaming cities, romantic scenes he had glimpsed and longed to revisit, until not even Herbert, not even a dashing blackeyed girl who had taught him to waltz, could hold Fremont Older in Hudson.

He left Hudson one morning when the thermometer stood at twenty degrees below zero, crossing the St. Croix River by sleigh on its bed of solid ice. He was going to St. Paul.

He had wired the foreman of the *Morning Press* that he was an expert printer in need of work. He had decided not to add that he was only fourteen.

The foreman had wired him to come on. Fremont appeared in the shop without a penny, half-frozen, intimidated by his first glimpse of a large city, and demanded the regular printer's wage of fifteen dollars a week. The door of the *Press* was slammed on his freezing nose.

The boyish arrogance that had carried him to St. Paul died as he stood alone and penniless in the strange city, the snow creeping to his knees, his shoulders cringing in his thin coat.

Late that afternoon Fremont Older crept timidly into a printing-office run by David Ramaly. He was blue with cold and weak from hunger. Ramaly asked the boy if he could operate a steam press. Too desperate to be truthful, Fremont replied that he could. He was promised six dollars a week, assigned to a large half-medium press with a legal blank on it, and ordered to print a thousand copies.

The boy's hands trembled. He forgot to adjust the grippers set over the type form. He switched on the belt. The crash of steel form on steel grippers could be heard three blocks away.

Ramaly stopped the press and knocked the boy to the floor in one movement.

"You damn fool," he yelled. "You've done a hundred dollars worth of damage!"

The boy was sobbing, his face to his worn sleeve.

"Take it from my wages," he wailed.

Ramaly seemed to choke down an impulse to murder. He ordered the boy out. Fremont had shuffled to the door when he felt a hand laid on his arm. It was Ramaly, with all the anger gone from him.

"You're just a poor, foolish youngster," he said gently. "Come on back and try it again."

The damage he had done was never mentioned. Fremont worked ten hours a day for his six-dollar wage and walked three miles each way between his boarding-house and the printing-office. He did not think of this as hardship. Since he was five he had regarded hard work as inseparable from living. Life was difficult for nearly every American boy after the Civil War.

Words could torture him, while physical hurts he bore bravely. One night his delicate right hand was caught between the tympan and the form. Letters printed into his flesh spurted blood, but he did not cry.

After a time he became a fairly proficient type-setter. The *Morning Press* that had once spurned the half-frozen country boy offered him ten dollars a week. In its press-room some of his confidence in himself returned. But all his spare time was spent on the river-front, watching the packets plying up and down the Mississippi.

Again his dark eyes filled with longing. He felt he had mastered St. Paul. Now his thoughts turned to St. Louis. Whatever interested Fremont Older became an obsession. He knew at last that he must go to St. Louis.

He left the *Morning Press*. He worked on small papers in small towns in the direction of St. Louis. He slipped aboard river boats and slept hidden in the cargo. Often he was reduced to the road, and one day he walked forty miles, carrying his trunk. At noon he asked for a meal at a farmhouse. The farm woman demanded payment.

The boy had nothing to offer but his copy of *Horace Greeley*.

"I tried to hold out Greeley's life that contained my dream," he wrote of this, "but the woman insisted on that or no dinner. It was a sad parting, but I gave it to her. After dinner I set out for Davenport with my trunk a little lighter and my heart a little heavier."

Fremont Older would collect many books in his full lifetime. He would love them with an almost personal affection, but he never attempted to find another copy of *The Life of Horace Greeley*. He would regret the loss of it all his life.

Working where he could, stowing away whenever he could, he at last neared St. Louis. He earned enough money to make the final stretch by steamer without berth or meals. As he slept that night on grain sacks on the packet's deck, someone stole his cap.

It was a new cap. The loss of it changed his destiny. For the engineer noted the boy's distress and gave him a soiled, torn, broad-brimmed hat of his own.

"I had no sooner put this old hat on my head than the boat landed," Fremont Older was able to write with an amused sympathy years after, "and I looked out from under its filthy brim and saw the magic city of my dreams."

He dared not face St. Louis in that hat. Wearing it, he could not enter a press-room and demand work. He could not remain in St. Louis.

That night he slipped between flaring torches on the river-bank and aboard a packet bound for New Orleans. Stories of the southern city had long entranced him. But not for many years would he see romantic New Orleans. The purser found the stowaway, and when at midnight the steamer stopped at a landing for wood, he shoved the boy down the gangplank and sent him with a kick into the darkness.

Clutching his trunk, the frightened boy stared into the night. Dimly he saw a road. It pointed, he knew, toward Illinois, and into that black moment flamed a memory of the strong and kindly patriarch who had shielded his childhood. Squire Augur had sold his house in Omro and put the money into a peach-orchard in Egypt, Illinois. In that despairing hour Fremont decided to walk to his grandfather's new home.

"I set out at midnight on a two hundred mile walk," Older wrote of this. "The road leading south from the woodpile passed through a dense forest. Looking upward through the tree-tops I could see dimly into the sky, but the road ahead of me was solid black. It was like walking blindfolded, or with my eyes closed. I stumbled along cautiously, stubbing my toes on rocks or falling flat over short stumps of trees that had been felled to make the road. I walked for hours before there was any sign of daylight."

His feet were swollen and his eyes bloodshot when he came to a village. A country inn spread a wide, welcoming porch for wayfarers.

The boy had not eaten for days. He went into the dining-room and ordered ham and eggs and corn-pone and coffee. He wolfed the food, his rough head lowered warily over the table. When the waiter was in the kitchen, he caught up his trunk and scuttled through the door.

Miles down the road the innkeeper, driving a wagon and lashing his horses on with a whip, caught up with the panting boy. Fremont cowered in the dusty road under the threatening lash.

"Why did you do that low-down, sneaking trick?" the innkeeper wanted to know.

The boy shuddered with fear. Sickness went over his bony body in waves.

"I was hungry," he muttered.

The man cursed him, turned the wagon, and drove back through the dust. Fremont crept to the side of the road and yielded up the breakfast he had stolen. "It was my last attempt at banditry," Older commented in later years. Often he carried points of honesty to an almost absurd degree.

The boy trudged on. He swam rivers with his trunk balanced on his head. He slept in haymows. He ate parched corn from the fields along the road. The soles were worn from his shoes, and his feet left bloody marks in the dust. One day he walked forty-five miles.

Late one afternoon he hobbled up to a picket gate before a poor little farm in Illinois. Squire Augur stood by the fence, shielding his hawklike eyes against the setting sun. He was a broken but still magnificent giant.

"My grandfather was stricken dumb when he saw me at the gate," Older wrote of this meeting. "He shaded his eyes with his hands and stared at me. I was far from being an impressive figure, covered as I was from head to foot with the dirt and grime of my two hundred mile walk. My story of why I left my job and why I came to him certainly did not make a hit.

"He had long since settled in his own mind what my future was to be. I had written him when I began learning to be a printer and told him what my ambition was and why I chose the printer's trade. In my letters I had reminded him of his own glorification of Horace Greeley in the war days and how he had transmitted to my childish mind my impressions of that great man. I had also written him that after reading Greeley's life I had decided to follow in his footsteps.

"I don't imagine my grandfather placed much faith in those foolish dreams of mine, but he had, no doubt, assumed that I would at least become a self-supporting journeyman printer and never again be a burden to him.

"Now, suddenly, out a clear sky, appeared before him, not a prudent, plodding young printer on his way to becoming a self-respecting citizen, but a dirty, ragged tramp boy, limping back to him for food and shelter."

The Squire and Maria Augur loved their grandson. They had done their best for all their children. But they had been swindled into buying the wretched malaria-ridden farm with its twisted peach-trees laden with bitter fruit. They had barely food for themselves. They were old. He was young.

Almost at once Fremont knew he could not remain with his grandparents.

It was cold the morning he left Egypt. Maria Augur

brought out a blue Army cape overcoat her son Duane had worn when he came back from the war to die. It touched the ground, it was heavy and queer, but part of his grandmother's heart was in the gift, and Fremont could not refuse it.

Wearing her parting gift while hunting for work in lower Illinois called out all his forbearance and courage. There were many Southern sympathizers in that locality who cursed the solemn youngster in Union blue as a "Damned Yank."

"Up to that time I had never doubted for an instant that we of the North, who had fought the great fight to free the slaves, were the salt of the earth, especially directed by the Divine Power to save the world," commented Older. "For the first time in my young life it gradually dawned on me that there are usually two sides to every 'great cause.'"

But the situation oppressed him, and he made his way back to Wisconsin, back to the village of Omro. Aunt Mary Augur, Duane's widow, lived there and was kind, but her household was teeming. She supported her family by dressmaking, and again he felt himself an intruder. In her home Fremont encountered again the savage and unforgiving God of his fathers. In answer to her sharp question as to whether he believed in God, he recalled the religion of the Terry's and replied that he believed in a God of love and not of hatred.

"I'm taking you to prayer-meeting tonight," she said, her lips tightening.

That night the thermometer was below zero, but there was no fire in the frame church. Heat and comfort were impious. Fremont found himself shivering in the front pew under the disapproving eye of his Aunt Mary. Slowly it dawned upon him that the eyes of the entire congregation were likewise fixed upon him, all equally disapproving.

Even the minister, droning through an interminable sermon, did not take his eyes from the apprehensive boy.

At last the sermon ended. There was deep breathing in the icy room. Everyone was looking expectantly at Fremont.

"All those who desire to be prayed for, come forward!" shouted the minister suddenly, glaring at Fremont.

"I was terribly embarrassed," Older wrote of this. "My face must have been flaming red, but I obstinately stuck to my seat. My aunt pulled me by the arm, angrily. But I still refused to budge. Again I was prayed for, even though I didn't assent to it by rising.

"Then we filed solemnly out into the freezing night air. Snow was banked four or five feet high on each side of the entrance to the church. My aunt, rigid with rage, grabbed me by the shoulder and pushed me over into the snow bank, saying: 'Fremont, you will live to be hanged!'"

That ended life at Aunt Mary's. Before dawn the next morning, having shamed her beyond all forgiveness, Fremont left Omro. But when at noon he sat on a drift by the road and opened his little leather trunk, he found within a lunch and a Bible.

"I knew then she did not think me utterly damned," he said.

He was a woeful figure, his face bitten blue with cold, trudging through the drifts of a road he did not know. In his desperation he was going to his Aunt Nettie Bowen, his father's sister, who lived on a farm thirty miles from Omro. He was not sure of the way. But he followed a heavy sleigh down the glittering white road, and that day, carrying his trunk, he walked the thirty miles.

Late in the evening he came to a snow-covered farmhouse. A woman six feet tall, a true Older woman, came to the door. The dark fire of her eyes was dimmed by years of suffering, for she had felt the full horror of the war years. But the weary lad saw in her the image of his soldier father.

"I'm Fremont," he faltered, "Emory's son."

Nettie Bowen folded him into her gaunt arms.

There was hard work and poverty on the Bowen farm. Fremont took his place in the family of boys, working in the forest cutting down trees as had his father before him, sleeping at night in the attic on a pallet of straw with a blanket over his head to keep out the terrible cold.

On this farm they were shut away from other human life. Fremont recalled forgotten flashes of life on the Fox and St. Croix and Mississippi. The latent quality in him that was poetry remembered rivers where torches flared and romance had whispered to a lonely boy. He remembered dream cities and towns he had passed by night and longed to return and explore. He remembered Horace Greeley and the clangor of presses and his long-neglected dreams.

He could not be content with the long, hard days and dull evenings of the farm.

But the Bowens were kind. Fremont was loath to leave the family who had opened their home to him in his need. Then his Aunt Nettie asked him to kill a chicken.

The ax swung in his limp grasp over and past the living feathered head. His muscles, he said later, just wouldn't let him kill that chicken. His aunt rushed from the farmhouse, grabbed the bird, and killed it with one competent stroke.

"Fremont, you'll never amount to a hill of beans!" she snorted.

The boy who could not kill a chicken was to become the editor who hounded a man into the penitentiary; who would write of himself: "I was ruthless in my ambition. My one desire—to develop stories that would catch the attention of readers, no matter what was the character of the stories.

"They might make people suffer, might wound or utterly ruin someone; that made no difference to me."

His cousins teased Fremont Older about the chicken. Their crude jesting turned his thoughts against the farm. Homeless again, he wandered back to Appleton, on the Fox, the village nearest the farm where he was born.

Aunt Nettie Bowen grieved at his leaving, but it was plain that she felt no good could come of a boy who hadn't grit enough to let a little necessary blood.

In Appleton, while working on the *Post* at three dollars and a half a week, he heard that Joe Hall, who owned the *Free Press* at Oconto on Green Bay, wanted a printer at fifteen dollars a month. The boy hurried there. Sitting again on a stool, a stick in one hand and the other busied with types, he knew once more determination and ease of heart. Fremont had returned to his long-postponed career.

Oconto was in a political turmoil entirely out of proportion to its size. Joe Hall was an old-fashioned fighting editor. He insulted his political enemies in ripe printed adjectives. He was found guilty of libel and sentenced to thirty days in jail.

"You'll have to get out the paper while I'm in jail, Fremont," he informed his new printer.

The boy's heart stopped. For a moment he was Horace Greeley.

For an entire month Fremont Older gathered all the news of the town and set it directly in type. Every day he went into the jail for the sizzling editorials Hall continued to write. He attended to all the rest of the copy, including the advertisements, did all the mechanical work of typesetting, made up the paper, and got it out on an old-fashioned Washington hand press.

Older wrote of this thrilling experience:

"Here I was, temporarily, an editor at fifteen. It was a great opportunity for me, I thought. My work must have been very crude, but Hall liked it, and that was enough for me. The day my editor's time was up, his friends made up a procession, headed by a brass band, and marched to the jail.

"The released editor came out, took me by the arm, and led me to the head of the parade, directly behind the band, telling his followers that I had saved his paper. We paraded through the streets and disbanded at Hall's residence, where an open-air supper was served. I sat on my editor's right. It was the happiest moment of my life."

The triumph left Fremont restless. He would again be an editor, he told himself. But in Oconto that time would be far-off indeed. He wanted wider fields. He could not bear waiting. He saved a little money and wandered on, through Milwaukee, to Chicago.

Chicago terrified the country boy. The great fire had swept the city only a year before, and the miles of broken walls under dingy snow filled him with a quaking sense of desolation. He worked for several weeks in the *Times* composing-room, but as he set type, his hands trembled. He had to go on.

He was hunting something through these restless, roving 'teens. What it was he did not know. But every week he wrote a long letter to his mother. His grandfather and grandmother had sold the sad little farm in Egypt and joined their daughter in California. Fremont dreamed constantly of making his way to them.

But the spaces between the Western cities intimidated him. He did not dare set out.

On a freezing winter day early in 1873 Fremont Older was the lanky young porter of a small hotel in Aurora, near Chicago. He carried baggage. He milked the cows. He was completely discouraged.

SQUIRE LEWIS AUGUR

CELIA AUGUR OLDER

A letter came from his mother in California. It contained a postal order for $125 from Squire Augur—Fremont's fare west.

Within an hour he had cashed the order and was riding to Chicago. All he had ever read of the West was rushing before his dazzled eyes. Greeley and Twain and Fremont the Pathfinder for whom he was named were part in his mind of the glamorous West. He was following them at last—his heroes.

He bought first in Chicago, fortunately, his ticket to Sacramento, and then such needful things as underwear and shirts and collars.

"Of course, I told the clothing salesman that I was equipping myself for an overland trip to California," he wrote of this imprudent shopping-trip. "It was an easy matter for him to flatter me into buying an overcoat. I would need it crossing the Rocky Mountains.

"It was the first overcoat I had ever owned. I put on my new clothes and overcoat in the shop where I had bought them, and walked proudly out into the street with my railroad ticket and ten dollars in my pocket. After paying my hotel bill I had six dollars left for food."

He bought a market basket and filled it with food. It would not last half the long journey across the continent.

At ten thirty on the evening of January 9, 1873, a tall and rangy sixteen-year-old country boy in a new overcoat, carrying a worn leather trunk and a large basket of eatables, climbed aboard the westbound train at Chicago.

It mattered nothing at all to Fremont Older that he would go hungry on part of his journey, or that his growing body was too large for the seat he shared with a stranger and he would have to sleep doubled up.

He pressed his high forehead to the window and watched the gas-lights of Chicago trickling past the slow-moving train. The railroad to the distant West had been completed less than four years before, its "last spike" driven in Utah in '69.

All his life Fremont Older had dreamed of California. Eastward, even into his lonely Wisconsin forests, its fame had trickled in a golden stream. The boy staring into the passing dark saw in vision long caravans of canvas-topped wagons winding over salt deserts. He saw Indians ahorseback, swarming by thousands, with blood-lust distorting their painted faces. He saw the great migration of '49, the gold-maddened hordes pouring into the mysterious West. He felt himself one of these adventurers, one with the Argonauts.

What did hunger matter? Or lack of sleep?

He would see his mother again. He would see California.

## Chapter IV

TRAMP PRINTER

HE WALKED up Market Street in San Francisco, bearing the worn trunk he had carried so many hundreds of miles through dust and snow and blazing sun. His eagerness was so intense that people turned to stare at the gangling youth.

The mark of the country was raw on his exterior. From the arms of the overcoat he did not need, for it was springtime in 1873, his long wrists dangled. Later Fremont Older would have coats and shirts made in Paris and London with sleeves extra long to fit his woodsman's frame.

As he walked toward the What Cheer House, his dark head turned with hawklike interest from side to side. He observed every race, every stratum of human life flowing through San Francisco's streets that warm evening. The richness, the crassness, the dignity of this strange and wonderful city were all he had imagined. In the famous What Cheer, after a ten-cent meal which included a mighty steak, he felt himself at last at home.

For several reasons the day had been momentous for young Older.

He left Sacramento because there was little printing work to be had there, he must repay his grandfather the money advanced for his passage west, and beyond all he longed to see San Francisco. He had worked a few days in the composing-room of the Sacramento *Union*, and that, his first Western newspaper, was, oddly enough, a crusading sheet famous throughout the United States for its fight against the railroad. The *Union* would die in the struggle, but years later Older would carry on its brave crusade.

Since 1850 the *Union* had formed public opinion for the West. It was incorruptible and universally trusted, "more valuable to California than an army corps." During the Civil War its editorials were copied from coast to coast. General John F. Sheehan wrote of its passing: "The railroad, while creating a transportation monopoly, destroyed a newspaper monopoly."

There had been two steamers at the wharf the morning Fremont Older left Sacramento. One, railroad-owned, was claiming the river monopoly. The other, owned by a man named Whipple, was fighting that monopoly and bore the banner "Friend of the People." Few people were aboard it, for the other boat, being richer, had cut its rate from a dollar to twenty-five cents.

"Here is where I first cast my lot with the minority," Older wrote of this. "I had very little money, but I admired Whipple's public spirit and paid my dollar and walked proudly aboard. Whipple's opposition didn't last long. The people wouldn't patronize him at a higher price, and he retired to private life with a very low opinion of the human race."

Early the next morning Fremont Older applied for work at the *Morning Call*. By noontime he was setting type in its dark and dirty composing-room.

Half a century later Older became its editor-in-chief.

"Somehow, through all the years that were to follow, I was drawn, as if by some invisible influence, back to the *Call*," he was to write in the editorialized version of his life in its pages.

Mark Twain, his latest hero, had worked on the *Call* as a green reporter a few years before. Climbing the ancient rickety stairs to the *Call* office, Older thought daily, "Twain climbed these—when he was unknown!"

Like Twain, the boy explored San Francisco. He even cultivated the friendship of a bartender who had mixed a certain punch for America's greatest humorist.

"All my idle time I spent in roaming around the streets of San Francisco," wrote Older. "I could see that the city was rapidly losing the flavor of its romantic past. A new generation had grown up, and the young people were not especially interested in the '49 stories told by their fathers."

Though only a boy, he was passionately interested in the stories and characters left over from San Francisco's early days. In '48, at the time of the gold discovery in California, San Francisco had been an adobe *pueblo,* founded in 1776 on the Spanish frontier. John Charles Fremont had first claimed California for the United States. American California was less than three decades old. The city was rich in newly minted legend which interested few of the Californians.

But these impressions were absorbed and stored away by the eager mind of Fremont Older until he himself became a bridge between the old California and the new.

He saw, on Montgomery Street, Pio Pico, who had once been the proud Governor of a proud Mexican California. He followed a strange, shuffling character that was the once-brilliant Ned McGowan, nearly lynched by the Vigilantes who took the place of law in the wild new gold city. He visited the grave of Casey, hanged by that dread committee and buried beside the crumbling adobe ruin that was Mission Dolores, founded when California had belonged to Spain. He lifted glasses with a broken old man, Sam Brannan, once the richest man in California, who had published in 1847 the first San Francisco newspaper, the *California Star.*

Out of his scant salary Fremont purchased drinks for that amazing madman Emperor Norton, who believed himself to be Emperor of Mexico and Protector of the United

States and who solemnly accepted the mock fealty of jest-loving San Francisco. Side by side the lanky, burning-eyed young printer and the dignified lunatic in shabby uniform and cockaded hat proceeded the length of the Montgomery Street bars heaped with world-famous free lunches. In grateful moments the Emperor often pressed upon his young friend a "million-dollar bond" with his imperial signature affixed.

Fremont Older was devouring San Francisco with an enthusiasm which would endure his entire lifetime, and in the meantime he was reading every book of Mark Twain he could borrow or buy, until *Roughing It* inflamed him beyond all denial and he knew that he must see the mines.

He left the *Call* press-room to follow the trail of Mark Twain to Virginia City.

Snow lay two feet deep on the silver city's hills when Fremont Older climbed their steeps to the amazingly garish International Hotel. A room there was thirteen dollars a week, but he knew that money was plentiful on the Comstock Lode. He found work immediately on the *Territorial Enterprise,* where Mark Twain had worked and first won his writing spurs under the editor Joseph T. Goodman.

He longed to know Joe Goodman. Years later when he did know that splendid editor, he realized that Goodman would have been his friend even then. At the time Fremont felt himself to be but a poor printer and the jovial editor far above him. But he haunted the saloons where Dan de Quille (William Wright) and Steve Gillis of the staff found their literary material and asked them endless questions about his hero Twain.

These, with Goodman, had been Twain's cronies, the founders of that Nevada writing group known as "the Sage-Brush School." Twain had first discovered he could write on the *Enterprise,* then rated one of the best newspapers in the West.

In Virginia City Fremont Older was still a boy alone, looking wistfully and from a distance upon the sort of men he wanted to know. He did not admire the suave and slippery-fingered gamblers, nor the gunmen, nor even the Comstock kings who swaggered behind fast horses and spent thousands in gambling and bought champagne by the truckload. He would never envy men who made money —only the men who could write, who could put their fellow human beings into a more permanent form than flesh itself, upon the printed page.

The boy found himself among jostling miners in the gambling hells. Next to the hotel was the El Dorado, like a palace to the dazzled lad. Shyly one afternoon he stood watching a game of faro, called in Virginia City "bucking the tiger."

"Suddenly I was seized with a desire to bet," Older wrote years after. "I put a dollar on the seven spot. I won on the first turn of the card. I went on playing and winning, rarely losing a bet.

"In a couple of hours I 'cashed in my checks' and the 'dealer' flipped me two twenty-dollar gold pieces. Here was an easy road to fortune! All my financial troubles were over. No more monotonous toil. I went happily to bed with my forty dollars.

"After a sleepless night, and without breakfast, I set out for the El Dorado with the two twenty-dollar gold pieces clutched in my feverish hand. The gambling madness had taken complete possession of my mind. Again I began to win, and at three o'clock in the afternoon the forty dollars had grown to one hundred and sixty dollars, a small fortune. I was warned by some of the players to stop before my luck changed. But, of course, I paid no attention to the warning, and at nine o'clock that evening I was flat broke."

Barring games of poker, Fremont Older never gambled again.

He was ashamed to return to the *Enterprise* office. The next morning he left Virginia City on foot, carrying his small trunk down the steep and seemingly bottomless Geiger Grade. After a while his foot hurt. He took off his shoe and found wedged against the sole a fifty-cent piece. He sat on a granite boulder and regarded it bitterly. It was all he had to show after months of work on the Comstock Lode.

He trudged through Carson, Reno, Bodie, and at the gold camp Sonora worked on the old *Herald* long enough to earn stage-fare back to San Francisco. It was now his chosen city, although it had no place for him as yet in its throbbing, excitable heart.

There, in a cheap boarding-house, he faced himself sullenly.

"My first year and a half in California seemed to me utterly wasted," he said. "I was nearly eighteen, and when I recalled where Horace Greeley was at that time, I became discouraged. There was nothing for me to do but to go on hunting jobs."

Then Older heard of an opening in Santa Barbara, a small town down the coast, and forgot his self-criticism. He left San Francisco on the famous old side-wheel steamer *Orizaba*, which in earlier days had carried the world-famous dancer Lola Montez from triumphs among the gold-hunters to her tragic death in the East.

Santa Barbara appeared to him first, and would remain to him always, an imperishable dream. A Mexican village with long gray mission sleeping against the hills, it held the song and ecstasy of the lost California. The young printer lived in an adobe hotel; he danced on Saturday nights at the Mexican fandangos with dark-eyed senoritas of secretive, generous glances; he learned to grin back, cheeks flaming with excitement, at swarthy caballeros glowering against adobe walls. There was danger in the adobe streets where guitars whimpered until the mission bells rang of Sunday dawn.

When he came back to San Francisco, he was nineteen years old, he was broad-shouldered and well-featured and six feet two, he was no longer a boy but a man.

Times were bad in San Francisco, those years of the mid-seventies.

Fremont Older stood impatiently before the job printing-shop on Clay Street where the idle printers waited for someone to offer them work. He felt like a slave waiting to go on the auction-block. Often he found only one day's work a week. Often he tightened his belt and went hungry. And many a night he walked the sidewalks of San Francisco, out Market Street and around the sand-lots, because he had no place to sleep.

Sometimes another jobless printer joined him, and the fog bit through their thin clothing as they walked.

After one midnight their feet lagged.

"Let's go to Portsmouth Square and sleep on a bench," suggested his companion.

"I will not!"

"Why not?"

"Because," said Older, "I've seen the men who sit on benches in the park. They've given up. I'll sit on the curb with you. I'll walk with you. But I won't sleep on a park bench.

When he spoke like that, his mouth was thin and grim as a sabre cut. His face had lost all its boyishness.

His thoughts as he walked the streets were restless and tormented. He was, he had to admit, a tramp printer. Like so many others he had met, from Wisconsin to Santa Barbara. Wandering, working, shifting, drinking, disappearing at last from the press-rooms.

Well, Fremont Older would not disappear, he told himself, his mouth that grim line. He was hunting a place to fit his questing feet. If he had dallied and adventured and grown curious along the way, it meant only time lost, not purpose.

He never once lost purpose. He still intended to be like Horace Greeley.

That confidence attracted Davison Dalziel, an adventurous young Australian who was later to become a great figure in Europe, when, in 1876, he decided to start a newspaper in San Francisco. Walking down Clay Street hunting a printer who would be capable and strong and enthusiastic, he recognized a fellow-adventurer. He pointed to the lanky young giant Older and grinned as he said, "I've a job for you."

Then there came into existence the maddest and merriest paper that ever sidled off a press, the *Daily Mail,* and Older first met men of the sort the gods of journalism intended him to be.

Because Dalziel was a young and glorified adventurer, he made Fremont Older, aged nineteen, foreman over thirty printers. As foreman, Older was on intimate terms with the newspaper men Dalziel chose, not for accurate reporting, but for brilliancy. They were the Bohemia of a young and excitable San Francisco, the first of a lusty race who were putting on record the West.

Not before nor since has a publisher gathered together such an epic crew.

For his newspaper Dalziel rented an immense suite of rooms near the water-front. They had been lavishly furnished by William C. Ralston, who built the world-famous Palace Hotel, for entertaining visiting notables. Later the rooms had passed to other hands and less moral uses.

Into these rooms Dalziel moved his newspaper paraphernalia. The presses of the *Mail* rested on rose-bedecked carpetings. The absorbed printers were reflected in imported French mirrors. The reporters used the drawing-room for their local room, tossed their hats on immodest marble statutes, and wrote their ornate tales on French tables no less ornate.

Not truth, but interest, was demanded by Dalziel for the *Mail*.

The brilliant reporter Arthur McEwen set the pace for the mad and merry paper with the lead story for the opening edition. Older told of it later in his autobiography.

"It assumed to be an accurate recital of an actual happening," related Older. "A young man, name fictitious, desperately disappointed in love, decided to kill himself.

"Providing himself with a rope, a pistol and bottle of poison, he went out to a cliff overlooking the Golden Gate, tied one end of the rope to a big boulder and fastened the other end around his neck. Then he stepped over to the edge of the cliff and swallowed the poison. As he jumped, in order to make his death certain, he fired the pistol at his head.

"The bullet missed the mark, but cut the rope. He dropped into the sea. The salt water acted as an emetic and his stomach rejected the poison. He swam ashore unhurt, but with the will to live reasserting itself."

The story, said Older, startled the city. The editors of the other newspapers, the *Morning Call*, the *Chronicle*, the *Morning Examiner*, the *Evening Bulletin*, the *Post*, the *Report*, and the *Alta California*, threatened to fire their "scooped" police reporters until they learned that the yarn was a hoax. It established precedent for the *Mail*, which for the rest of its short life was to contain very little truth but a great deal of drama.

The days on the *Mail* were the most interesting the young foreman had ever known. McEwen, lounging into the composing-room with his neat pages of handwritten copy, was amused by the eagerness of the tall, awkward young country fellow with the long arms and burning gaze.

McEwen also was over six feet tall, a sandy Scot with a whip-lash tongue. He later became William Randolph Hearst's leading editorial writer.

The two young men were not unlike. There was about one a blazing Yankee sincerity. And to the other belonged that untamable quality born of long generations of Highlanders. Their friendship became the deepest Fremont Older was ever to know.

After the *Mail* went to press, McEwen and Older joined the other newspaper men in the near-by mirrored saloons where congregated, in the seventies, the light-hearted knights of the Press. Older was accepted as one of them. They called him "Free." They opened to him new channels of thought.

Some of the new ideas he absorbed puzzled the young man reared under the thumb of Maria Augur's vengeful God.

There were nights when, with McEwen, he watched dawn creeping down the clammy darkness of the waterfront. Once, homeless, he had slept unsheltered on that water-front. Now, safe in the intellectual and financial security of the *Mail*, Older could tramp it like a conqueror.

Once, on the Embarcadero, they met a bundle of human flotsam, filthy and unglamorously drunk. McEwen, arguing a point in philosophy, tossed the man a half-dollar.

"Don't do that!" protested Older. "Can't you see the man's unworthy?"

McEwen teetered on the edge of the wooden sidewalk. His sharp eyes twinkled maliciously.

"To be poor and worthy is bad enough," he observed. "But to be poor and unworthy, Free, that's hell!"

Older absorbed that precept. Half a century later he would wave away charity solicitors with the comment, "I'll let you handle the deserving cases. My hands are busy with the undeserving."

McEwen was a sardonic iconoclast. Once he met in a Turkish bath a judge he was opposing politically.

"Ah, at last we meet on equal terms," he chortled to the reddening jurist. "Stark naked—as God made us."

Older had kept his resolve not to become too good a printer. But he did not confide even to McEwen his dream of becoming an editor. What right had he to such aspirations, a man with but three years of schooling, who was reading Sir Walter Scott for the first time? But he was secretly determined to make his way from the composing-room to the local room, and he knew that if the *Mail* survived, his chance would come.

In the meantime he was reading with the insatiable greed of a man deprived of a longed-for education. He had discovered the novelist Charles Dickens. He would read Dickens to his last hour with never-diminishing enjoyment. He knew every character. He could finish every line. He met and recognized with chuckling amusement Dickens' characters in his everyday life.

He read Thackeray, the lives of William the Silent and Napoleon, and many histories.

In August, just before Fremont Older's twentieth birthday, one of San Francisco's rare sultry days dropped over the city like a warm blanket. Citizens nourished on wind and fog collapsed under the unusual heat.

Nemesis, in the person of one of the gayer reporters on the *Mail* staff, pranced into the brightly carpeted local room. He carried a three-gallon bucket, ice, four quarts of claret, a dozen lemons, a pound of sugar, and a tin dipper.

"Nothing like punch on a hot day!" he chirped.

He set the bucket on an ink-stained marquetry table. The staff gathered about, helping to squeeze and stir and taste.

Someone observed that it needed brandy. The "devil" was hurried downstairs for three quarts of Martell. This was being solemnly stirred in and sampled when the magnificent Dalziel strolled in, adjusting his monocle.

He brightened, beholding the punch.

"A little champagne—" he murmured, sipping at the tin dipper.

He sent the "devil" back for three quarts of champagne. This was added to the punch, and the bucket, as Older later described it, was brimming with dynamite.

"Not a line of copy was written that afternoon nor in the evening," said Older. "One by one they succumbed to the influence of the punch and eventually passed out. At dusk the staff was strewn around the local room like poisoned flies—dead to the world."

Older realized that the future of the *Mail* rested with him, as head of the composing-room. He shook a snoring reporter into semiconsciousness. The staggering newsman groped blindly for a scissors and slashed columns of news out of a heap of papers he found on the exchange desk.

"There was nothing for me to do but put them in type and publish them," wrote Older. "Ordinarily the printers would have edited them, but the composing-room was not entirely free from the influence of the tin bucket. Not a line of local news appeared in the *Mail* next morning.

"I think that hot day and that bucket of punch finished the *Mail*."

The paper perished shortly after. No one had been paid. The brilliant staff scattered. Dalziel carried his strange genius to another continent, where he became a great financier, garnered more than a hundred million dollars, and was knighted by the King of England.

McEwen left temporarily for the East and better journalistic prospects. Fremont Older was on the sidewalks again —his world collapsed.

To join once more that dreary throng of jobless printers

in Clay Street seemed unbearable to the young man who had been foreman on a brilliant, if short-lived, paper.

"Life seemed to have failed me," Older wrote of this unhappy period. "I had passed twenty and none of my dreams had come true. I had wanted to be an editor, and my sudden rise at nineteen to the position of foreman over thirty men, and my intimate contact with those brilliant writers on the *Daily Mail,* gave me hope. The crash of the paper left me utterly discouraged and with a longing to go far away from the city, back to the land where I had begun life."

Older did what he would always do in bitterness. He turned to the hills.

His stepfather's brother owned a ranch in Mendocino County in northern California. He had told of rich forestland to be had for the taking. Like an inspiration it came to Fremont Older that he would be a pioneer, as his forefathers had been on the dangerous frontiers of the East.

Horseback he rode into the redwood forests. He preempted one hundred and sixty acres, dark and beautiful with virgin timber, in Sherwood Valley. In a space by a fern-rimmed stream he built his cabin.

He split boards and shingles from a fallen redwood for walls and roof. He stripped redwood branches of their soft tips and built his mattress high from the earth floor. He built a stove of stones and mud, he raised vegetables before his door, he worked in a lumber-mill when he needed money, and felt, he said, like a king.

Peace soaked into him; restlessness died. At night, watching the pines tossing between the stars and his paneless window he knew he was supremely happy.

By December of 1878 the Indians of Sherwood Valley were starving over their fires. And Fremont Older, who had turned his back on the world, found that he too was starving. Not for food—there was plenty of that in his snug cabin. There was another and as deep a hunger, born of the newspapers and magazines his mother sent from Sacramento.

Life called him to return. He had finished his preëmption time. He owned one hundred and sixty acres of California.

He forgot the hardships and disappointments he had endured in San Francisco. He remembered men like Arthur McEwen, the sort of man he wanted to be like. He stopped remembering himself as a printer. He wanted to be an editor. He wanted first to become a reporter. That way led to the top.

In his sorriest moments he had not forgotten the peaks.

He said farewell to his friends the Indians, crouching around their fires.

"They were facing months of famine with no more apparent realization of it than their neighbors, the birds, the squirrels, and the jackrabbits," he wrote of this parting.

"In contrast here was I, my preëmption time finished and the owner of a hundred and sixty acres of land, setting out for the city to renew the old struggle with its worries and failures."

With fresh awareness on his stern young face he was back in San Francisco early in 1879. He was again eager and determined.

His clothing was outdated and worn. Printing work was harder to get than before. Within a week he was forced to sell his claim to a land speculator. For his hundred and sixty acres of redwood forest he received one hundred dollars.

At the end of the week Older owned an overcoat and two new suits, shoes and underwear and half a dozen good shirts. He had indulged in several memorable meals and theaters. And he had not a dime left.

# TRAMP PRINTER 63

He was back on the sidewalk again with the hungry printers, in his fine new clothes, drearily waiting for someone to give him a job.

That experience terrified Older.

"I'm twenty-three," he told himself harshly. "I'm a wastrel. I'm a tramp printer going nowhere."

He swore that the next time he found work he would save.

On the heels of his resolution came a job as type-setter for a printing firm. He made twenty-two dollars the first week. He hurried to a Market Street bank and opened an account with eight dollars.

Many times a day he paused at the case to open the little black book.

"Next week I'll deposit ten," he promised himself.

Instead, he turned twelve dollars over to the bank on pay-day. Now saving was his entire career. He moved to a cheap dark room. He was shaved twice a week. He ate doughnuts and coffee twice a day.

He thought constantly, "Soon I'll have a thousand dollars!"

Next to him worked a miser printer who rumor said had a thousand dollars in the bank. Older happened to glance at him one day, noted his broken shoes and ragged coat, and thought suddenly, "God, I'm going to look just like him!"

He dashed out of the printery to the bank.

"I had already discovered that I could do nothing reasonably and temperately," Older explained later. "I was sure to overdo whatever I became interested in. So I broke my resolution as suddenly as I made it. I had one hundred and sixty dollars in the bank. I put a man in my place and took a vacation.

"I drew out my entire savings, bought two new suits of clothes, shirts, scarfs, in fact everything necessary to make a good appearance. I got a shave and a hair-cut, a French dinner, and a dress-circle seat in the old California Theater.

"That resolution made so many years ago has remained *broken*. Since that time I have never tried to accumulate money. Often I have shuddered at the life I escaped, limited and smothered by petty economies."

Older would never regret not saving, nor suffer thereby. All the rest of his life he lived richly and easily and without counting the cost. He was never burdened by the niggling economies that oppress most men.

A few days later, as penniless as the day he left his grandfather's farm, Fremont Older was on his way to join the idle printers. His feet dragged reluctantly up Market Street.

When he left Market Street for the printer's hang-out, he had invariably turned into Clay Street. But this morning, without reason, the long-legged young printer turned into Sacramento Street.

As he turned this unaccustomed corner, his life turned at last in the direction he had wished it to go.

## Chapter V

### THE REPORTER

WHEN Fremont Older turned that corner, he was twenty-three. He would never again go hungry or walk the sidewalks with no place to sleep. That autumn morning he met the beginning of a future which would be tremendously lived.

"I have always felt that the entire course of my life was changed by that turn into Sacramento Street without any reason or object known to me," he wrote in the story of his early struggles. "I had never done it before.

"When I reached Leidesdorff Street, I saw a well-dressed, handsome man standing on the corner, intently looking about him. He acosted me:

" 'Perhaps you can tell me where the idle printers congregate.' And then, giving me a sharp look, he added:

" 'Perhaps you are a printer out of work?'

"This man was R. G. Rowley, an attorney from Redwood City, San Mateo County. When I told him I wanted work, he said:

" 'I am about to start a weekly newspaper in Redwood City and I am looking for a good all-around printer who can run a cylinder press. I can only pay $12 a week at the start, but if the paper succeeds, I'll pay more.'

"For some time I had been earning nearly twice as much, but I accepted his offer instantly, with no more understanding of why than I had when I turned into Sacramento instead of Clay Street. Was it fate?

"In later years I connected this incident with my boyish

ambition to become an editor, and I still believe by that thoughtless turning of a corner my life was turned in the direction I wanted it to go. I was never again compelled to hunt for a job."

Rowley was a belligerent attorney of Revolutionary stock. He was founding the *Weekly Journal* to fight the bosses of Redwood City and their speaking-trumpet, the *Times-Gazette*.

There was room in that town of fifteen hundred souls for two papers. But the rivalry between them mounted at once from political wrangling to personal insult. Their front pages boiled. Rowley spent all his time thinking up insulting editorials and left the rest of the paper to his printer.

This gave opportunity to Older. He was always eager to take on extra work. He planted himself firmly in the life of the pretty suburban town. He skated at the whitewashed rink, drank beer at the saloons, visited quiet country homes at evening, was called "Free" by everyone from the police chief down, and presently knew all the happenings of Redwood City.

These events he set up in type without first writing them down.

Rowley was delighted. But when his twelve-dollar-a-week printer made a few corrections in his own articles, he was furious.

"I thought I was improving them," apologized Older.

He knew, by Rowley's silence, that he had been right. With three years of schooling, with little knowledge of grammar and only a printer's knowledge of punctuation, Older had improved the writings of a man with a classical university education.

It was the sight and sound of words he knew. He sensed without formal learning whether a sentence was right or wrong.

Rowley had started an earlier newspaper and wearied of

fighting the bosses. Soon the bosses learned he was tiring of the *Journal*. They dared not approach Rowley. But they sent, according to Older, a spy named Ward to the innocent Older.

"I'm a newspaper man looking for a paper," he said.

Older did not know Ward was lying. Ward suggested they offer to buy the *Journal*.

Older rushed off to Rowley. He was jubilant when Rowley agreed to sell them the *Journal* for six hundred dollars, nothing down, payments to begin in six months.

As Older set up the front page of the next week's *Journal*, his long hands hovered over the type. It stood in print, at last, his own name: "Ward and Older—Editors and Proprietors."

He mailed the blurry first edition to his mother in Sacramento.

Horace Greeley had served well as an ideal. Fremont Older was at last part owner of a newspaper.

Early the next morning he went feverishly from store to store, asking support from the merchants. Nearly every advertiser in the town promised to use the *Journal*. The future of his little paper seemed assured.

When he returned to the *Journal* office, Ward was not there. That worried Older. But he had to trust his partner. He could not afford to doubt.

The paper went to press and was sold in the streets. He walked about the town with the newsboys, anxious as if his life depended on the number of papers sold. That night he returned to his home with his head aswirl with plans.

He woke from a sound sleep. Ward had somehow found his way into his bedroom. He was leaning over the bed.

"I've been to the bosses, Older," he whispered. "They say if we'll let the *Journal* die, they'll pay us each a thousand dollars."

In that blinding moment Older knew he had been betrayed. Worse, he had betrayed Rowley. He had Rowley's name on a contract. If they let the *Journal* perish, Rowley could not stop them.

"I'll not do it!" he cried, struggling up. "It's dishonorable!"

The *Journal* was his. He could not let it die.

Ward furiously demanded the bill of sale. Older heard himself saying that Ward could kill him before he would give it up, and then in the darkness he was fighting Ward with an animal fury he had not known since he was a little boy in Appleton and the children had laughed at his cut-down clothing.

But even while his fists flailed, he sickened. Ward was but a tool. Hatred Older could feel, but not blood-lust. When he had Ward down, he struck no more, only carried the spy to the door and tossed him out into the night. Older never saw him again.

It was humiliating to go to Rowley the next morning and reveal how he had been trapped. It was heartening to hear Rowley's indignation and feel the clap of a friendly hand on his shoulder.

"We'll lick 'em together, my lad," boomed the belligerent attorney. "After this it will be 'Rowley and Older, Owners.'"

So their names stood together the next week when the paper went to press. And Older's wages were raised to eighteen dollars a week.

But Rowley was tired of the hopeless battle. He went back to law practice. He sold the *Journal* to the very bosses he had created it to fight, on the condition that they give Fremont Older a place on their *Times-Gazette*.

Older went to work for the bosses.

"I was not yet an editor," he commented, "but the road I had so longed to travel was opening at last."

It was during this time, while Older was still in his early

twenties, that he contracted a youthful marriage with a Miss Emma Finger of Redwood City. It appeared to be soon regarded by both as a mistake, and they separated and later were divorced. Political enemies would spread dark and unfounded stories regarding this closed chapter in Fremont Older's life, but he suffered such attacks, as he did all attacks, in silence. Divorce was rare in the seventies and eighties, and professional scandalmongers made the worst of it. Older himself never referred to this episode, and few in later years knew that it had taken place.

Older as business manager of the *Times-Gazette* received eighteen dollars a week. He attended to advertising, watched circulation, and drove around the hilly countryside collecting subscriptions. But much of his time was spent in the office.

The editor was given to long absences. At such times Older collected news stories and set them directly in type. He never resented doing another man's job as well as his own.

Once when the editor was missing, W. H. Lawrence, one of the owners of the paper, dropped into the press-room. Older was setting up a story.

"He was much disturbed over his editor's neglect of the paper and asked me what had become of him," related Older. "I told him he was visiting a friend in Oakland."

Lawrence answered testily that he thought the editor had better remain in Oakland. Then, looking fixedly at Older, he demanded sharply, "Whom would you suggest for his place?"

Older said later that a lump rose in his throat which nearly choked him. He managed to bring out the remark that he had been writing the paper while the editor was away.

"Why not give me a chance?" he gulped.

"That is just what I wanted you to say," answered

Lawrence with a broad smile. "You are now the editor and manager at a hundred and twenty-five dollars a month."

Older's first big local story was the drowning of Sheriff Green. One Sunday morning Green was giving his wife and two small children a boat-ride on the creek near the town, and he took along a prisoner named Jim who happened to be spending ninety days in the jail at Redwood City for stealing a clock.

The boat capsized. The Sheriff and Jim managed to put Mrs. Green and the two children on the bottom of the upturned boat, struggling to keep them there as they slid off again and again. Sheriff Green became exhausted, sank into the water, and drowned.

"Here was Jim's chance," was Older's version of the tragedy. "The shore was only thirty feet away. A few strokes and he would be safe. But it never occurred to him to save his own life. He went right on placing the woman and children back on the bottom of the boat, until finally they remained. Then Jim went down and joined the Sheriff.

"Sheriff Green's funeral was the largest ever known in San Mateo County. It seemed as if every inhabitant was in the procession. It was two or three miles long.

"While it was passing I thought of Jim over in the morgue. It suddenly dawned on me that he was the real hero. Not Green, who died trying to save his wife and children. He couldn't do otherwise. Jim had nothing to lose and everything to gain by swimming ashore and saving his own life. But evidently it never entered his head. He gave his life that others might live.

"I drifted over to the morgue where I thought the real story was. Jim was lying on a board, white and silent. Not a soul in the place.

"I made him the feature of my story, and by so doing angered the widow and half the people of the town.

"To the potter's field with Jim. He was only a common thief."

Older the journalist had at last come into his birthright. But the young man who a year before had been a jobless printer was not content. There were larger vistas beyond this charming suburban town. Again he looked to San Francisco.

He felt he was ready at last to take his place among the sort of men he had known on the *Mail*.

He began sending small items of local news to the city papers. He received small sums in return. Then the San Francisco *Call* offered a ten-dollar prize for the best story of each county bordering on San Francisco Bay. After a great deal of thought Older composed an essay, "Suburban San Mateo."

He won the prize.

"I have had many great moments in my life," Older wrote of this triumph. "As I write these lines my mind runs over them all, and I now decide that finding my article, just as I had written it, in the city paper with my own headlines and my name at the top, was the one greatest moment.

"I took the paper to my room and read it over and over. I laid it aside and tried to forget it. Then I would pick it up and pretend I had just discovered it, hoping to again enjoy the big thrill. But it did not come, nor has it ever come during the many years that followed.

"No doubt there is a supreme moment for all of us that only occurs once in a lifetime."

He was now even more determined to attain the city. He became the San Mateo County correspondent for the *Chronicle,* and later for the *Alta.* When a big story broke in the county, he struggled to scoop the "big-town" reporters that came down from San Francisco. His persistent quality as a news-getter attracted the attention of the city editor of the *Alta,* and word was passed to Older that, if he liked, the country correspondent might try his hand in the *Alta* local room.

This was in the summer of 1884. Older was off overnight to San Francisco.

"Try getting a start first on a small-town newspaper," he would advise would-be reporters who came to him in later years. "Don't attempt to break in first on a large daily. You get a closer and more intimate touch with life in a small town."

Older stepped from a quiet country town into a world he had never known existed, not even in his days as a tramp printer. On his first night on the paper he was assigned to the police beat to be "broken in."

Later he would grow familiar with a world of steel cages filled with drunken women and men, with "stiffs" lying on marble slabs in the grotesque postures of sudden death, with jailers who held power of life or death in the filthy ancient prison under the old City Hall. But that first night, he said later, was one of horror. He wrote of it:

"Suddenly I faced my first story.

"It was about a gun fight in a Barbary Coast dive. One of the 'duelists' had been shot through the leg and was brought into the hospital for treatment. All the reporters gathered around him to get the story, but he was in too much pain to talk. He could only yell, 'For God's sake, give me something! Give me something!'

"He was evidently a morphine addict and wanted a shot of the drug to deaden the pain. Prison Keeper Lindheimer's answer to his appeal was, 'What the hell do you want? Ham and eggs?'

"There was general laughter at this bit of heartless humor. The wounded man was given nothing. A surgeon dug out the bullet, bound up his wound, and he was packed off by 'trusties' and put to bed.

"I felt that my entire future was at stake in this first police story, as the city editor would be sure to judge me by it. Nervous and excited as I was by the ghastly surroundings, I pulled myself together and wrote what I thought was an interesting story, quoting Lindheimer's remark about the ham and eggs."

Fremont Older had forgotten—he would not remember for many years—how wildly he had wept when another boy killed a forest squirrel that had trusted its life to them. He had forgotten the passionate hatred of injustice that had swept him when his grandfather preached against slavery at the Lincoln rally in the clearing.

But these emotions were part of him as, in the dingy hole that served as reporters' room in the City Hall, he wrote of the outcast writhing under the probe and the heartless laughter. The scene, not the actual shooting, was news to his country-bred mind.

The next day the city editor said to Older, "You're all right."

That story was read in the local room of the *Morning Call* by one John Pratt, a city editor with a nose for genius. He was a little soft-voiced Englishman who had known Dickens. He sent word down the police beat to the new reporter. The next Monday Fremont Older was working for Pratt, one of the most remarkable newspaper men, Older often declared, of his day.

There were six dailies in San Francisco. The *Call* was one of the leading money-makers. Older had worked on it first as a printer, now as a reporter, and he would return to it as editor. In the *Call* he had found the right newspaper, as in Pratt he found the right editor.

Older knew nothing of writing. Pratt took a kindly interest in the green reporter and criticized and advised.

"Never say a woman is beautiful," he would comment in his soft voice, pencil poised over Older's copy. "Describe her, and then let the reader judge if she's beautiful." And again, "Don't sit around waiting for an editor to think up ideas for you. He has enough work of his own. Think up your own assignments."

Older acted on that advice. Never again did he loaf around the local room waiting for a big story to be dropped in his lap. He was out ranging the city, and he managed to be wherever anything happened. He talked with everyone he met. He was eager, enthusiastic, interested. He grew a mustache. He began wearing his hat pulled low over his burning eyes, and he puffed an up-tilted black cigar. He might have been astonished to learn how strikingly he patterned his appearance upon that of the saloonkeeper of the Omro of his boyhood.

Arthur McEwen of the old *Mail* days was in San Francisco again, and the two became inseparable. In this year McEwen founded the *San Franciscan* with Joe Goodman, upon whose *Enterprise* Older had worked in Virginia City. At last Older met Goodman, the editor who discovered Twain. He found a bushy-bearded and baldish man with a delightful and kindly wit, a fit working companion for the rapier-tongued McEwen. McEwen's satire, however, was directed solely at pretense and pettiness. He was as truthful as he was vigorous.

Again Older and McEwen, ablaze with maturer dreams, tramped the water-front till dawn, talking loudly of philosophy and economics and women and song. As they walked, the long arms of these six-foot journalists waved wildly in the fury of argument. McEwen at times spouted lines from a poem Joe Goodman had written upon the death of Abraham Lincoln, which he and many others considered a masterpiece; and in other moods the dynamic friends argued the merits of that amazing new book *Progress and Poverty*, written by McEwen's friend Henry George, who had begun a newspaper career in San Francisco as a compositor and started the *Post* in 1871. Older's first city editorship would be on the paper founded by the famous economist.

Older met through McEwen the sardonic Ambrose Bierce, who gored San Francisco with his pen and it was said, could make or unmake a man or woman with a word. Bierce, like McEwen, was a columnist and editorial writer. In a few more years he would be one of the earlier stars to brighten the pages of Hearst's *Examiner,* but he attained his literary fame as a writer of short stories. Gertrude Atherton said of Bierce that he had the best brutal imagination of any man of the English-speaking world.

McEwen's influence was strong upon the receptive Older. McEwen wrote for his *San Franciscan* a story called "A Dream of a Tramp." It told of Christ, in the guise of an outcast, wandering from door to door, from minister to minister in San Francisco, asking help in His own name. His own representatives on earth turned Him from their doors.

Years later the editor Fremont Older galvanized the city by sending a woman reporter, pretending to be a prostitute, from minister to minister in San Francisco asking aid. Certainly he never recognized the resemblance in the stories, but the grip his long-dead friend McEwen held upon his way of thinking was still strong.

Older was completely at home now in the convivial, deep-thinking, prankish, poetry-loving newspaper life of the city, and in the *Call* local room. He entered it always with a sense of triumphant home-coming. He was never without a story. On the ocasions when, like all other young newspaper men of that bibulous era, he failed to show up for office duty for a few days, he invariably returned with at least one sensational "scoop" that won him forgiveness and reinstatement. After his writing was done and more and more often his stories made the front page, he read every one of the other city papers and all the out-of-town papers on the exchange desk. Ideas swarmed to him, and he began helping out his driven city editor with suggestions for other members of the staff. He could not handle alone all the stories he thought up.

Pratt thought all his ideas good. He would ask Older which reporter he thought could best do a suggested story. Finally Pratt discussed with him many of his problems relating to staff members and asked his opinion of various men.

One raw cub baffled them both. He had been put on the staff by the owner of the paper, and he sat hopelessly all day, without an idea, without a gleam.

"What can I do with him?" babbled Pratt.

Older had an idea. The Salvation Army had just been formed.

"Send him out with the Army," he suggested.

Pratt sent the cub on a three weeks enlistment with the savers of souls. At the end of that time he produced two deadly columns. Pratt read the story and groaned.

"You were with the Army three weeks, weren't you? Eating and sleeping and singing with them? Now listen! When they came back into barracks at night, where did they hang the bass drum?"

The young man didn't know. Pratt fired him.

Older probably told that story to every reporter he ever hired.

"Where did they hang the bass drum?" he would boom, after criticizing a story for its lack of detail.

Older got along so well with Pratt that within a year he was given the stellar assignment of the Bowers murder case. He was now the acknowledged star reporter of the *Call*.

"It was the most interesting crime story I have ever known," was his comment on this assignment.

For two years he would write a daily story concerning

the mysterious Dr. Bowers, and for nearly six years thereafter he was still working secretly on the Bowers case.

Everyone in San Francisco was certain that Dr. Milton Bowers had murdered his wife. The elegant medico had fed his spouse phosphorus poison in small doses, sitting the while by her death-bed and stroking her hand. Her brother, Henry Benhayon, testified to that.

Ced Dr. Bowers had political influence. In spite of it he was sentenced to be hanged. They built his scaffold outside his cell window.

"They'll never hang me," he told reporters in the jail, smiling and stroking his beard.

One morning Benhayon, his wife's brother, was found dead, laid out neatly in a rented room. Later it was discovered that the room had been rented the day before by two men who often visited the doctor in his cell. Beside Benhayon's body was left a confession, declaring that he himself had poisoned his sister.

Older was one of the first in that room. On a table near the body, but out of reach, were three bottles. They held whiskey, chloroform, and cyanide. The confession was propped among the bottles.

Older picked up the pen and the inkbottle. He turned them over in his fine, long hands. He knew then that he had not been wrong. The pen was unstained. The bottle had never been opened.

The confession, then, had been written elsewhere. Benhayon had been killed elswhere, Older wrote he was convinced through the plotting of the condemned Dr. Bowers, and brought after death to this room.

Older told Pratt he was positive Dr. Bowers had engineered his second murder from his cell.

"Get the story!" ordered the editor tersely.

Older worked desperately to uncover the truth. Despite all his sleuthing, Bowers on retrial was found not guilty and won a suit giving him his dead wife's $17,000 of insurance. But Older continued in secret to hunt evidence and probe witnesses for half a dozen years.

"After Bowers was given his liberty I continued to work on the case," Older wrote. "The desire to fathom this mystery took complete possession of me and I thought of it day and night.

"Six years passed. Interest in the case gradually died out, and I finally reluctantly gave it up as a mystery that could never be solved. Bowers had evidently caught up the broken threads of his life and had gone with it nearer to his heart's desire. With his purse comfortably fattened with insurance money, he married the woman he loved.

"One Sunday morning in 1893 I met Bowers walking down Market Street. I hadn't seen him since the coroner's inquest on the body of Benhayon. He had changed very little. The same cold blue eyes, the same long beard slightly streaked with gray. His new wife was walking by his side. Bowers was faultlessly dressed in the mode of that day, black Prince Albert coat, striped trousers, patent-leather shoes, and a glossy silk hat. One hand was resting between the buttons of his coat and his wife's arm was linked in his. Bowers, with his other hand, stroked his beard slowly, exactly as he did in his cell when he was under sentence of death.

"Apparently he was calm, serene, and at peace with the world. His wife was smiling pleasantly. Possibly they were on their way to church, since it was the hour of Sunday morning services. He knew I had been on his track and I thought his eye caught mine for a second. Did I imagine it, or was he laughing behind that mask of a beard?

"For a moment I fancied he was saying to himself, 'You tried to get me, didn't you? But I fooled you!'

"I never saw him again."

The boy who had not been able to kill a chicken had followed a six-year man-hunt. It had not been Dr. Bowers, but justice, that Older wanted. Justice seemed to him now the most precious thing in the world.

The dearth of it he rediscovered daily in his reporting. There was one fight in the direction of justice which went on for years that Older as a *Call* reporter was obliged to watch wistfully from the side-lines. This was the astonishing single-handed crusade the boyish blue-eyed giant William Randolph Hearst, newcomer on the journalistic horizon, was waging with his newspaper, the San Francisco *Examiner*, against the Southern Pacific Railroad.

"In the early eighties the political power of the railroad became absolute," wrote Older of the situation.

"It controlled both political parties in California. Its power had superseded all law, all government and all authority that had hitherto been exercised by the people. The real capitol of the state was moved from Sacramento into the railroad building at Third and Townsend Streets, San Francisco.

"There, in a magnificent office, sat the big railroad boss, who dictated public policies and appointments not only in this state, but throughout the entire West. This stupendous organization became an overshadowing influence in all walks of life. It held the future of every ambitious young man in its grasp. It could make or ruin anyone, politically. The Press was practically silenced. Here and there, a feeble note of criticism broke loose occasionally, but whoever had the audacity to make it was soon silenced by the big boss."

Then out of Washington came an investigation. A congressional committee demanded to know what the railroad had done with the millions advanced by the American people toward building the road. It was hinted that the Contract and Finance Company, a corporation within a corporation which had been organized to construct the Central Pacific, the parent line of the Southern Pacific system, had stolen millions through false entries.

The man in charge of the railroad construction was a San Franciscan. The congressional committee from Washington appeared suddenly in San Francisco in 1887. Fremont Older was assigned to report for the *Morning Call* the investigation conducted in Parlor A of the Palace Hotel.

Reporting was never a job with Older. He threw himself completely into any story he covered. He felt he was part of the investigation, and he attended the proceedings with an almost fanatical interest. He was certain the steel band of the railroad would at last be filed from the neck of California. Older confined his written words to stately, crisp paragraphs in the newspaper fashion of the times, but the blaze of his interest shone through.

Attention was centered on the books kept by the Finance Company. Scandal hinted that two sets of books had been kept, one for the corporation itself, the other, a false set, used to collect the government millions.

Older, selecting a red-plush upholstered chair in the sedate parlor on the opening morning of the investigation, found himself sitting next to Dennis Kearney. Kearney was the well-known "sand-lot agitator" who was whipping California to fury against the Chinese. He whispered grimly behind his hand to Older:

"If they really want the truth about the false books, let them subpœna John Miller."

Older snapped at the tip. He scribbled the information on a sheet of copy-paper and shoved it across the table to Congressman Anderson of the committee. Anderson looked up from the note and nodded meaningly to Older.

It was a chance word tossed in the air. But it blossomed. One of the first questions asked the impressive Governor

Leland Stanford when he was summoned to the witness-chair was:

"Do you know a John Miller?"

Stanford was one of the "Big Four" who had built the Central Pacific Railroad, and they now owned between them more than a hundred million dollars, five thousand miles of railroad track, and fifty million acres of land presented to them by the United States Government. He admitted to knowing a John Miller who had been a book-keeper for the Finance Company, and Miller was summoned before the congressional committee.

"At the opening of the session next morning, in walked John Miller, protected by body-guards," related Older.

"Trailing behind him was a group of the toughest-looking human beings I had ever seen. Such ferocious faces couldn't easily be found outside of a rogues' gallery. They had been hand picked by the big boss to follow Miller into the room, line up against the wall, and glare at him when he took the witness-stand. After Miller had been sworn, these strong-arm men shot glances at him that would make an ordinary man quail."

But, to Older's admiration, Miller told all he knew. There had been a set of false books. Miller had seen the president of the company pack them in a box and nail down the cover; the next day the secretary of the company had left unexpectedly for Europe, and the books were never seen again.

Some said they had been dropped into the Atlantic Ocean, others believed they had been burned. After hearing Miller's testimony the committee from Washington were certain the false set had existed but had been destroyed. They shifted their questioning to an attempt to discover what had been done with large sums of money drawn and spent without vouchers. One entry in particular interested them. Stanford had at one time drawn out

$150,000 without a voucher, in Sacramento, California's state capital.

Under pressure on the witness-stand Stanford admitted a vague memory of having drawn such a sum.

"The State Legislature was in session on that date, wasn't it?" Congressman Pattison demanded.

"I believe it was," replied Stanford.

"Then what did you do with it?" snapped Pattison, certain he was at last nearing the truth.

The tense listeners were likewise certain. But they reckoned without Stanford. He refused to answer.

The congressional committee immediately carried the matter before Judge Sawyer of the Federal court, in an attempt to force Governor Stanford to answer. Older walked beside Congressman Anderson of the investigators to the Federal Building. On the way he remarked to Anderson that all they would get for the walk was fresh air.

"What do you mean?" demanded the man from Washington.

"I mean," answered the reporter who by now knew his city, "that Judge Sawyer is an intimate friend of Stanford's and frequently dines at his home on the hill, and he'll never compel him to answer."

Older was right. Stanford did not answer. The investigation fizzled out. The railroad was left brightly whitewashed. Nobody seemed to mind very much.

But Fremont Older cared. The tyranny of the railroad, which he had resented when as a youth of sixteen he first entered California, seemed to him as criminal as the murder Dr. Bowers had committed. He was only a reporter and could not write what he wanted to write of the fiasco. But his long lips gripped on questions under the bristling mustache.

Why should a millionaire not be compelled to answer on the witness-stand, like any common man?

Why should a railroad control the voting powers of men put into office by the people?

"If I were an editor," Older found himself thinking savagely, "I'd fight the railroad."

## Chapter VI

### MANAGING EDITOR

FREMONT OLDER was now rated one of the best reporters in San Francisco. Sometimes he served as assistant city editor on the *Morning Call*. Sometimes he "sat in" as city editor. As its star reporter in the early nineties Older made top wage—thirty dollars a week.

He was sent to Sacramento in 1893 to report the Legislature. He was not amazed at the amount of skulduggery going on in that august body. Since a boy of sixteen Older had watched the railroad spreading its steel claws in the West. He had no illusions regarding politics.

But this session the red and white camellias spread their scentless glory around the old Capitol building. He loved Sacramento, warm in sunlight, set in magnolias, camellias, and palms. Here he had come upon his arrival in California as a wandering printer boy. Here had lived his mother, and his grandfather the Squire—in his eighties now, but a giant still. And here Fremont Older met the woman who would hold his closest friendship as well as his love.

They met at the home of a mutual friend who had written a play. It was being produced by a group of amateurs, and Older's opinion as a "big-city" newspaper man was asked. A girl from Clyde, New York, a student of Syracuse University vacationing in Sacramento, was in the amateur cast.

Her name was Cora Baggerly. She had the face of a Madonna, a glance spiritual and deep, a nature so sensitive that it appeared to the casual aloof and even cold. She wore her dark hair like a crown. Beneath the dignity, rare in so young a woman, was illimitable gentleness.

She read her few lines with an ingenuous gusto that amused and charmed Older. He would tease her for years about that quaintly sincere impersonation.

The droll little play that brought them together grew into many acts and years. Their stage widened, showing both camellias and clouds. Many of the scenes Fremont and Cora Older played together might be sensational and strange, but always at the back of the stage a clear light burned. It was romance. It was friendship. It would light the way through bitterness and despair. It cleared away much of darkness for the passionate idealist Fremont Older, who without it might have died of disillusion.

It was perhaps his salvation.

Cora Baggerly did not return to college. They were married a few months later in San Francisco.

Another type of woman might never have permitted Older the crusader to exist. But Cora Older was of Fremont Older's stern background of pioneer America. Alike they had been bred in traditions of honesty, of law for and by the people, of justice for all. Older's maternal grandfather had once owned the site of Madison, Wisconsin, and Cora Older's people had owned part of the Capitol grounds at Washington. The Baggerlys had settled in Maryland and Virginia two hundred years before. Some were ministers who preached against slavery, as had Older's people. Her great-great-grandfather, at a time when George Washington kept Negroes, had freed his slaves.

When the Olders had been married a month, Fremont enthusiastically said to his bride:

"Cora, I want you to meet Pat Sullivan."

"Who is Pat Sullivan?"

"He's the man they're going to hang!"

Cora Older was gentle, though inclined to austerity. She

would always fall in with her tempestuous husband's enthusiasms. But nothing in her Presbyterian life had prepared her for this experience.

Demure in navy-blue tailored suit, white shirtwaist, and sailor hat, she followed Older into the ill-smelling gloom of the City Prison. There, shaking the iron bars of his cell in a maniacal rage, was Pat Sullivan the murderer, waiting to be hanged.

"I just wanted you to know the truth about him," Older explained to her.

The truth about Sullivan was not pretty. But he was the first prisoner to stir the attention of Older, and out of this interest would grow a crusade that reformed prison conditions from San Quentin to Sing Sing.

Pat was a victim of love.

He had come, Older told his wife, from Ireland as a stoker, saved his money, and bought a small dive on the Barbary Coast. He fell hopelessly in love with one of his own percentage girls, a woman with a child, whose husband had divorced her for infidelity. Pat gave her child a home, he forgave the woman many sprees and many men, until in his dumb despair he joined her in drinking that ended in delirium.

He lost his dive, his home. The woman left him.

Again and again he found her, brought her back, patiently tried to redeem her. Older first met Pat in the "DT" Ward in the Emergency Hospital, when as a reporter he covered that beat. Through many years he watched Pat's attempts to save the woman. Pat caught up with her the last time in a dive on the Barbary Coast.

"I asked her to come home with me," Sullivan told Older, when he visited him in prison after the killing.

"And she laughed at me! She threw back her head and laughed at me, and went on drinking with the men. She

THE REPORTER
OLDER AT
TWENTY-EIGHT

CORA BAGGERLY
OLDER
IN HER EARLY
TWENTIES

said, 'Go on, you drunken bum!' She went on laughing at me.

"So I went out, and went up the street, and waited for her in a dark doorway, and when she came by I killed her."

Yelling, shouting, with eyes bloodshot under matted hair, Sullivan shrieked demands to his jailers that he be swiftly hanged.

"I went to the office and wrote what I knew of Sullivan's life," said Older, "and how many times he had forgiven the woman, and tried to make a decent life with her, and how many times he had failed, and still tried.

"It was a sympathetic story, and at that time, nearly thirty years ago, a sympathetic story about a murderer was nearly unknown."

There was no psychiatry, no attempt to explain crime, in the nineties. Older, puzzling over Sullivan's case, fumbled with the idea of circumstance. Men went wrong, he decided, defeated by an unbeatable combination of bad upbringing and bad luck.

Later Older would revise that theory.

Cora Older, a few days after her first visit to any jail, was horrified by receiving a printed invitation to Pat's hanging. The West was opening startling vistas before this conventional Eastern girl. She would march into them with a courage that would be a source of wonder to Older and his friends. Whatever he might do, whatever risks he might take, she would be with him.

There would be times when she would weary of Older's fighting, when she would sicken as the waves of a city's hatred went over their heads.

"Cora, if you wanted peace," he would tell her then with his marvelously tender smile, "you should have married a minister."

But she would walk composedly by his side in a city street where stones were flying. She would stand with him while a mob beat in their windows. She would face social ostracism with Fremont Older.

Her world had been narrowed and beautifully fitted to comfort and simplicity. The girl from the puritan East had married into another existence. She had scarcely realized there was poverty and crime. Yet at eighteen Cora Older plunged into newspaper life as her husband's aide when the great chance came to him.

This was shortly after their marriage.

In appearance Older was still a man of the country, long-legged, lanky, with heavy black hair beginning to desert his high forehead, a dominant nose, mouth firmly contoured under the sweeping Western mustache, and deep-set dark eyes which smoldered and were tender, benign, or without mercy, flashing the signal-lights of his multitudinous moods.

A friend of Older's once said he looked like a cavalry officer. Someone else, less friendly, declared he looked more like a buccaneer.

After his marriage, it was noticed, Older by degrees took on a new distinction. Cora Older always dressed simply and well, in the tailored suits and shirtwaists fashion then decreed for day wear. Later, when their fortunes improved, she would be referred to as "the best-dressed woman in San Francisco." And Older, to the astonishment of the careless journalistic crew who were his cronies, began paying attention to his appearance. He was utterly without personal vanity and while still in his thirties wore the attire of a rather negligent old man—cutaway coat, bulging trousers, and slouch-hat. He was meticulous only in well-cared-for hands and well-glossed boots.

Urged on by his young wife, Older patronized a good tailor and developed an unsuspected talent for selecting scarfs. He had always been handsome. Now he developed in grooming and dignity.

Older had been for many years a star reporter. He had served in every newspaper capacity, as apprentice and printer's devil, type-setter, press-room foreman, circulation manager, business manager, and all-around news reporter handling water-front, City Hall, and police beats. He had been telegraph editor, drama editor, assistant city editor, and for a short time city editor.

"There are detours in life that cannot be avoided," he commented once in a letter, "but they need not make us lose sight of the final goal.'

The untrained Older's schooling had lasted many years. He was ready for the great matriculation when R. A. Crothers sent for him.

Crothers was part owner of the *Morning Call*. Older, who had left the *Call* soon after his marriage, had been for a few months city editor of the *Post* when Crothers offered him the city editorship of the *Call*, at forty dollars a week, Pratt having long since departed.

The newly married pair moved into the historic old California Hotel. They lived frugally; only on Sunday evenings might they have been seen dining at the gayer restaurants, feasting on duck and salad and baked potato, at fifty cents a dinner.

At the end of the year their world caved under them. The *Call* was sold.

Again Older faced the haunting question, What next? And again Crothers, who had sold his share of the *Call*, made an offer to Older.

Crothers had bought the dying *Evening Bulletin* for $65,000 for the estate of his sister, Mrs. Rose Pickering. Eventually Crothers assumed half interest.

There were in San Francisco, in this year of 1895, the *Chronicle*, founded in 1856 by Charles and M. H. de

Young, a prosperous morning paper which had begun as an advertising theater program; the *Morning Call,* founded in the same year and named after a farce of that name played by Lola Montez, the dancer; the *Morning Examiner,* founded in 1865 and taken over by William Randolph Hearst in 1887; the *Evening Post,* founded in 1871 by the economist Henry George; the *Evening Report,* founded in 1863; and, most historic journal of all, the fading *Bulletin.* The *Alta California,* which had been created of San Francisco's first two newspapers, the *Californian* and the *Star,* had given up the ghost in 1891.

Older, as a wandering reporter, had worked at one time or another on every newspaper in the city except the railroad-controlled *Report* and the *Bulletin.*

The *Bulletin* was one of the first newspapers in the colorful gold-hunting West, having been founded in 1855 by the pioneer crusader-editor James King of William "His paper brought about the reformation, but the reformer lost his life," was written of this intrepid editor. The *Bulletin* fought the gamblers and politicians and gangsters that ruled early San Francisco. The blood of James King of William cleansed the crime-ridden city, for when he was shot to death before the *Bulletin* office by James Casey, ruler of the underworld, the wild young city of San Francisco gave birth to the Vigilance Committee. Casey's body dangled from a rope, and the *Bulletin* as a memorial to its martyred founder carried on his crusades for many years.

But its valor had waned.

"The paper was at very low ebb," wrote Older of the *Bulletin* when Crothers bought it, "having a circulation of perhaps nine thousand, and advertising insufficient to meet the expenses. I think it was losing about $3,000 a month.

"It was necessary to turn this deficit into a profit, in order to save the capital invested. Crothers offered me the managing editorship, which I acepted."

There was no time, no money, to be lost. The *Bulletin* had to be put on a working basis overnight. There was a saying in the city that every time a pioneer died, the *Bulletin* lost another of its few remaining subscribers. Only the old-timers read it.

Crothers was willing to take a chance on Older. He would win beyond his wildest hopes.

How unlike they were, this pair destined to be working companions for a quarter of a century! Crothers, so sedate that he had been known since youth as "the Old Man," was a college graduate, an attorney with a classical education, fond of quoting the Odes of Pindar.

"He had little respect for any man not a university graduate," Older said of Crothers.

But Crothers knew that, despite only three years of schooling, Older had a nose for news. In his desperation he gambled everything on that.

Older had the chance he had been awaiting for thirty years. For he was nearly forty when he caught up with his boyish dreams of Horace Greeley and stepped into the decaying offices of the tottering *Bulletin* as its managing editor, at forty-five dollars a week.

The San Francisco directories of those years tell the story of his sudden rise. In 1893 he is listed as a reporter, in 1894 as city editor, while in 1895 he is listed: "Older, Fremont, Mgr Ed Evening Bulletin, California Hotel."

It was a disheartening prospect he faced with such boyish enthusiasm and courage. The *Bulletin* was housed near the water-front, in a building with in-caving walls. Cobwebs and dirt darkened the rooms, and the files were yellow with four decades of dust. There was no reportorial staff and no money to hire anyone.

The solitary and inadequate press could not produce more papers if circulation should increase. The type was set by hand. There was no money to buy another press.

"It was up to me to change this situation quickly or fail miserably," commented Older. 'Here was a fighting chance for me to make a success. Perhaps it was the only one I would ever have. So I decided it was not a time to concern myself with the ethics of journalism. That could be considered later when the paper was on a paying basis."

The *Bulletin's* failure would be Older's. Its success would establish him.

He received unexpected encouragement. His young wife shared his ambition.

"I can work in the office with you," Cora Older offered. "That will save a salary."

She was inexperienced, still in her teens, but she saved several salaries. She wrote half-page interviews with celebrities, half pages of book reviews, society news, and drama criticisms. Her enthusiasms were as keen as Older's.

Then her young brother, Hiland Baggerly, came from Union College to share the adventure. He also proceeded to hold down three jobs. Having played on the college baseball nine in Schenectady, the sports section fell to him. Baggerly wrote knowingly of "Gentleman Jim" Corbett and "Ruby Bob" Fitzsimmons, of the latest peccadilloes of that brawny and bull-headed ex-champion John L. Sullivan, of boat-races on the bay, bicycle-races, and a smoldering new invention with a steering-bar known as the "petroleum bicycle." In his spare hours the smiling collegian went the rounds of the police beat and the City Hall.

Baggerly eventually developed his sports page into the most distinctive in the West. He discovered for it such talented cartoonists as "Tad" Dorgan, Rube Goldberg, Robert Ripley, Herb Roth, Peter Llanuza, and Dan Leno. Years later Ripley wired on "Hi's" birthday, " 'Believe it or not,' I once worked for Baggerly at two fifty a week!" Charles Van Loan began writing on the *Bulletin* sports sheet, covering baseball. Eager youth would clamor at the *Bulletin* doors to work with high hopes at low salaries.

Fremont and Cora Older and Hiland Baggerly were in the beginning the major part of the *Bulletin* staff. There were three other members. The Olders left the California Hotel and took a flat which Baggerly shared with them. Mornings the three walked together to the office, they returned home weary and late each evening. Their lives centered in the moldy rooms where they were building with their very souls a newspaper for another man.

The *Bulletin* was not dying without reason. Older first scanned its pages with dismay. It was the dreariest sheet ever hawked from a street-corner. The dull news was printed in small, close type and with single-column heads. There were no illustrations to brighten the leaden news.

Older was not only managing editor but also city editor. He was like a core of radium throwing off power. He gave out all assignments, searched other papers for news leads, chose subjects for editorials and hovered over the man selected to write them while they were written, selected lead stories and "grape-vine" and telegraph news, and wrote the headlines. These headlines by degrees, not to agitate the dignified Crothers, he broadened from one column to three.

"I worked hard to make an attractive, readable newspaper," Older said. "While limited to a small staff, I kept every member of it combing the city night and day for interesting news, which I sensationalized as much as I dared."

And again, with his astounding faculty for honesty, he wrote:

"I lived, breathed, ate, slept and dreamed nothing but the paper. My absorbing thought was the task of making it go.

"I was perfectly ruthless in my ambition. My one desire

was to stimulate the circulation, to develop stories that would catch the attention of readers, no matter what was the character of the stories. They might make people suffer, might wound or utterly ruin someone; that made no difference to me, it was not even in my mind. I cared only for results, for success to the paper and to myself."

Crothers liked restraint in a newspaper. He was horrified as his dull *Bulletin* turned sensational. But the booming circulation closed argument. Crothers gave way before the dynamic Older with admiration and dismay.

The *Bulletin* steadily brightened. Feature stories, symposia, and illustrations gave it appeal. "Do You Lace?" "Should Women Wear Green?" "Why Do Women Submit to the Fashionable Razor-toed Shoe?" Its feminine readers were asked such questions on the nucleus of a woman's page.

Even on the front page Older revealed his serious nature in questions asked the readers. The news-story heads required answers. "What Is the Railroad Saying to the Assembly in Sacramento?" "What Is President Grover Cleveland Planning in Washington?" "What Is Being Done about Rebuilding the City Hall?"

From the beginning the *Bulletin* provoked thought in its readers.

Also from the beginning did Older's editorials hold the attention of the city. He seldom wrote one himself. But he inspired them, poured them verbally into his writers and let them write his thoughts. He was too restless to stop and pin his own ideas on paper.

The *Bulletin* pages glowed with personalities, of local or world-wide fame. Items concerning Harriet Beecher Stowe, Queen Victoria, James McNeill Whistler, and Lotta Crabtree were written as intimately as if these celebrities were next-door neighbors. Older liked stories written that way. When the widow of Robert Louis Stevenson returned to San Francisco after the death of the famous author in the South Seas, Older, without vanity but knowing that he himself could best write the story, went out on the pilot-boat to meet the ship and bring back the interview.

Circulation stirred feebly, and rose . . . fifty . . . a hundred . . . a thousand!

"It was not long before the paper began to respond to the strong pressure I put upon it," wrote Older. "We had only two competitors in the evening paper field, the *Post* and the *Report,* and I had the satisfaction of seeing our paper slowly creep upward, until we had passed the *Post* and were becoming a serious rival of the *Report.*"

He owed the first encouraging results to a contest. Every day a ballot ran on the front page to be filled in with the name of "Your Favorite Teacher." Thousands of school children filled in the ballots. The contest swept the schools. The prizes were tours, and twenty popular teachers were sent by the *Bulletin* that summer on trips which ranged in length from a near-by resort to Europe. The winner of the grand prize departed with impressive publicity to France, and her travel letters were printed in full by the *Bulletin,* under such descriptive heads as "Some of the Many Inconveniences Experienced in a Pullman Sleeper."

Older's idea of the contest was a new stunt, and so successful was it that when the time came for allotting the expensive prizes, the *Bulletin* was able to bear the cost. Circulation rose until the old press would no longer serve. For many reasons Older had been urging Crothers to move the plant. He hated feeling "out of things," and the office on the water-front was far from the center of the city. As there was no money to waste on hacks, the reporters walked miles for their stories. An expense-account was unknown.

When the press failed, Older gloated.

"Now we'll have to move," he told Crothers.

They left the caved-in building on May 18, 1895. The

editorial Older ordered written that day revealed his jubilation. Discreet headlines chortled:

"New Bulletin Ready to Move! Goes Uptown, and in the Swim. A Matchless New Plant All in Position. A New Press, New Type-setting Machines, and a New Dress, and It Takes the Lead!"

The editorial rushed into the frank sentimentality of the last century:

"On deserting the old quarters its makers leave many reminiscences of the days that are gone. The dust of decades is there gathered on wall and desk, traditions hover in the old atmosphere and every turn brings memories of monster events of the old days, when the paper proudly held its well-earned place of champion of the just and righteous cause. It will be a severing of old ties, and the grave editor will feel that he is leaving something behind him. But he will feel that he is going to a better state and while he may sigh for the old he will welcome the new, for in the rooms uptown he will have many things for which he has yearned for years. He will be in the midst of the swim, more closely in touch with the world whose throbbing pulses he may feel, and above all he will be relieved of the necessity of trudging weary blocks between office and the center of population in the city. The old location has been a drawback to editor and reporter."

So Older took his readers into his confidence, showing them his problems and moods, as would always be his way.

But new press and plant must be paid for. Older was daring, but wary as a soldier in action. He had shown his mettle these few short weeks. In the new offices he redoubled his ardor.

Within a few weeks he was able to run in a box on the *Bulletin's* front page, "Actual increase for months of April and May, 6,873 copies." He bought white hats for the newsboys. Boldly he adopted a front-page slogan to serve as prophecy:

"Largest circulation of any afternoon paper west of Chicago!"

The new plant boasted "a complete zinc etching department with a full corps of reliable artists."

"In my ceaseless efforts to make the paper attractive," wrote Older, "and to do unusual things, I undertook art work on chalk plates, which was a novelty at the time. A plate of chalk was used, the artist making his drawing upon it with a steel tool. With Will Sparks as artist, we produced some very good effects. This was before we were able to install a photo-engraving plant."

Sketches of the wives of the "Bonanza Kings" and other social leaders, of prominent citizens or even a scene, daily adorned the front page. Even spot news was not neglected, for Older would send out an artist to sketch a shipwreck or burning building. The front page of the second section bloomed with "French Fashions," sketches of wasp-waisted ladies with immense puff sleeves and larger skirts. The "Woman's Fancies" page showed such attractive art tidbits as "Last Word in Beach Wear," portraying hour-glass beauties in balloon-sleeves bathing-suits, long stockings, mop-caps over pompadours, and laced boots, ready for the sea.

With the development of art the headlines grew in size and emotion. "Oscar Wilde the Dainty Sweating on a Prison Treadmill." "Poor Marie Michel—Why She Suffocated Herself with Gas." An account of a missing girl was captioned "Hattie Is Missing!" A reader might not know Hattie, but after such an introduction he would feel concern for her safety.

There were five new linotype machines in the new plant. They did the work of twenty-six hand compositors. The saving in their wages would help pay for the machines. Someone suggested that they could save more money by hiring girls, who worked more cheaply than men.

Older was anxious to save money. He was in this great adventure on a shoe-string basis, and any saving meant much to him. But he had been a printer. He had stood in line with the jobless on freezing sidewalks. His brother, Herbert, was a printer, and for many years a proofreader on the *Bulletin*. And at this suggestion of saving, Older's jaws clamped.

"We keep men on those machines!" he said, and when Older's mouth locked in that grim line under the sweeping mustache, not even the owner of the paper dared dispute him.

Older's name, as managing editor, did not appear on the editorial page. But he did not mind the omission. His pride was not personal; it lay in workmanship, and his life work was to be the building of the *Bulletin*.

But for the first time he had an office of his own, a closet-like hole which spilled proof-sheets and old papers like a never-emptying magic pitcher. Crothers took refuge in a large office and bought himself a shining mahogany desk. He suggested mahogany for Older. He felt his managing editor was earning his right to dignity.

Older scorned such display. In his home he would accept simple luxury, but in his office he would have his way. His one office extravagance was cigars. Their ashes carpeted the floor. On many evenings the janitor collected as many as twenty Havana stubs that Older had laid, still burning, around his scarred desk.

Older smoked one cigar after another. One could tell his mood by the tilt. He laved in mellow smoke, using perhaps an inch of each cigar, putting it aside, forgetting it, lighting another. Havana in hand, Older stressed and punctuated his remarks.

His cigar was his solace, his scepter, and his ferule.

Everyone Older met yielded up a story. There was a story, he often said, in everyone. One of the amazing stories he uncovered in those early days concerned the minister of a fashionable church, named Brown.

"Brown had been accused of having improper relations with a young woman, a member of his church, and we made quite a scandal about it," wrote Older of this case.

"The preacher, of course, denied the story, but I was able to stir up enough discord in his church to cause some of the members to ask for an investigation. The investigation resulted in a trial of Brown by a jury of preachers from other churches.

"I made desperate efforts to get condemning evidence, and succeeded to quite an extent, running big stories with flaring headlines daily during the trial. During this fight Brown, in order to frighten me into abandoning the fight against him, caused to be written to me a forged letter signed by John J. Valentine, the manager of the Wells Fargo Express Company and a prominent member of his church. The letter asked me to drop the matter, saying that Brown was a very fine man, and undoubtedly innocent and persecuted.

"As soon as I received the letter I immediately rushed down to Valentine with it. He said that it was a forgery, that he had never written it. This made what I considered a great story. I published a facsimile of the letter, with a heading across the page, 'Brown, the Penman,' and a handwriting expert's testimony added.

"Brown was acquitted by the friendly jury of preachers, resigned and went east, and nothing was heard of him for more than a year. Then he reappeared in San Francisco, hired a hall, and in a public speech admitted his guilt. No one seemed to know why he made the confession."

"A great story" this seemed to Older. He did not see at

the time a human life ground to pulp and spewed forth in headlines. He was giving his own life to the *Bulletin*. Why not, then, the reputation of a minister who had broken the rules of church and man?

"The Church Scandal" and the "Teachers' Popularity Contest" brought the *Bulletin* to life. But it needed a mightier fillip to send the circulation soaring. That fillip came in Holy Week.

At Easter time, as in Christmas week, all old newspaper men say, nothing ever happens. There is no news. The passions of mankind are ennobled and fixed upon matters higher than earth.

Yet it was in Holy Week of 1895, shortly after Fremont Older took over the destiny of the *Bulletin,* that "the Crime of the Century" was committed.

## Chapter VII

### OLDER THE SENSATIONALIST

"THE DURANT MURDER case, which broke in the spring of 1895, helped us very much," Older wrote of his early fight to build the *Bulletin* circulation. "Every man, woman and child in San Francisco followed the absorbing story of the Durant case and quite naturally they were interested in whether or not Durant would hang."

Not only in San Francisco, but wherever the annals of crime were read, men wondered and would always wonder whether Theodore Durant was "the perfect young churchman" or "the monster of the belfry."

On the third of April in that year, a few months after Older became managing editor, beautiful twenty-year-old Blanche Lamont waved goodby to her fellow-students at the Normal School. She carried her school-books to the car line, where she was joined by a young man later identified as Theodore Durant.

Then Blanche disappeared.

This was at three o'clock in the afternoon. Two hours later George King, organist of the Emmanuel Baptist Church on Bartlett Street, was sitting before the organ playing when he saw Durant stagger out of the door that led to the belfry. Durant, King said later, was white and seemed on the point of nervous collapse. He explained to King that he had been fixing the gas-pipes in the belfry and had been overcome by gas. Later it occurred to King there were no gas-pipes in the belfry.

Durant was the type of young man mothers point out to their worldling sons. He was good-looking, mild in appearance, always quiet and with beautiful manners, and came from a respected San Francisco family. He was studying medicine at the Cooper Medical Institute. His spare time was taken up with church activities, for he was a leading spirit in Emmanuel. He was assistant superintendent of its Sunday-school and secretary of the Christian Endeavor, and as he had a flair for mechanical matters, he attended to all the electrical and gas equipment of the church. In the choir his voice was indispensable, for he sang either bass or tenor. On holidays he worked in the Golden Rule Bazaar.

Durant was also a member of the Signal Corps of the Second Brigadiers.

Good Friday of 1895 was celebrated on April 12. Blanche Lamont was still missing, and the *Bulletin* and other papers made much of the mystery. In the early dusk of that evening Blanche's "closest friend," Minnie Williams, who was nineteen and, like the missing Blanche, a girl of unusual beauty, was seen to enter the Baptist Church on Bartlett Street with Theodore Durant.

Durant and Minnie were both active in Christian Endeavor work. That evening they were expected at a business meeting and sociable of the Endeavor at the home of a member. Minnie did not arrive. Durant came very late, too late to take charge of the business meeting as was his custom. He was overheated and seemed rather "jumpy," his friends noted over their coffee and ice-cream. But he was in time for the sociable and took part in all the games.

At nine-thirty the next morning, Saturday, a group of young girls of the church entered it to decorate the altar with calla lilies for the Easter services. One, in playful curiosity, opened the door of a small room off the library.

Before them lay the body of their friend Minnie Williams. The girls fled screaming from the library without noting that the entire floor of that room was carpeted with blood.

Minnie, the coroner found, had been strangled, her breasts and wrists severed, stabbed many times in the heart, and violated after death. A knife broken in five pieces lay on the library table. The tip of it was found later in the dead girl's brain. An intimate piece of her clothing had been forced down her throat with a pointed stick.

"It was an immensely interesting story and sensational angles were breaking every hour of the day," wrote Older. "Every new angle was made the occasion for an extra. During the running of this story street sales grew rapidly."

Older detailed men to run down every angle and clue on the Durant case. He hired reporters he knew were like bloodhounds. His staff grew with the story. He sent out artists to sketch the church, the belfry, the beautiful Minnie and her still missing chum Blanche Lamont, and the dapper, mustached, bovine-eyed, lank-haired, bored-looking Durant.

For the name of Durant was beginning to be heard in the case. That Saturday Durant left the seething city and went to the camp of the Signal Corps on Mount Diablo, across the Bay from San Francisco.

The *Bulletin* shrieked over the discovery of Minnie Williams' body. It demanded in widening headlines, "Where Is Blanche Lamont?"

Blanche's aunt, on this morning when Minnie's body was found, received a package in the mail. Wrapped in a newspaper were three rings that had belonged to Blanche. On a margin of the torn paper were written three names—those of Blanche's music teacher, King, the organist, and Theodore Durant.

The police said this meant that Blanche was hiding for some reason and had sent the package to her aunt as a sign. But the aunt wept to a *Bulletin* reporter:

"Now I know my poor girl is dead!"

All that gruesome Saturday the police searched the church. Under pews, behind the altar, through the library, the search went on. Crawling among the foundations under the church with lighted candles, they found the schoolbooks and shoes of Blanche Lamont.

They were certain then that somewhere in the church she lay dead.

All that night, carrying candles, the police climbed and crawled in silence into crannies black with the dust of years.

Morning crept over the breathless city. The bells of other churches rang out, for it was Easter Sunday. Within the church on Bartlett Street the lilies shone white on the altar. Crowds began gathering in the street outside. It was within an hour of morning service.

But the church doors were sealed. The steeple bells were forbidden to ring out their message of life rerisen. Before the church police fought back the crowds to make room for the death-wagon driving up to the arched doors. The body of Blanche Lamont had been found.

Found, under such awful conditions that women fainted in the street upon hearing the story. On this morning of Holy Easter a cry went through San Francisco such as had been heard before in the days of the Vigilantes.

For Blanche Lamont had been strangled as had her chum Minnie Williams, probably in the same library, and dragged up steep flights of stairs to the uttermost platform of the belfry. There her body was stripped of clothing and left naked to the winds and the rains that blew through the open steeple. Her clothing was found stuffed in the very apex of the sharp spire.

The police who discovered the body said that they had never seen anything more shocking or more beautiful. She was a girl of marble, lying under the mute iron bells, the whiteness of her body softened by the dust of eleven days.

Blanche, in the belfry tower, had been visited many times after death.

Hiland Baggerly, Older's brother-in-law, was covering the case for the *Bulletin* and was in the church when the body of Blanche was found. He rushed to the California Hotel with the news, and Older hastily summoned a working crew and brought out a Sunday edition.

Now a name burned every lip—Durant.

So respectable was Durant, of so impeccable a family and reputation, that the police hesitated. The *Bulletin* and other newspapers bayed them on. Finally the chief of police sent the order for Durant's arrest to the Signal Corps camp on Mount Diablo. It was said that Durant himself was operating the heliograph that day and received the message ordering him to be held for the murders of Blanche Lamont and Minnie Williams.

Durant, taken from the Ferry to the prison by an army of police to guard him against mob violence, remained calm. Evidence was rolling up against him. His handwriting was similar to that on the newspaper that had enclosed the rings. King, the organist, recalled seeing Durant come from the belfry shaking with nervousness the night Blanche disappeared. The girl students at the Normal School remembered his meeting Blanche after school. Someone else had seen him at the Ferry Building waiting for Minnie, who lived in Oakland, the Friday she disappeared. That same Friday Durant had asked a fellow-student at medical school to answer to his name at afternoon roll-call.

Durant had answers for these.

"The organist is a liar," he told reporters in prison. "It is the minister who should be under suspicion! As for the girls who say they saw me with Blanche, they are mistaken." But all that night, on his prison cot, he moaned in the grip of nightmare.

On April 16 thousands of San Franciscans filed past the funeral parlor where the bodies of the two beautiful girls lay under masses of heliotrope and lilies, and Fremont Older ran a four-column headline in the *Bulletin:*

"Durant's Fetters Are Forged!"

It took six weeks to get a jury. No one wanted the responsibility of passing judgment on "the Crime of the Century," as the Durant case was called. Nearly four thousand men were examined before twelve could be found willing to try Theodore Durant. The trial lasted many weeks, and the *Bulletin* ran every word of the testimony. Older sent a cartoonist to the trial each day to sketch the leading characters slightly caricatured, with small bodies and large heads. This was before newspaper photography was perfected. Older had "strips" drawn showing Durant in every courtroom attitude.

"The Crime of the Century" had many angles. Older played them all.

Women flocked to the courtroom to see Durant. Many protested love for him. One became famous as "the sweet-pea girl." Every day she brought into the courtroom a bunch of sweet peas to lay at the defendant's feet. Another woman appeared before the bar and proclaimed herself the "Female Messiah" come to set Durant free. A madman interrupted proceedings with the announcement that he had murdered the two girls.

In the courtroom, as a spectator, was to be seen the stately though youthful figure of William Jennings Bryan, campaigning in the West for free silver.

Durant's fellow medical students testified that in autopsy classes he was a "slasher of dead bodies" and was given to devouring books on abnormal passions.

A pretty, trembling girl from the Baptist Church whispered from the witness-stand that a few days before Blanche Lamont disappeared, Durant had suggested that she submit to a medical examination and that the church was a quiet place where they would not be seen. After that, said the girl, she avoided Durant.

Older adopted a thrilling new word for the front page, "Extra." Every new development in the Durant case served as excuse for an extra. He began using six-column headlines on the seven-column front page. The circulation grew by thousands.

"The Crime of the Century" paid for the *Bulletin's* new presses.

"The case went to the jury about three o'clock in the afternoon," related Older. "Of course, no one knew definitely what the verdict would be, but I was prepared for whatever decision might be rendered. I had three stories written, put in type, made up into page form, stereotyped, and laid alongside the press. One story was headed 'Guilty,' another 'Jury Couldn't Agree,' and a third 'Acquitted.' Believing Durant would be convicted, I had the 'Guilty' page placed on the press ready to start at a second's notice.

"I sent Henry L. Brooke, an experienced reporter, to the courtroom to telephone the result. The telephone was kept open with a man at each end. When the foreman of the jury said 'Guilty,' Brooke rushed for the door and got out just as the court ordered the door closed. Brooke was wise. All the other reporters were locked in.

"Our press started instantly and we were all over the city before the other papers knew anything about it.

"I used the same method when Durant was hanged. I had a man in the gallows room show a handkerchief at the window when the trap fell. A man on the hill saw the handkerchief and waved one himself, which was seen at the warden's office, where I had a telephone open.

"Again we 'scooped' the town and our circulation went permanently past the 20,000 mark. This put the *Bulletin* in the lead."

The man who kept the telephone open in the *Bulletin* local room was Older. Tense with nervous interest, he mounted guard over the wooden box with handle that was the telephone of the nineties. The transmitter and receiver were the same, and Older alternately shouted into it and listened to the reporter at the other end of the line.

Crothers, the classical scholar, watched his booming newspaper with deepening dismay.

"There's not a thing in it I can read," he complained plaintively.

But for the first time, now that the *Bulletin* was living up to its boastful slogan, "The Greatest Evening Paper in the West," he ordered his name onto the editorial page: "R. A. Crothers, Editor and Proprietor." It was an enormous relief to know that the presses were paid for at last and the *Bulletin* would not be his financial ruin. But the means to the end oppressed Crothers. He would have preferred a less sensational success and an editor who had at least a smattering of Greek.

Older could overlook Crothers' disapproval in his own elation. In the *Bulletin* offices he seemed to be everywhere.

"I visited the pressrooms every afternoon and watched the newsboys buy their papers," he wrote. "I asked them what they thought of the headlines and often followed them to the ferry to see how the papers sold.

"Circulation. Circulation. There was no room in my mind for any other thought."

He listened at street-corners, in lobbies, street-cars, for comments on stories. He haunted the news-stands.

Although the staff was enlarged, everyone on the paper was working harder than ever. That January of 1896 the Saturday edition of the *Bulletin* consisted of twenty-four pages of bright and sparkling news, articles, poetry, editorials, and the paper's first novel, complete in one edition, *The Purple Emperor*. The Saturday *Bulletin* was like a magazine, but bursting with news of the hour.

In March Older began his first continued serial, a chapter every Saturday, *Weir of Hermiston*. It was the last work of Robert Louis Stevenson. By the opening of the following year he had launched the sentimental serials he would develop as circulation-getters to such a tremendous degree. The first of these was "Comfort Pease and Her Gold Ring," followed by "The Price She Paid."

Growing troubles in Cuba were overshadowed in the *Bulletin* by any local scandal. Older believed that the heart affairs of a Market Street chambermaid were more interesting to San Franciscans than any historical event in another part of the world.

The woman's page developed in interest. "How to Make Tissue Paper Lamp Shades" and "Tomorrow's Menu," which cited the colossal menus of the nineties, held the attention of women readers. A new game, golf, was described on the society page instead of in the sports section. Mrs. John Jacob Astor had taken up the fad and was planning a golf-course at Newport. In San Francisco a dozen daring society women were "studying" golf, costumed in bell-bottomed skirts, tight shirtwaists, and blow-away sailor hats.

Every corner of every page had Older's scrutiny. Some editors stress news, some specialize in editorials or features, but his interest was extended to every department—art, sports, editorials, even advertisements. He introduced a box in the classified section: "A First Class Novel Given to Every Person Inserting a Classified Advertisement in the *Bulletin* Three Times." He drove every department in the paper with all his energy, just as he drove every force in his powerful frame.

The "Teachers' Popularity Contest" was so successful that Older repeated it the second season, and another selected group of teachers won trips to Honolulu, the East, and Europe. Children sending in the most votes won prizes.

From the beginning Older stressed the value of editorials. That first January he ran a squib on the editorial page:

"Editorials . . . are the special excellence of the *Bulletin*. Its timely utterances, vigorous, comprehensive and pointed, ever sounding the note of warning and jealously guarding the interests of the people, make the *Bulletin* the terror of evil-doers and the shield of the citizens."

The editorials were fierce and protective, straight-spoken and kindly, interested in matters vital or small. They were the voice of Fremont Older.

When the *Bulletin* began to pay, Older knew a great triumph. He was able to hire Arthur McEwen, his friend and literary mentor since the days of the mad and merry *Mail*. McEwen was to write politics, but he dressed them with pith and seasoning unlike any political dish ever served to an astonished public. He hung many of his satirical political opinions upon a mythical cobbler that made the lordly politicians of San Francisco and Sacramento writhe. Other political wisdom, McEwen informed his readers, he gleaned from a cab-horse.

"For several nights," the horse remarked, according to the sardonic McEwen, "I was dragging Governor Budd around. [Budd was the Governor of California.]

"The whip was going constantly, and I learned from conversations which the governor, his head out of the cab window, held with a number of queer persons, that he was dashing about fixing things for the removal of a man called Weaver from some exalted public position or other. The speed we went and the company we kept were enough to disgust a decent horse."

It was nonsense, but barbed. *Bulletin* readers might laugh, but they learned to know and resent the politics that were. In the wake of the editor Fremont Older, whose name was not on the *Bulletin,* grew a following.

Older revealed his respect for William Randolph Hearst as a newspaper man in a front-page article on April 18, 1896. Hearst, after his sensational success with the San Francisco *Examiner,* had gone to New York and an even more spectacular success with the *Journal.*

Hearst returned to his home city on a visit, and Older's article said in praise of this owner of a rival San Francisco paper:

"When Mr. Hearst went to New York to undertake the founding of a newspaper which should attract the attention of all Gotham, there were those who looked upon his venture almost in the light of foolhardiness. The then leading metropolitan papers seemed so firmly entrenched in their stronghold that for a new man to attempt to compete with them seemed like madness. Yet Mr. Hearst went ahead, and the predictions that the New Yorkers would not know he was in town were not verified. They found out in a very short time that he was there and they have been battling ever since to keep him from hiring all the newspaper talent in the city. Today the *Journal* is a worthy rival of the New York *World.*"

Later, in the competition for circulation between the *Bulletin* and the *Examiner,* Older would fight Hearst politically, but never without admiration for Hearst the editor.

Hearst, in the late eighties, had begun the struggle against the railroad, which by then had consolidated its tentacles in the vast Southern Pacific system. He was now engaged in an almost hopeless battle against the railroad's attempt to repudiate the Central Pacific's debt to the Government, and it was finally won. Charles Edward Russell wrote in his *Stories of the Great Railroads* that this was "as wonderful a victory as was ever achieved by one man."

Now, as Older's power grew with the *Bulletin*, he became obsessed with the longing to share the fight against the railroad. The election of 1895 was coming on.

"From the beginning of the campaign I felt that it would help the *Bulletin* tremendously if I could win a political victory in which a mayor would be elected," he explained.

"The entire state at that time was politically controlled by the Southern Pacific. In order thoroughly to dominate the state it not only controlled the Legislature, the courts, the municipal governments, which included coroners, sheriffs, boards of supervisors, in fact, all state and county and city officials, but it also had as complete a control of the newspapers of the state as was possible, and through them it controlled public opinion."

The *Bulletin* was not exempt. Every month a check for $125 came to the *Bulletin* office, a good-will offering, from the railroad.

Many times, said Older, he made desperate efforts to free the *Bulletin* from this influence. But the owner did not think the paper was strong enough financially to refuse the railroad subsidy.

It was up to Older to make the *Bulletin* powerful enough to break the railroad shackles.

"What I wanted was a fight against the machine, and it must be a winning fight," he explained.

"Earnestly considering the situation, I thought of James D. Phelan. He was rich, which gave him leisure and made him independent of money considerations; he was of Irish stock and a Catholic. I thought that if the *Bulletin*, which had been a very solemn, conservative paper under the old management, were to take up a political fight for a popular, clean young rich man, it would help the paper enormously."

Older impulsively took matters into his own hands. He rushed out of the *Bulletin* door one morning, down Market Street, and into the building owned by the popular Phelan.

The reserved Phelan stood by his polished desk in polite astonishment as a strange powerful giant, six feet two inches tall, rushed up to him with out-thrust hand. Phelan was small, intelligent, alert, always well-groomed. He was interested in poetry, the arts, and his fellow-men.

"I'm Older of the *Bulletin*," boomed Phelan's visitor with a winning smile. "Mr. Phelan, why don't you run for mayor?"

"What put such an idea into your head?" began the startled Phelan.

Older permitted no more. Hunched forward in a chair, his fine hands waving with the momentum of his oratory, cigar clenched, eyes narrowed, he poured forth his argument. He told of graft, of corporations, of crime robbing a city. A man was needed, cried the persuasive Older, a young man with a fine, clean name.

He left the thoughtful Phelan contemplating his duty of running for mayor of the city he loved.

It was even more difficult to persuade Crothers. The *Bulletin's* owner was a staunch Republican, and he objected violently to having his paper snatched away for the Democratic Party. But in California the Republican Party was the railroad, and it was the railroad Older wanted to outwit.

In the end he won over Crothers. He was allowed to support Phelan with the *Bulletin*.

That, to Older's mind, was the real victory of the election.

## Chapter VIII

### TASTE OF POWER

OLDER ordered written the first article naming James D. Phelan as candidate. In January of 1896 he had the satisfaction of seeing Phelan take office as mayor of San Francisco, and again in 1898, and again, under a new charter, in 1900. Later Phelan would be the first United States Senator from California to be elected by direct popular vote.

The editor who had taken over the destiny of the *Bulletin* one year before had chosen well. Phelan's administration was a firm and beautiful civic revolution. Supervisors were found willing to defy the railroad bosses. The city turned from graft to economy and pride. An honest man sat in the City Hall.

From his pioneer parents Phelan inherited his love for beauty, and this he impressed upon impressionable San Francisco. He dreamed of a city lovelier than Paris or Athens. He planned and beautified streets. Parks, buildings, public statuary, playgrounds, sprang under his able hands. Out of his poet's soul was later to come the Civic Center, that place of clear-cut public buildings framing a fountain where doves are fed by leisurely San Franciscans and flowers bloom the year around.

The way was not easy for the earnest young mayor. Phelan was bombarded by scandal-dipped pens hired by the bosses. For every improvement he was compelled to wage a new war against graft. The gas company charged excessive rates for lighting the streets. Phelan cut their rates, and for this saving of the people's money he was ostracized by certain wealthy men in his fashionable clubs.

During these years—happy years for San Francisco—the *Bulletin* edged slowly "out of the red." It had grown from quaking failure to dazzling success. The mayoral victory had added much to the *Bulletin's* prestige, and to Fremont Older's. Crothers raised his salary to sixty dollars a week.

Subsequent increases in salary were due to Hearst. The publisher several times offered editorships to Older. These Older rejected, for he was having far too much fun on his shoe-string *Bulletin,* but each offer brought him a rise of salary from the protesting Crothers.

The *Bulletin* developed a Sunday Magazine, lurid with tales of mystery, love, drama, science, romance, and religion. It was a frank appeal to the women readers. Women ruled the home, and the *Bulletin* was a home paper. Masculine San Francisco, however, swore by its sports page and editorials.

But Older did not relax. He watched every department, constantly criticizing and thinking up new improvements.

Older's passion now was for headlines. He had gradually accustomed the shocked Crothers to larger type. At times he gave half the front page to double-deck heads in two-inch type, with boxed excerpts from the story that ran in smaller type below. Sometimes he split the headline, alternating two-inch and one-inch Gothic type.

As a one-time type-setter he enjoyed playing with letters, trying out new varieties and combinations of type in the composing-room. It was a game he played with never-failing zest. He used different type for different stories. Sometimes he ordered a special font made to suit a particular story. He winced at a typographical error. He wanted, and would achieve, the "cleanest" sheet, freest from typographical errors, on the Coast.

The broken headline never seemed as effective to Older

as the full-page head, although it piqued curiosity. One of his specialties was the "dingbat head," made of one large line and two small, which was a certain circulation-getter. But his favorite was a "stepped" or double head in two-inch type running the full width of the page, as startling as gun-fire.

Older began using single-column subheads under the scare-head, as many as five to a story. Any news of special interest served to bring the glowing word "EXTRA" to the streets.

Every front page attracted new readers. Every page was a carefully planned triumph. Older was master of the sensational lay-out.

Around this time Arthur McEwen left him to work for Hearst on the New York *Journal,* and during the Spanish-American War in 1898 he made use of a cunning trick Older had invented when city editor of the old *Post,* a few years before. The opposition San Francisco paper the *Report* had been stealing Older's news stories, and Older devised a news item the lead initials of which, in reverse, read "The Report Steals News."

McEwen used the trick with resounding success. He trapped the *World* into printing in code, "We Pilfer the News."

The Spanish-American War marked the definite turn of the *Bulletin's* fortunes. Troops poured through San Francisco, the channel of war. Gigantic headlines and dramatic war stories were meat and drink to an excited city.

The century turned.

The *Bulletin* adopted a new slogan: "Always Fourteen Hours Ahead!"

There was beginning to gather around Fremont Older an amazing group of youthful hero-worshipers. Many would become famous editors, writers, attorneys, artists. They idealized the dynamic editor with the eternal cigar who charged out of his denlike office and through the local room as if he intended to rip down the building. They preferred working for Older at low salaries to working for any other editor. They warmed to his enthusiasms. They made his ideas their own.

People said he made writers.

"That's impossible," was his answer. "Writers are born. They either have talent or they haven't any."

But he had a way of noting some small item in the paper and demanding, "Who wrote that?" Then he would send to the local room for some dazzled young cub, tell him to pull up a chair, and, leaning back until his dark head bumped the wall, talk to the young fellow about himself, his thoughts and work and point of view, with an intimate interest that was the highest flattery. He would send out a newly-made follower treading on clouds.

Older was the driving urge behind the art department. When the nineteen hundreds began, a good photographic reproduction in a newspaper was still due to accident, and he preferred good drawings to poor photography. At one time he had twenty-five artists at work on the *Bulletin*, and all were good.

He introduced women artists on newspapers. He gave women writers the fairest chance an editor ever gave women. Older opened up the *Bulletin* pages to the suffrage fight, but long before women had the vote, they had every suffrage right in the *Bulletin* office.

He often recalled with a smile the lone woman who had occupied an unenviable position on the *Post* when he was its city editor in the early nineties. Every afternoon at a certain hour Older would take a long look around the local room. Everyone seemed to be miraculously busy. But

Older would catch some unfortunate reporter's eye, signal him, and to this elected one fell the solemn duty of seeing Nellie home.

No lady, not even a newspaper lady, could be permitted to walk home unescorted in the nineties.

Now Older made Virginia Brastow city editor of the *Bulletin*.

"The men were furious at first," he said, "but they soon learned to respect her judgment."

Older was by instinct more chivalrous than a Southern gallant, but chivalry, he believed, was best shown by giving women a fair chance. He put his women writers on equal terms with the men. He had faith in their ability. He forgot they were women. If he had a story to be written, the person best fitted to write it, man or woman, got the assignment.

"Editors make a mistake in not hiring more women," he often said. "They are the best possible business investment. They work harder, don't drink, and give more to their jobs."

He believed in stressing a paper's appeal to women. He gave particular attention to the "woman's interest." It was his ambition to make the sports page so interesting that even the women readers would demand it.

In 1901 Governor Gage appointed Older a member of the Special Health Commission, on which he also represented Mayor Phelan in Washington. In 1903, so well on its way to success was the *Bulletin,* the Olders went to Europe on their only European holiday.

On the boat going over they met William Randolph Hearst and his bride, Millicent Hearst. Hearst and Older had met in the late eighties, when Fremont Older, wandering journalist, had been one of the first reporters to work with young Hearst on his new *Examiner*. Older had scored a sensational scoop, and Hearst came into the local room to congratulate him. Older shied from his praise and a few days later left the paper. In that era, when he had so recently discovered the gaily drifting, roistering newspaper world, Older avoided responsibility. Hearst had intimated that he might go far on the *Examiner.* As an independent reporter Older had dreaded being tied down, preferring to work when and where the mood turned him.

For years Hearst and Older had fought in print. Older fought Hearst as represented by the *Examiner,* the powerful morning paper that perpetually menaced his own ambitious sheet. Older was doing his best with what poor materials were given him, trying to make a paralyzed paper pay, struggling for circulation against a Hearst paper backed by millions.

Now the rivals met, talked with enthusiasm together, found to their mutual astonishment that they liked one another.

For as strong-natured a Yankee as Older the European trip was a mingled delight and annoyance. He was impatient, wanting to dash from one spot to another, while the studious Cora, who spoke several languages, wanted to linger and enjoy.

"I'll never enter another museum as long as I live," he vowed.

He did enjoy England. He formed what would be a lifelong friendship with the London editor Alfred Harmsworth, afterwards Lord Northcliffe, who later visited the Olders in California. With Harmsworth, another devotee, Older followed the paths of his beloved Dickens through England. But on the opposite side of the Channel he was lost.

Gregarious as a bartender by nature, Older was the loneliest figure on the Continent those few months. His joy when in Italy he found a waiter who spoke a broken English was the high spot of the trip. He spent hours at the table discussing the affairs of the world with him.

Once, too, in Italy, he heard a voice in the night that sang gloriously in passing. Tears filled his eyes. Whose voice was it? Greater by far, he often said, than Caruso's.

Whenever Europe was mentioned, Older spoke wistfully of the voice singing in the Venetian night. He loved music passionately, but his sole contribution toward it was whistling the first line of "Believe Me, If All Those Endearing Young Charms."

He whistled this enthusiastically, walking or driving.

No one ever heard him get beyond the first line.

Europe was a respite in his hard-working life, but Older was glad to be home. Back before the doors of the *Bulletin* delivery rooms, he watched the damp editions rolling off the press and was again at peace. He loved spot news, excitement, being where things happen.

A few months after his return the Japanese fleet fired on the Russians at Port Arthur. Two *Bulletin* men, Grant Wallace and Lowell Otus Reese the poet, who later married a niece of Older's, were dining together the evening San Francisco learned that the Russo-Japanese War had begun.

"We rushed out and got Older on the phone," is the way Wallace tells it. "Older was that kind of editor, you could haul him out at any hour if you had an idea or a story. I told him the war had started and I wanted to go as correspondent. I can hear him now yelling over the phone.

"'God, what an expense—the paper can't stand it!' Older bellowed, and a second later, 'How soon can you go?'"

Wallace went as war correspondent for the *Bulletin* at forty-five dollars a week and expenses, and three novels were written around the romantic battlefield adventures of this tall, Hamlet-like reporter. Wallace said he was first hired by Older with the words:

"I've seen your copy. I know what you can do. Go ahead and do it."

After that introduction to office, Wallace, like all good *Bulletin* writers, was left strictly alone. Only the printers saw the stories they wrote, heads and all, until they made the page. Older trusted the judgment of his fellow-workers. He demanded the utmost of his reporters in enthusiasm and time. In return he gave them all his trust, his kindly attention, his glowing, heartfelt praise.

As the staff grew in size and competency, Cora Older's work lessened. For years she had come daily, in simple tailored suit and sailor hat, to work beside her editor husband. Now she wrote only special Saturday articles. She covered prison life on Alcatraz Island and the start of the horses at the race-track. She went by train to the state line to meet Sarah Bernhardt, interviewed the famous tragédienne in French, and sat up on the train the rest of the night to write her story. She reported the tragic scenes in the hop-fields when the pickers struck. She interviewed the ex-champion, John L. Sullivan. They discussed greatness.

"I could have been as great as Napoleon if I'd wanted to be a soldier," the Strong Boy of Boston told her modestly, "but that wasn't my line."

Cora Older's loyalty to the paper was so intense that when she developed ptomaine poisoning from eating a canned soup whose makers had refused to advertise in the *Bulletin*, she moaned in the hospital to Older:

"Jimmie, if I die, be sure to sue them! They didn't advertise with us."

In that dramatic city of lovely women and handsome men the Olders were an outstanding couple. Both loved social life in its gregarious, not snobbish, sense. Both loved the opera, the theater, the rich pageantry of San Francisco society "before the fire."

"Quite the handsomest couple in San Francisco," Gertrude Atherton said of them in her autobiography.

The Olders moved downtown to the Palace Hotel, the most famous hostelry in the world. There they gave dinners and gathered about them gay and interesting groups.

Against the dominant stress of her "Jimmie's" life Cora Older built her own, beautifully and with a calm strength. Her gentleness soothed his wild, nervous unrest. Through the stormy scenes that were to follow, she would fight for serenity, clinging to her books, her flowers, her friends. In the Palace Hotel she tended pots of geranium on a window-ledge and dreamed of someday owning a garden.

Cora Older would have her garden, after many years. In the meantime she was being rushed with her turbulent husband into a torrent that would buffet them cruelly and nearly carry them under.

For the *Bulletin* had become after ten years the most powerful newspaper in the West, and Fremont Older was the West's most powerful editor. He was nearing fifty, but he looked younger by fifteen years.

The *Bulletin* was sensational, beyond a mere yellow. It was vermilion.

But it had a conscience and a soul. The *Bulletin* was Older. Its building had been the great romance of the fighting editor's life.

But his real career was just about to begin.

## Chapter IX

### THE POLITICIAN

THE NEW MAYOR was selling out to the grafters! Eugene E. Schmitz was mayor. Phelan, three times mayor, had refused to run again. Schmitz, the suave, bearded orchestra-leader of a local theater, had been swept into office on the Labor ticket.

Memories of his election tormented Fremont Older.

The *Bulletin* had been left straddling the fence. There had been another candidate, the conscientious Joseph S. Tobin, and Older wanted to bring the paper to his support. But Crothers gave way to the railroad. After all, he owned the paper. He accepted $7,500 from the railroad, according to Older, and the *Bulletin* was forced to support its candidate.

The *Call* stated with amusement:

"Boyle is out for Schmitz, Older is out for Tobin, and Crothers is out for the stuff."

As a result Schmitz was mayor.

For the first time Older had not taken a definite stand in the *Bulletin* office, and for the first time he had failed. He felt that his paper had betrayed the public. He tortured himself with accusations. For everyone in San Francisco knew that the affable Mayor Schmitz, elected on the Labor ticket, answered to a little attorney with hair parted in the middle and handle-bar mustache who was frequently seen around the City Hall. This man, who looked like the original flying-trapeze hero, was the political boss of San Francisco—Abraham Ruef.

Older, recovering from the disappointment of the 1901 election, sent a message to the new mayor.

"You have the greatest opportunity any politician has had in years," ran the Older manifesto. "If you will be true to Labor, and not associate with the evil forces of San Francisco, there is nothing in the United States you cannot achieve politically."

This was at the same time a warning and a promise. The affable musician mayor ignored both. Schmitz answered Older, thanking the editor for his advice, but adding that Abe Ruef was his friend and they would stick together.

"This was the beginning," wrote Older later, "of the struggle that led into every corner of San Francisco life, into the depths of the underworld, to attempted murder and dynamiting and assassination, that involved some of the biggest men in the American business world, and wrecked them; that ended by filling San Francisco with armed thugs and overturning the Southern Pacific rule of California."

From the hour Schmitz sent that message to Older, the editor was out to "get" the grafters in the City Hall.

After Schmitz' election, graft mounted in the city like an ill-smelling tide. Older heard rumors of it everywhere. He was a man of the world now, well-dressed, a *bon vivant*, fond of good food and fine wines, belonging to clubs and very popular.

There were some who suspected him of being an agitator, not content to leave well enough alone. Their numbers would increase in those startling years "before the fire."

Older had forgotten much of the burning idealism that had once fired him. It had been submerged in the effort to make the *Bulletin* pay. In spite of the paper's astonishing growth, its expenses had likewise grown, and the margin between profit and loss was hair-line. It could not afford to take chances.

But the rumors of graft challenged Older.

"Scraps of talk, small bits of evidence, little intimations came in to me at my office," he wrote. "I heard of bootblack stands, houses of prostitution, gambling joints, that were being forced to pay small graft money. Nothing definite, merely hints here and there, a glimpse of something not quite clearly seen, an atmosphere that began to envelop the city.

"The big graft did not develop at once, but the times were ripening for it."

He had his reporters run down every hint of graft. He printed all they uncovered. For four years, with black headlines and flaying editorials, he would excoriate Mayor Schmitz and his money-grabbing crew.

But San Francisco was a light-hearted city. It shrugged gay shoulders at Ruef. It frowned lightly on the *Bulletin* that was violating the primary code in the West—not to question one's neighbor.

"Times are good," people said. "Why stir up trouble!"

But Older continued to write accusing headlines:

"Governor's Friend Has Fat Job." "Use Knife on City Payroll." "Sins of a Corporation Exposed."

These flamed with a passion as sincere as the more human headlines:

"Bloody Fight for a Woman's Love." "Drunken Policeman Stands on Corner Insulting Women." "Shot in the Back."

Crothers continued to be bewildered by the antics of his lusty newspaper. In his clubs his conservative friends taunted him about its radicalism. He shared their disapproval, even while he basked in its growth.

"There simply isn't a thing in it fit to read!" he complained with growing peevishness. Then he would add with amazement, "But, do you know, people seem to like it!"

But the *Bulletin,* Older argued, appealing to Crothers'

respect for tradition, had begun as a crusading sheet. He was determined that it should continue as one, to atone to the city for the mistake of the Schmitz election. Crothers would wilt before Older's persuasive arguments and retire to his own office, to solace himself with the Odes of Pindar.

Flushed with such small victories, Older swung against the corporations that were buying the good-will of the *Bulletin* with monthly donations.

He was finding it increasingly difficult to uphold the banner of civic decency over the *Bulletin* with one hand and accept corporation money with the other. He felt he could not fight the graft iniquities with a paper that accepted graft.

There was also petty grafting in the *Bulletin* offices that angered him.

"The fact that we were taking money from the railroad, the gas company, and other public-looting corporations was known in the business office," wrote Older. "As a result that department had become permeated with an atmosphere of chicanery and dishonesty. There was petty graft in the circulation department as well as the business office. *Bulletin* men, by various shady pretexts, were getting rugs, pianos, bicycles, furniture, jewelry, everything they could get hold of, in trade for advertising. The books were juggled.

"That this was a more or less common practice at that time made no difference to me. I was intensely desirous of cleaning up the whole office, in all its departments, so that I could go after Schmitz with clean hands."

The chief of a telephone company called on Older.

"We're planning to spend a whole lot of money on advertising," he told the editor with a beaming smile. "But we don't want ads. We want reading matter."

Older's glare was terrifying.

"You'll take ads!" he growled, his jaw clamping on the

nineteenth cigar of the day. "You'll not get one inch of reading matter!"

It was a show-down. Older called in Crothers, who wavered between the telephone subsidy and the best managing editor a newspaper-owner had ever the luck to acquire. He decided it was of greater profit to uphold Older.

Emboldened by this victory, Older slashed off the subsidy of the gas company. Not for many years would he be able to wipe out the railroad shame. But he stormed through the *Bulletin* offices, knocking out graft where he found it. "I hoped and struggled to make an honest paper," he explained.

Every step he took was protested by the owner.

Some of the *Bulletin* employees demurred. One of the redeeming features of working on a paper, they argued, was the perquisites enjoyed. But perquisites, Older answered, were bribes. There was some dispute with the local theaters, and Older ordered the *Bulletin* staff not to accept passes. Months later Cora Older discovered that she was the only person on the paper paying for her own tickets.

For himself, he refused in a thousand ways to accept money. Years later, during the graft prosecution, a man who attempted to bribe Older at this time would take the stand and testify to the editor's honesty.

In the meantime Older was hovering over the civic grafting like a taloned hawk. Scandal uncovered scandal. He wrote of them all—the hints of the liquor-license graft, the French-restaurant graft, the street-repairs graft, the Chinatown graft, the theater graft, the dance-halls and houses-of-prostitution and gambling-houses graft—all grist, he knew, to the pockets of the men in power. When the complete proof eluded, Older asked questions of his readers: "Who Owns a Certain House of Ill-Fame on Jackson Street?" "Who Received the Money for the Street Repairing Job?"

These were printed in large type for a city to answer.

Ruef the boss, in the shelter of the City Hall, grew angry. He was retained by rich corporations to secure franchises from the city. He ruled the political ring and the underworld of San Francisco. He unleashed both against the editor who couldn't be bribed. He made the saloon men take their advertisements out of the *Bulletin*. Other persons were incited to bring civil or criminal actions against Crothers or Older, who were arrested during this period seventeen or eighteen times.

Crothers, always shy and sedate, did not approve of anything the paper was doing and was reduced to despair by every new attack and arrest. Older, waiting in the Hall of Justice with Crothers to arrange their bail, would horrify the dignified newspaper-owner by glancing down the police line-up and remarking, "Well, Crothers, it looks as if we are the oldest offenders!"

But there was even more dangerous plotting.

One Saturday night Crothers crossed the dark alley between the business office and the press-room. He was struck over the head by gangsters, beaten, and left for dead.

When Older reported the slugging, the police refused to investigate. They were Ruef's police.

Ruef had put them on the force, one by one. Ruef publicly made fun of the attack on Crothers.

"I don't know what they want to attack me for," Crothers said plaintively. He was like a lamb in a tiger's den. His slugging in the alley was Crothers' greatest contribution to the cause.

Police, while on their beats, canvassed against the *Bulletin* and solicited subscriptions for a rival newspaper. They had orders from Ruef to treat the *Bulletin* as an outlaw.

But Older was in the excitement of his first great crusade.

He stormed at Ruef with new fury. He gave a new name, "boodlers," to the officials who were bleeding the city.

Mayor Schmitz and his crowd found that word plastered over their photographs in the *Bulletin*.

Out of the City Hall came a secret order:

"Get the *Bulletin!*"

Ruef's hand was closing down on the troublesome paper that threatened his reign with Schmitz. He had at his command not only the police, but powerful gangs from the Barbary Coast. They framed the "newsboys'" strike against the *Bulletin*.

It was called at delivery hour. The papers were rolling from the presses. The wagons were waiting at the doors. Older looked out of his office window to see Market Street black with men. They pressed forward, into the offices of the *Bulletin*.

"They descended on us, a storming mob, breaking our windows, attacking our clerks, besieging the office," wrote Older. "Policemen stood idly on the corners and watched this, doing nothing, under orders.

"It was impossible to get a *Bulletin* out on the streets for sale. Gangs cut the harness from the horses on the delivery wagons. They stormed our drivers. Professional thugs broke the arms of loyal carriers, beat up our solicitors with brass knuckles.

"Word had come down from above that the *Bulletin* must be forced to stop publication in San Francisco.

"It did not take me long to suspect the origin of this trouble. It lasted, however, for several days before I was able to get hold of the men who could stop it. On those days, coming out of the office, I was met by a storm of stones, bricks, bits of wood, everything that could be found and thrown. Whenever I appeared on the sidewalks I was surrounded by a clamoring mob, and had to fight my way through it at every step."

But he added that he enjoyed the situation immensely and was having "the time of his life."

When the attack began, Older rushed through the offices shouting encouragement. Champing his cigar, mustache bristling, he looked more than ever like a brigadier. Glancing through the broken windows, he was not surprised to see groups of grinning police stationed at the street-corners. He knew the strike had been organized in the shadow of the City Hall.

The rioters were not newsboys. The leader was the owner of a dice game protected by the police. The half-hundred lieutenants who led on the "boys" wore brass knuckles and had never sold a paper in their lives. They were paid hoodlums from the Barbary Coast.

Older made his way, late that afternoon, through threatening crowds before the *Bulletin* offices. The sidewalk he stepped upon was carpeted with blood and broken glass. He was not armed. All his reporters, even the minister who wrote his editorials, carried guns, and some wrote their stories with loaded guns on their desks; but Older refused to carry a revolver even when his life was at stake.

But the expression on his face was savage. The hoodlums fell back before that look. Stones were thrown, but fell short, after the tall form striding fiercely away in the gas-lit dusk of Market Street. Men were awed by Older.

Glowering, he strode at the head of a mob to the Palace Hotel. In the hotel suite Cora Older had fitted with the intimacy and charm of a home, he telephoned to a power in the underworld.

This man, one of the stanchest friends Older ever had, was known everywhere as "the Kid—King of the Pickpockets." Once, visiting Chicago, he was mistaken for a stool-pigeon by gangsters and beaten nearly to death. He was brought back to San Francisco and placed in an insane asylum.

The Kid's hallucinations were terrifying. In his dementia the mobs of gangland were still out to get him. His dazed brain recalled Fremont Older, the fighting editor who was respected and feared even in the underworld.

"Older could call off the mob!" he told a friend who visited him in the asylum, and the friend told Older.

Older, good-natured, always ready to do anyone a kindness, paid a visit to the asylum and assured the "King of the Pickpockets" that he had attended in person to calling off all enemies; the "King" would be molested no more. The Kid's mind seemed to clear. He left the hospital. He resumed his kingdom in San Francisco's subterranea. His respect for Fremont Older developed to a form of worship.

"The Big Fellow," he named Older. The name carried everywhere.

This was the man to whom Older telephoned the night the newsboys' strike began.

"All I want are the names," Older pleaded. "The names of the men who framed the strike!"

Within the hour the Kid called back and in low, furtive tones gave Older the names.

"They were well-known tenderloin characters," wrote Older, "inspired by Ruef and Schmitz."

In the meantime, as the city's police stood by laughing, Older hired police of his own. Mounted guards patrolled the streets while the more courageous carriers delivered papers. The framed strike cost the paper $25,000 in money, and Older was never able to estimate how much in business loss.

Then he swung into a counter-attack on the underworld. He sent for the four gang-leaders who had framed the strike.

They filed into his office, sullen and belligerent. They did not know whence came the tip to Older, who was frequently said by the underworld to possess second sight, so keen a knowledge he had of their most secret affairs. But there was murder in their hearts for the rat that had squealed as they faced the flashing-eyed giant who glared at them through the smoke of Havana cigars.

"Twenty-four hours," were his opening words, "and a thousand dollars, to break the strike!"

Their glances sidled together. No one knew how much power Older possessed. He had a look about him of holding their very lives in his hand.

"It'll take longer than that," said the ringleader uneasily.

Older smiled at the gangster. That smile was sardonic, ruthless. He had found out all about the man—his carefully hidden life, his affiliations, the things he needed to fear—before he sent for him. Older had the edge. How much he knew was revealed in his smile, and how much more he knew the man dared not guess. But he cringed.

"Twenty-four hours!" repeated Older between his teeth.

That night it was the turn of Abe Reuf, boss of the city, to stare appalled out of the windows of his home upon what appeared to be the unleashed hordes of hell. A thousand "newsboys" yelled and hooted at his door.

"Lynch the boss!" they howled all that night.

The four gang-leaders Ruef had hired to frame the *Bulletin* threw in this gesture of ill-will against the boss to please Older.

The next afternoon the *Bulletin* wagons tore unmolested about the city. The white-capped newsboys shouted extras again at their corners. The strike was broken.

It had done more harm to Ruef than to Older. The spirits of the fighting editor's warrior ancestors were set marching. Older was more than ever determined to lick the men who were running San Francisco.

## Chapter X

"AN ENEMY OF THE PEOPLE"

THERE were many forces in San Francisco fitted together for good or evil. The political, social, tenderloin, business, and labor worlds all touched secretly. The tenderloin looped the water-front and faded into the downtown business section. Its stench seeped into the courts and Federal buildings, the Hall of Justice and the City Hall.

For some time Older had been hearing rumors that Ruef, Mayor Schmitz, and the Chief of Police took hush-money from the houses of prostitution and the gambling-houses. He had printed these rumors in a fashion far from veiled, but the actual proof eluded him.

The town was wide open. Business was soaring. Along the Barbary Coast entire streets were given over to women, who were passed from fashionable houses to cheap cribs and on to the hideous short existence of the streets. They were last seen in dreadful rows in the women's court, in prison wards in the county hospital, in cheap wooden boxes bound for the potter's field. Money earned by their bodies was paid into the City Hall.

Older particularly hated one enterprising citizen. This was Jerome Bassity, the "King of the Maquereaus," one of the six political bosses of the city, who handled money earned by the women of the underworld. This man was massive, porcine, dark-jowled, perfumed, with small, greedy eyes. It was said that the opium-pipe he smoked was set with diamonds and rubies. He sent the women of his own particular "string" to hospitals to be operated upon that no money need be wasted upon them for illnesses or lost time.

Older printed articles flaying the maquereau king. He printed a life-size picture of his porcine countenance. Without mincing words he described the way the money was earned that this man was feeding into the coffers of the City Hall.

"But business is good," protested the average citizen, frowning at the poor taste displayed in such articles. They regarded Older's harping on the gambling and prostitution evils as bad manners. Everyone knew such things existed, but why bring them into the light of day? It was poor publicity for glamorous San Francisco.

Older got up a page. Under a banner line, "Houses of Ill Fame," were photographs of houses. Under each was told the story of the lurid life that went on inside. Under that were printed in large type the names of the proprietor and the owner of the property. And Older demanded to know what evil power permitted these places to run wide open in respectable neighborhoods.

He turned the spotlight of the *Bulletin* on the gambling evil. He needed proof—proof that showed bribery looped like an octopus around the City Hall, that would stir the Grand Jury to action. In his hunt for proof he flayed the gambling interests.

Dr. William A. Mundell distinguished himself in the gambling exposé. He later gave up reporting to become a detective and was head of the Burns Detective Agency in San Francisco. Every night "Doc" was up until three or four o'clock, drifting around the saloons and gambling-houses, drinking little, hearing much. "Doc" was born with a hand cupped to his ear. He came into the local room early, turned in three or four columns that included a list of the protected gambling-houses running wide open, which were mostly in Chinatown, and went home to sleep all day.

The city editor complained to Older of "Doc's" peculiar hours.

"Let him go ahead," answered Older. "I don't care if he never shows up in the office as long as he gets the story."

The *Bulletin* was like a tornado blowing dust out of the corners of a dirty room.

Older ran a front-page lay-out of Chief of Police Whitman, Mayor Schmitz, and Boss Ruef. Their faces were surrounded by pointing hands. Below ran the accusing words:

"One or More of These Men Are Taking Bribes in Chinatown!"

That charge brought Older a subpœna. He would receive many a summons before the Grand Jury. Each time, he always said, he was treated as if he were the guilty party. His mistake, he explained, was in attacking the big fellows who stood behind the little fellows.

On this occasion he faced the Police Commission. He was shown his printed accusations. The police wanted to know how Older knew they were taking money.

"I can't prove it now," he said ominously, "but I will!"

Older learned that a Chinese, Chan Cheung, was paymaster to the police for the Chinese gambling interests. Ordinary police who patrolled Chinatown were given $40 a week by the gamblers. Sergeant Ellis, in charge of the Chinatown squad, received $200 a week, Older learned.

"Before putting the screws on Chan Cheung," related Older, "I determined to work on Ellis."

By putting Ellis on the *Bulletin* payroll for two years at $125 a month, he persuaded the Sergeant to go before the Grand Jury, lay on the table before them $1,400, and say:

"I received that from Chan in Chinatown. That's seven weeks pay to overlook Chinese gambling."

Older waited, expecting the lid to blow off Chinatown while the city shared his indignation. Nothing happened.

"That was the end of that," he wrote. "I had not Schmitz or Ruef or Whitman or any one of the commissioners. I had simply landed $125 a month on the *Bulletin* payroll.

"Then I determined to get the truth out of Chan."

Older baited a trap in Chinatown to lure Chan out of hiding. He hired a friend of Chan's to entice the wily payoff man from his den and had him brought to the Grand Jury room. Then, with his friend and Grand Jury member Ed Bowes, he staged a "Belasco drama" which was in all probability the first amateur performance presided over by the man who would become the celebrated Major Bowes of radio. In the Grand Jury room the silent Chinese was faced with highbinders he had hired to commit various murders. As each soft-footed highbinder crept into the room, the district attorney asked him solemnly:

"Is this the man who hired you to kill?"

Each highbinder nodded. Chan stared back at them blandly. But his thin body trembled in the black satin suit he wore, for Older had ordered his opium taken from him.

Then the district attorney stormed over Chan.

"You can hang for this! In prison—with a rope around your neck!

"Or . . . you can go back to China . . . live in peace and plenty with your children and your ancestors.

"Who takes the protection money? Tell us that and we'll let you go!"

Chan answered blandly, "No sabe."

The Grand Jury gave up.

"And all the while," wrote Older indignantly, "Chief Whitman and Ruef and Schmitz were smiling around the streets of San Francisco. They knew the Oriental. They knew we could boil him in oil and he would not talk. They knew the Oriental, and I didn't.

"But I learned to know him then."

Older, determined to find evidence that would convince the Grand Jury, returned again to the prostitution evil.

"I thought that if I could only link the administration up with taking money from the women at 620 Jackson Street, at last I would have something to wake up the people of San Francisco. They surely would not stand for a mayor who took money from prostitutes.

"This house, that I called the 'Municipal Crib,' had been built by Schmitz contractors, Schmitz had been interested in the construction of it, and there were all the earmarks about the whole affair that would indicate that the administration had knowledge of the use of the place, and would also have some control over the revenue. There were sixty or seventy women in the place, and I was positive they were all paying revenue to Schmitz.

"But all my efforts at getting positive evidence were fruitless."

He made the "Municipal Crib" a byword. He kept it before his readers. He had the place raided and attempted to persuade girls to go before the Grand Jury and disclose to whom they were paying money. They were afraid.

Then the graft heads who had failed to silence Older with the framed "newsboys'" strike organized a boycott against the *Bulletin*. The head of the Building Trades Council declared the paper unfair.

"This charge was absurd," Older said. "Every employee on the paper belonged to a trade union. But unions representing 60,000 members were forced to boycott the *Bulletin*. Any member caught reading the paper was fined $5.00."

The boycott lasted many months. During that time the curly-headed Ruef held meetings and made the vilest personal charges against Older and Crothers. The audience cheered Ruef and hissed the *Bulletin*. Older, who had stirred up matters the city thought better left hidden, was railed against as a public enemy.

In vain the *Bulletin* protested that it was not trying to break up unionism and that the false politicians were selling out the unions. Restaurants, saloons, and stores were coerced into withdrawing advertisements and subscriptions. Circulation and advertising, twin arteries of a newspaper, were left bleeding.

The city was against Older. He overrode its hatred. He surmounted the attacks and the calumnies. For during the boycott people canceled their subscriptions, but they bought the *Bulletin* on the street. The *Bulletin* delivered at home cost sixty-five cents a month; at five cents a copy it brought a dollar and a half. So while subscriptions died, the street sales sky-rocketed.

People "bootlegged" the fearless newspaper that thundered and accused. And what people read, advertisers must utilize. Despite the boycott the advertisements sneaked back into Older's paper. He had not won, but he had not yielded.

Suddenly his bribe-hunt switched to Sacramento, the state capital. Two building-and-loan companies were being investigated by a Senate committee. Older learned that four committee members would vote to whitewash the companies for $1,650.

Older marked the bills himself, in his own office. He had them photographed, the marks showing. A man carried the bills to Sacramento in place of other bills that had been provided to bribe the four senators.

The next morning in the Senate the four sat well-groomed and smiling at their desks, the marked money in their pockets. They wondered at the appearance there of Fremont Older, the fighting editor, and his friends Franklin K. Lane, who would later be Secretary of the Interior, and the writer Arthur McEwen. These three sat directly in front of the four senators and did not take their eyes from them.

The Senate opened with prayer. Then Frank Nicol, a prominent attorney, arose to a question of privilege.

While the faces of the four senators whitened, Nicol read aloud a detailed account of the bribery. Meanwhile editions of the *Bulletin* with a four-page lay-out of the bribery story, featuring pictures of the four bribe-takers and the bills Older had marked, were rushing by train to Sacramento.

The senators were trapped. One fled to Mexico. One was acquitted. Only two paid for their bribe-taking with sentences in the state penitentiary.

Older had tasted blood. He was gloating, victorious. He did not see, as he would later see with an almost unbearable clarity, the tears and heartaches and broken homes attending upon those four indictments. Men who betrayed their trust, he felt, were criminals, and he believed in punishing crime.

His reverence for honesty was almost fanatical. It had been ingrained in his spirit on the harsh Wisconsin frontier.

He rushed back to San Francisco to find that public opinion had shifted in his favor. He had successfully trapped his men, and it was success the public wanted.

Another election was coming on, that of 1905. Older was determined that the handsome Schmitz should never again be mayor of San Francisco. He had fought Schmitz with accusations for four years, and the entire state knew what was being done in San Francisco's City Hall.

As he prepared to fight the reëlection of Schmitz, Older found to his astonishment that the elements who had opposed him were now on his side. Even the railroad felt that Abe Ruef was growing too powerful, and a new mayor would break the power of the Ruef machine.

This theory, Older found, was shared by both Republicans and Democrats. They were willing to unite against the laborites to prevent a three-cornered election fight which by dividing their strength would enable Schmitz to remain in office.

Because of Older's public service in trapping the Senate bribe-takers, his was the power of fusing the anti-Schmitz factions. Railroad, Democratic, and Republican representatives would unite, and Older the iconoclast, who had fought them all, was given the task of welding them together.

Older was also to have a veto power in choosing the candidate for mayor. They agreed not to select a candidate he did not approve.

But whatever man one faction suggested, the others refused. Older was driven to making his own selection. He thought of "Honest John" Lackman, who had been a supervisor and sheriff.

He called Lackman by telephone and asked the startling question he had once asked Phelan: "How would you like to run for mayor?"

All sides agreed upon Lackman. Representatives appeared in Older's office with a typewritten list of names. They had agreed among themselves upon a man to fill every office the mayor could appoint, and they wanted Older's preëlection promise that Lackman, if they elected him, would appoint every man on the list.

Older looked up from the list. His expression was volcanic.

"A preëlection bargain is a felony!" he stormed.

That finished Lackman as a candidate. A few hours later Older was told that the Democratic forces were planning to break from the reform league and nominate a candidate of their own. That night, sleepless, he tossed in his bed at the Palace Hotel.

He was up, as usual, at dawn. That habit, born of his farm training, was never to be broken. At an early hour he sent a message to a young attorney he knew, John Partridge, to hurry to the *Bulletin*.

Partridge, looking puzzled and rather sleepy, came into his office. Older was tilted back in his chair drawing at a newly-lit cigar. With the unstudied dramatic explosiveness that was one of his most astounding qualities, he shouted when he saw his young friend:

"John, it's you for mayor!"

Partridge was dumfounded. His political experience was sketchy, but he could not withstand Older's enthusiasm. He sat in the messy, littered office, listening while the flaming editor called the railroad representatives and got them to agree to support his new candidate. And then Older ordered an editorial written.

The editorial exposed the politicians' attempts to control a candidate's appointments. Older had it set up, and then he called in the men who had demanded the appointments and showed them the proof-sheet. He watched their faces blanch as they read, and he leaned across his battered desk.

"Either Partridge is nominated by two o'clock today," he told them grimly, "or this story goes on the street!"

By two o'clock Partridge was selected by the Republican League. "That foul bird," his enemies called him bitterly. That night the Republican convention met for the formal nomination.

"The convention met in old Pioneer Hall," wrote Older. "When it assembled I was walking up and down in a dark alley beside the building. Through the window I saw hats going up in the air and heard a roar of cheers, and I knew Partridge was in."

Now to put Partridge under the Democratic wire! If the Democrats refused to accept him as coalition candidate, the fight would be three-cornered and Mayor Schmitz would retain his power.

Older worried out a plan to bend the Democratic faction to his will. That night, in their rooms at the Palace, Cora Older watched her husband with anxiety. She knew his moods, and this was one of desperation. Finally he stamped to the telephone and summoned a friend who was well-grounded in politics.

"I want you to take a message for me," Older told this friend.

He was manipulating wheels within wheels. He had a weapon, and this was complete knowledge of the bribery case in Sacramento that had resulted in the trapping of the four senators. Older knew more about that bribery than he had printed at the time. Now he sent word to a certain powerful Democratic leader that if Partridge was not accepted, the entire truth of that bribe-taking would be told and names never before connected with the case would be printed.

Older had an answer back immediately. Most of it was unprintable.

But at eight o'clock that night John Partridge was indorsed by the Democrats as their reform candidate for mayor.

"That was a jubilant night for me," commented Older. "The *Bulletin* next day was full of rejoicing in the prospective victory of right over all the powers of graft and corruption. And this was sincere on my part, for I honestly believed that Ruef and Schmitz were the bad forces in San Francisco, and that when they were eliminated we could have a clean city.

"I plunged immediately into a most malignant campaign against Schmitz. The *Bulletin* was filled with cartoons showing Schmitz and Ruef in stripes. Our editorials declared that these men should be in the penitentiary and would be put there eventually."

One cartoon showed Schmitz as a dummy sitting on the knee of ventriloquist Ruef.

Partridge made speeches exposing the graft that was shaming the city. The campaign for the 1905 election was at its hottest.

Older began hearing queer rumors to the effect that the very political parties that had accepted his man were plotting against his election. His contempt for such rumors was magnificent.

"Everyone who was deaf, dumb and blind should have known the truth," he later commented sadly. "I went to my office on election night confident that we would win."

That night Fremont and Cora Older sat in the *Bulletin's* local room surrounded by friends who had dropped in to help celebrate the victory. Men raced in turn from the telephones, checking up the returns and writing out bulletins. As the different precincts were reported, Cora Older held herself ever more proudly. Her eyes were fixed on Fremont Older in perfect sympathy and understanding, but his expression was black.

"We're licked!" he admitted harshly.

One by one friends left them. There would be no celebrating that night. Only Arthur McEwen, back again from New York, remained, his clean Scots wrath unleashed on the mobs swarming under the *Bulletin* windows and hooting at the returns that counted Partridge out.

"I'm going back to New York tomorrow," McEwen stormed. "I won't stay in a town as rotten as this."

For, after all the fighting and exposure, the suave musician Schmitz was elected for the third time to the mayor's office, by 42,000 majority, the largest count he had yet received. And Schmitz carried the entire Ruef ticket with him, including eighteen Ruef-selected candidates for the Board of Supervisors. The crusaders had been wiped out.

Below the *Bulletin* windows the crowd was growing. They were for Schmitz, and they had whistles and horns. They shouted. They sent up rockets that threatened the business section of the city. Nobody cared.

By ten o'clock the crowd was mad with victory. They pressed up to the *Bulletin* offices and hammered in the windows. Rocks flew into the local room and into Older's little office.

The shouting redoubled, and Older and his wife and McEwen, looking through the broken windows, saw Ruef, the little curly-headed boss, being carried by in the center of a great mob, carried on the shoulders of cheering men. From their shoulders Ruef spoke, hurling insults against the *Bulletin,* against Older.

"He's not an editor—he's a raving anarchist!" Ruef jeered.

Rockets flared. Men and women cheered the boss and hooted the editor. The mob swept on with the dapper figure of the little boss swaying aloft.

"Let's get out of here," said Older shortly.

He strode out of the building with Cora Older walking proudly beside him. The mob washed around them like a clotted liquid. Thousands, drunk with triumph, blew whistles and horns and shouted insults. Older pushed his way between yelling men as if he saw and heard nothing.

Down Market Street that regal couple walked without hurrying their pace, and none could read the despair possessing both of them. And while men shouted and jeered, none dared molest the scowling giant Older. He was never known to lift his hand against any man, but men feared him.

Years later a play, Ibsen's *An Enemy of the People,* would recall that night to Older.

He was rated an enemy by the city he was fighting to save from national disgrace.

Tossing restlessly in his bed in the Palace, he sensed for the second time in his life the heartlessness of the human race. Once before, as a tiny lad in Appleton, Wisconsin, he had felt that deathlike revulsion against his fellow-beings. His mother was ill, and Fremont was told she was dying and he must run for the doctor.

As he sped through the village street, people laughed to see a bare-legged little boy running so wildly, with his face streaked with tears. Their heartlessness while his mother, as he thought, was dying made life unbearably hideous.

This mood would creep over Older with growing frequency. He felt it now while the crowds roared on and rockets soared over Market Street.

So they wanted to be robbed, those people in the streets, Older thought stormily. They wanted graft and prostitution—even murder—to serve as pillars for their city! They wanted crooks in power!

When Older finally slept, he was tormented by terrible dreams.

One of the election rockets set fire to an office-building near the Palace Hotel. Older wakened to the roar of flame and the screams of fleeing people. City and sky glowed like an evil pit.

"It seemed to my exhausted brain that all the powers of hell had been unleashed," said Older.

That night, he often said, was the bitterest in his life.

## Chapter XI

### THE GRAFT-HUNTERS

IT WAS NOT in Older to stay beaten. Something in his nature rose recharged and in need of more action. He would not, like his friend McEwen, leave San Francisco. Older received New York offers, but San Francisco was his chosen city and the *Bulletin* his life-work. He would continue with the paper and his fight to make the city clean.

Ruef, after the 1905 election, boasted everywhere that he would smash the *Bulletin* with libel suits. The *Bulletin*, someone wrote later, was "the most consistent and fearless critic of the Ruef-Schmitz régime." The contest was narrowing down to Ruef and Older.

Older had to get Ruef.

It was a man-hunt, relentless as that Older had prosecuted with the doctor he believed had killed his wife. Then he had followed clues, tracked down witnesses, pursued a scent years after Bowers had gone free. He was as ruthless now.

Behind Older's hatred of graft was the pioneer's belief in honesty. He had come from a world where men did not cheat one another. Never in his life did he take advantage of perquisites. He even refused to buy, through the paper, anything at wholesale.

San Francisco read Older's flaming editorials with admiration and sympathy. But while it condemned and resented graft, it tolerated. Graft had always existed. Graft was in the clean salt air of the city, it was in every breath one drew. Older must make it tangible. The public must be made to believe his graft charges.

This problem became his obsession. A sharp line drew down his high forehead in those years, born of constant tension and watchfulness.

He carried his problem one evening into a French restaurant.

The French restaurants were the city's delight and scandal. Not even in Paris, said gourmets, did one find better food or finer wines—California, Italian, French, Spanish. Their sea food, chicken, crêpes Suzette, and champagnes had made the French restaurants of the harbor city famous around the food-loving world.

But above their public dining-rooms, where the men took respectable wives and sisters, were other rooms. And these upstairs dining-bedrooms caused many rumors.

One restaurant possessed an elevator large enough to hold an automobile. Car and passengers boarded the elevator and were whisked to the mysterious regions above stairs. Red plush and secrecy held inviolate the indiscretions of San Francisco's flaming youth.

Older, as became a *bon vivant,* was often to be seen dining in the French restaurants. On this pleasant evening in 1905 he entered one of the most celebrated.

The proprietor greeted Older, not with his customary effusiveness, but with Gallic despair.

"Meestaire Ol-daire," he wailed. "I am ruin!"

Because of their upstairs dining-rooms and a growing hostility on the part of the respectable, the French restaurants were in danger of losing their licenses.

Older studied the bill of fare.

"Why don't you see Ruef?" he suggested sardonically, for the notorious boss was ever in his mind.

Several nights later he again dined at this place. A beaming host thanked Older for his splendid suggestion.

"I call on Ruef," purred the grateful restaurateur. "He feex everytheeng!"

This was the most definite proof of bribery yet discovered. Older's hopes flared. He printed the story headlined as a challenge to the city. He waited for it to rise against Ruef.

As usual, nothing happened.

Older knew then that nothing could be expected from a graft-ridden San Francisco accustomed to its shame. He said to his wife:

"Cora, I'm going to Washington."

"To Washington?"

"Yes, to get help from Heney."

Even Cora Older thought the trip would be fruitless.

Francis J. Heney had won the attention of the nation as prosecuting attorney for President Theodore Roosevelt in the famous Oregon "7–11" land-fraud cases. Some time before, he had made an election speech in San Francisco.

"If I had control of the district attorney's office," Heney had said in that public address, "I would indict Abe Ruef for felony and send him to the penitentiary. I personally know he is corrupt.

"If you elect these people, the graft of this city will become so great that the citizens of San Francisco will ask me to come back and prosecute him. When the time comes I will do as the people request as a matter of civic duty."

Ruef had limited his answer to calling Heney a liar.

There had been no actual proof then against the grafters. Now Older had this one clue, one fragment of bait, to tempt Heney—the French-restaurant bribe. Armed solely with it, he left in secret for Washington.

It was not his first trip to the East since he had left it as a wandering printer boy. In 1895, when Older first took over the *Bulletin* and tasted political power, he went to

Washington to urge upon President William McKinley the appointment of a friend of his, Judge James A. Waymire, as Secretary of the Interior.

McKinley, Older wrote, proved affable and bland. He protested his love for the dear judge. The trusting editor from the West was given in Washington what is known today as the "run-around," made up of easily broken half-promises. For the first time Older watched the oiling of political wheels. He returned home with a wavering faith in any political honesty.

During the graft prosecution many truths and many lies would be raked up against Fremont Older. He smiled at them all.

"They haven't discovered my real past," he would retort. "I voted for McKinley!"

At Washington he talked with Heney and Detective William J. Burns of the Secret Service, who was helping Heney with the land-fraud cases. Both were instantly responsive to Older's suggestion that they investigate the graft on the west coast.

"It will take at least a hundred thousand dollars to begin the investigation," mused Heney.

"You'll have it!" promised Older, rashly.

He was asked to the White House to meet the President. Roosevelt bared his immense canines at Older's revelations. He promised to bring down the weight of the "Big Stick" on the looters in San Francisco's City Hall.

"When?" Older wanted to know.

When, Roosevelt could not say. Heney and Burns were still occupied with the Oregon scandal. But "Teddy" promised action, and Older rushed back to San Francisco with his mighty secret, to the task of raising a hundred thousand dollars.

His thoughts flew ahead to James D. Phelan. The former mayor was a millionaire who dearly loved his city. Under his calm hand the city had been honest. Would Phelan give a fortune to have it so again?

Also there was Rudolph Spreckels, another young millionaire who had made an intelligent campaign for an underground-trolley system to help beautify the city. His campaign failed when the street-car company used bribery to fight it, embittering Spreckels against prevailing politics. Phelan and Spreckels were two of the largest landowners in San Francisco.

Older called on Phelan and Spreckels. Both came wholeheartedly into the plot, though neither had a whit to gain by it—beyond satisfaction. They promised to underwrite Older's scheme to the amount of fifty thousand each.

Now Older was ready. He wrote Heney to come west. He waited, fuming with impatience.

While he waited, his grandfather, Squire Lewis Augur, died across the Bay from San Francisco at the age of ninety-eight. The patriarch who had preached against slavery had lived to see the little boy he had reared in hero-worship of the editor Horace Greeley himself a successful editor. He was alert and intelligent to the last. Older on both sides of his ancestry came of long-lived stock. Older and Augur men lived to be seventy-eight, ninety-eight, one hundred, and several well over a hundred.

Older's mother had died in 1895, shortly after her son became managing editor of the *Bulletin*.

The year turned while Older impatiently waited word from Washington, and it was April, 1906. Caruso was singing in San Francisco. Cora Older gave a supper in honor of the great tenor. The ladies came late into the patio of the Palace Hotel, where the dining-tables were placed around a circular carriage-way, and braziers warmed the crisp spring air. Older and Enrico Caruso sat alone at the table, waiting.

Social grace with Older was something that came and

went with the tides of mood. He could be marvelously winning, charming a roomful of people with his warm, all-conquering personality. He was never known to be rude to anyone who might rank as a social inferior. Yet he could be almost magnificently rude.

This evening his mind was with the graft-hunt. Cora Older, rustling into the patio with her other guests, felt her heart sink. Caruso was dolefully drawing a cartoon on his menu-card. Older was smoking, hunched forward, scowling blackly into space. They had sat half an hour without speaking.

"What was there to talk about?" Older stormily apologized later. "He can't even talk English!"

On another evening that April Caruso appeared on a balcony high over the patio and sang. His golden voice poured through the rotunda where the carriages circled, where the braziers glowed. On the night of April 17 he appeared for the last time in San Francisco. He sang Jose in *Carmen*.

The Olders heard him sing Jose that night. Upon returning to the hotel Cora Older left an early call. She was going to Stanford University to a lecture on philosophy by William James.

At five the Olders wakened. So did all the trembling terrified city. It was the earthquake of April 18, 1906.

Cora Older stood braced, California-fashion, in the doorway, her bare feet gripping the floor. Older remained in bed, refusing to budge for a mere earthquake. The entire hotel seemed to circle on its axis, settle and shake violently, heave again. The floors rocked like decks at sea. The crashing in the sitting-room of a life-size bust of their novelist friend Gertrude Atherton gave the impression that the walls had fallen.

"This isn't fair!" Cora Older found herself repeating wildly. "We're too young to die."

They struggled somehow down the shuddering stairs, pulling on the evening clothes they had worn the night before. Their dressing was completed in a street that had upheaved and split and turned over, tossing office-buildings, hotels, restaurants, street-cars, telephone poles and wires, into a confusion that was nightmare. In near-by Union Square they found Caruso sitting on a park bench and singing to see if the shock had harmed his voice. "I shall never return to this city," he vowed, and he never did.

Thousands of white-faced men and women and children, half-dressed, homeless, milled past them, fleeing to the ferries. The Olders joined the procession and that evening were safe in the hotel at San Rafael, a fashionable resort where they had spent several summers. San Francisco's "best people" had hurried across the Bay to San Rafael, and the hotel was crowded with society refugees dressed in a Mardi-gras assortment of evening dress, bath robes, night clothes, top-hats with bedroom slippers, fur coats, and even blankets.

The next day Hiland Baggerly arrived with bulging suitcases. As a newspaper man he had been able to make his way through the police lines into the blazing Palace Hotel and rescue their clothing. Less fortunate guests wore evening dress to the breakfast-table and silk hats on the tennis-court.

Early every morning Older hurried to San Francisco and toiled to save the *Bulletin*. The newspaper plant was a heap of cinders and twisted machinery, but he gathered his staff together across the Bay in Oakland and brought out the paper temporarily in the plant of the Oakland *Herald*. Amid the roar of the flames as for three days San Francisco burned, amid the cries of the lost and bereaved and dying, the *Bulletin* marched with flying headlines.

"San Francisco was destroyed," wrote Older. "I was in the midst of the cataclysm, working, as all men did in those feverish days and nights, first to save what I might of the *Bulletin*, and later to help others who needed help.

"But my mind was so filled with one idea that even in the midst of fire and smoke and heaps of ruins, I thought of our plans to get Ruef and Schmitz, and mourned the delay I feared the fire had caused. I worked frantically, feeling that this overwhelming disaster must be met and handled, so that we could go on with our hunt of the grafters."

The *Bulletin* files had burned in the fire. Advertising was wiped out, for all business was destroyed in the ravaged city. Among the many things lost in that desert of ash and smoking ruin was, temporarily, the graft prosecution.

Within a few days Older found temporary quarters for the paper above the old ice-house at the foot of the Telegraph Hill cliffs, near the water-front. He brought his staff back to the ruined city. The reporters struggled through miles of desolation and questioned the soldiers, for the city was under martial law, for tragic reports of the vanished. The *Bulletin* ran a daily "Missing Friends Column," where people asked information of friends or relatives lost in the earthquake and fire.

As the task of rebuilding the city began, Older began that of rebuilding circulation, rebuilding advertising, building, in short, another *Bulletin*. Before long he was able to establish the paper in a well-equipped modern plant on Market Street in the very heart of the city.

Older unfurled larger headlines. Looting was rampant in the ruins. Thousands living in shacks and tents were in terror. *Bulletin* headlines excoriated the robbers and the inadequate police. Older demanded news, more news, hot news, spot news, well played. He drove his staff in that broken shack of a press-room as they had never been driven before. And they, hot-blooded young enthusiasts all, worked as though their very souls were lashed to Older's. He himself did the work of many men.

He played stories to the limit of their human appeal. During those nerve-racking days he sent a reporter to Honduras to find a missing San Francisco embezzler. The discovery of the man in hiding and his confession to the reporter filled a half-page box on the front page.

"Mitchell in Honduras with $40,000!" shrieked the head. And under that, in the seven-column box, were the remorseful words of the embezzler, beginning:

"My God! How I have suffered! If ever a man went through hell on earth I have! I can't stay in any place long. I must keep traveling all the time. I am restless. My thoughts torment me, but I cannot get away from them. It is awful to be under constant suspicion, to know that men do not trust and believe you!"

A few weeks after the fire, Older, striding down the gutted canal that had been Market Street, met Francis Heney, the man he had gone to Washington to see. Heney was paying a flying visit to San Francisco. Older pumped his hands.

"God, I'm glad to see you!" he said earnestly.

"Where can we talk?" answered Heney.

They found an empty tent and two boxes for chairs. Hunched together, surrounded by miles of ruin, they spoke in low voices.

"I'm through with the land frauds at last," said Heney. "I'm ready whenever you are."

Older pledged the hundred thousand to underwrite the graft investigation.

In that moment, in a tent in the still-smoldering city, was launched the crusade that would shock the continent.

Heney said he would not accept a penny for his services. Nor did he.

"This is my city," he said as they left the tent together. He looked out over dark acres of broken, charred stores and homes, tents that housed fugitives from earthquake

THE GRAFT-HUNTERS

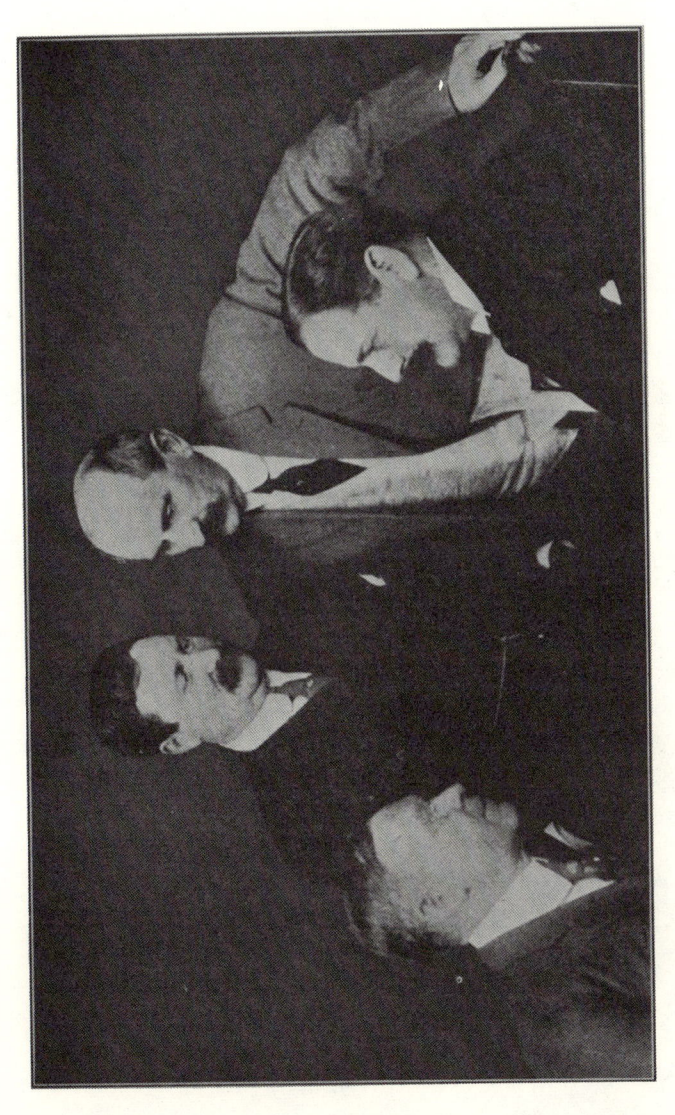

Left to right: Francis J. Heney, William J. Burns, Fremont Older, Rudolph Spreckels.

## THE GRAFT-HUNTERS

and flame, soldiers patrolling with drawn guns, homeless families huddled like gipsies around camp-fires. Heney added, "I can do this much for her."

Then there moved quietly into San Francisco William J. Burns of the Secret Service and his group of detectives who were to investigate the inner workings of the city. They established secret headquarters. Night and day, for months, detectives followed every move made by the boss, the mayor, and the police chief of San Francisco.

The government men worked in secret. Only Theodore Roosevelt, Burns, Heney, Older, Spreckels, Phelan, and Burns' detectives knew of the graft-hunt. But their quarry was "tipped off."

"At this time knowledge of the embryonic investigation was closely guarded," Cora Older revealed several years later in her article, 'The Story of a Reformer's Wife," in *McClure's Magazine*.

"Not more than eight men in the United States knew of it.

"In those days the character sifting of the citizens of San Francisco had not begun. Too often the worthiness of associates had been insufficiently tested. So it happened that one of the little band of reformers confided to a close friend the purpose of the men allied in secrecy.

"Within twenty-four hours the information came straight to Mr. Older that Ruef knew of the intended inquiry; the railroad knew of it.

"The little boss, enmeshed in crime, was terror-stricken. Who the confidant was that turned informer is an interesting question.

"The answer is even more interesting: a justice of the Supreme Court of California!"

Years later this Supreme Court judge who acted as "tip-off" for Abe Ruef was exposed by Fremont Older as a bribe-taker in a sensational litigation.

But before the grafters knew they were being stalked, Heney had completed the study of Older's evidence in the several French-restaurant briberies Older had uncovered, and found it a legally sound case. The Grand Jury had previously refused to investigate this evidence.

The graft prosecution found a powerful ally in William H. Langdon, the new district attorney, who brought a copy of the Penal Code into Older's office one day, thumped it on the desk, and exclaimed, "I mean to enforce that!"

While the detectives were piling up evidence against Ruef and Schmitz, Older was whetting the indignation of the city with headlines. The *Bulletin* scored the lawlessness running unchecked in the fire-swept city. "The political boodlers and highway robbers" were denounced as brothers in crime. Charges were brought by headlines:

"Police Protection Purchased." "Gas Pipe Thugs Permitted to Rove Ruins by Lawless Police." "Hoodlums Rule City."

The front page of one extra was flooded with five headlines and a box:

"Policeman Caught Robbing Dying Man."

The *Bulletin* flayed the police force. It charged wholesale burglary by men in uniform. Ruef had placed men with criminal records on the force, and the *Bulletin* exposed these, giving the name and record of each man. It charged that Ruef had placed certain "jail-delivery judges" on the bench and that a nod from Ruef would set any criminal free. It charged that the police chief, owned by Ruef, controlled the saloon vote and that the chief took licenses away from saloon-owners who didn't swing votes the Ruef way.

The *Bulletin* charged that Ruef was planning to take $10,500,000 from the treasury of the helpless city to use for purposes of bribery, of which three millions would be used to bribe the city supervisors and fix the voting-machines for the coming state primary election of 1906.

And politicians, roared the *Bulletin,* were driving the refugees from the parks! Where were the homeless thousands to go? To whom did the parks belong, if not to the people?

The homeless were permitted to live on in the parks.

And politicians, bellowed the *Bulletin,* were protecting the wreckers who out of greed were dynamiting the good houses left standing.

Since the earthquake nineteen thousand revolvers had been sold in San Francisco. Every night had its quota of sluggings and attacks and robberies.

"This is a carnival of crime!" Older's paper screamed over the ruins.

The city by the Golden Gate was compared everywhere to wicked Port Saïd. In distant cities ministers declared from their pulpits that San Francisco, like Sodom and Gomorrah, had been punished with disaster for its sins.

When election-time came, a judge made a costly error. He sent to the penitentiary a man caught stuffing ballot-boxes. It was said by the *Bulletin* that Ruef attended in person to the fixing of the voting-machines in use, paying heavily for the right to rig them with rubber bands so that the votes of those not "in the know" did not register, and that Ruef punished the judge who punished the ballot-stuffer by removing him from the bench.

"Why prolong the farce?" howled the *Bulletin.*

"Let Ruef cast the ballot! Why have an election? Why bother about voting machines? . . . One is sufficient! Let it be made of gold and inscribed with the King's image and coat of arms and let it be set up under the remnants of the blasted dome of the City Hall, and in the presence of the majority of voters—the majority, mind you—let Abe Ruef cast one ballot for the people and let them say a loud 'Amen!'"

This was Older's voice, trumpeting his fury. Ruef, frightened, made a show of reform. He removed the chief of police and put in another.

"Both corrupt!" booed the *Bulletin*.

In the midst of scorching charges and the struggle to rebuild the city came another catastrophe. The street-car men struck, presumably for three dollars a day.

But the real cause of the strike was far more sinister.

## Chapter XII

### BLACK FRIDAY

FREMONT OLDER charged in the *Bulletin* that the United Railroads strike was "framed" by the president of the railroad, the Eastern capitalist Patrick Calhoun, to distract public attention from the graft discoveries.

"Sooner or later the trail of graft we were uncovering would lead to Calhoun," explained Older. "Ruef was attorney for the United Railroads; Calhoun its president. Calhoun was the big fellow behind the little boss.

"The street-cars were tied up. This second calamity, falling upon the disaster of the fire, halting the city's attempts at rebuilding, infuriated the business men and property-owners of San Francisco.

"Calhoun knew the city; he knew what would influence the powerful men of the city. He knew San Francisco was in ruins and that the business men above all things wanted the street-cars to run, otherwise they would be utterly ruined."

Calhoun answered the strikers by sending three trainloads of strike-breakers headed by James Farley, professional strike-breaker, from New York to San Francisco. When the men arrived after having been hissed in the cities en route, the fire-littered streets of San Francisco grew sodden with the blood of strikers and strike-breakers and police. The strike-breakers took over the street-cars and ran them through mobs of protesting men.

"Rioting broke out on the streets," wrote Older, describing the situation. "Men were beaten, crippled, killed. The city was in turmoil."

Then Calhoun arrived in San Francisco. Older greeted the railroad president with triple headlines in three-inch type:

"Calhoun Refuses to See Carmen!"

Up and down Market Street in his shining automobile, a hero to the nervous city, rode magnificent, silvery-haired Calhoun. Around him men rioted; sixty were maimed, five killed. In reality Calhoun had nothing to fear. He was surrounded by armed guards, and he had paid $700,000, it was charged, to the city administration. But he was creating the effect he desired.

"There goes a man who isn't afraid of anything!" men said admiringly, pointing after the smiling capitalist in his expensive car.

Older, certain that the strike had been planned by Calhoun, certain that men were struggling and rioting and dying because of Calhoun, pitied the families of the strikers. He had tried to prevent the strike. Now the labor leaders who with Older had striven to avert it informed him that the strike would end if they could not raise $5,000 by noon. The money was to feed the hungry families of the men who were striking for three dollars a day.

Older's mistakes were of the heart. He thought of the sacrifices the men had made and the sufferings of their families, and he knew all their struggles would be in vain if the strike failed. Out of pity he raised the money to feed the women and children.

That would be held against Older

His headlines slashed on. The Grand Jury cleared the United Railroads in a street-car accident case. The *Bulletin* shouted:

"Underlings of Ruef Whitewash Company."

Older no longer hinted; he knew, and he printed all he

knew. In spite of the street-car strike, bitterness grew against Ruef and Schmitz.

Phelan, the ex-mayor, brought the serious charge in the *Bulletin* that San Francisco had burned because of its inadequate water-supply. There had not been enough water to fight the fire, he said, because the water company had bribed away the city's rights. As a result three hundred and fifty millions had gone up in flames.

Schmitz' insulting answer to his honest predecessor hid panic: "Since the fire Phelan hasn't been in his right mind."

Gigantic headlines in the *Bulletin* drove home Phelan's charges:

"Administration Betrayed City by Its Scandalous Water Deal." "Schmitz Lives in an Atmosphere of Graft." "City Is Betrayed."

Such charges twisted the barb in the ruined city. The tragic losses of the taxpayers were painfully new. The phenix city under the ashes was at last aroused.

The *Bulletin* stormed on:

"How long will citizens tolerate the rule of the gas-pipe, the fenderless cars, impassable streets, criminal police and corrupt administration of affairs?

"How long will it tolerate Abe Ruef—boss of three political parties and the ruler of the city?"

Older would write his own answers to these questions, for the graft-hunters were ready at last. The French-restaurant briberies had been worked into a well-grounded case by Heney. Older had uncovered new evidence, a $20,000 bribe Ruef had accepted from promoters for prize-fight permits. Daily, Burns and his men were turning up fresh evidence against the "unsavoury boss" and the musician mayor. District Attorney Langdon had all the evidence in his office. In Washington President Roosevelt read with vigilance the secret reports being sent him on graft in California.

The *Bulletin* gave the first public hint of the graft prosecution. It announced that Francis J. Heney, the fraud investigator, had been made a deputy district attorney by District Attorney Langdon. Wise ones, reading between the lines, knew this meant a prosecution.

Mayor Schmitz promptly shook the ashes of his native city from his glossy boots and fled to Europe. He sailed after a wine party which lasted all night through. The *Bulletin* compared it to Belshazzar's feast when that doomed king saw the handwriting on the wall. It also charged that Schmitz left for Europe not only to escape investigation, but to sink his "political loot" in European bonds.

The Mayor's departure left the city in the hands of Supervisor James L. Gallagher, under the guidance of Abe Ruef. It left Ruef alone facing his enemies.

The little boss with the high forehead was a shrewd attorney. He knew that Heney's appointment as deputy district attorney was the first threatening step in his direction. Ruef made a desperate countermove.

He removed District Attorney Langdon from office. He made himself district attorney. It was the act of a cornered man.

His next step was to dismiss Heney.

"The brazen effrontery of this staggered us," wrote Older. "Immediately, however, we perceived the danger in which we stood.

"With Ruef as district attorney, our chance of getting a friendly Grand Jury was removed from the realm of the possible into that of the fantastic."

Older, by confiding to Judge Thomas Graham the secret plans of the graft-hunters, had persuaded him to dismiss what Older insisted was a Ruef-selected and crooked Grand Jury, and he was demanding that a new Grand Jury be drawn.

The night Abe Reuf made himself district attorney, the news was telephoned to Older at the San Rafael Hotel. Older left for San Francisco at dawn, driving the large new White Steamer, brass-glinting, snorting, terrific, that was his pride. It was one of the first cars in general use in San Francisco, and it won several silver racing cups. Usually, however, it was to be seen in tow of horses on its way to one of the blacksmith shops that served as early-day garages. A hundred-mile drive without a serious breakdown was a miracle.

On this morning Cora Older, in goggles and veils, sat by the side of her grim-lipped husband. Whenever anything happened of particular interest or excitement, Older wanted her with him. She was to miss, however, the events of this day that would be remembered for years in San Francisco as "Black Friday."

On the highway en route to the Bay the bearings flooded in the steam vaporizer. The car stopped. There was no smithy within miles. Older stamped on strenuously to the ferry. For six blazing hours Cora Older waited in that topless open car.

"I intended to send a machinist over to change the vaporizer," Older later explained, "but something exciting had happened in the graft prosecution and I forgot that I even owned a car. I was in a whirl until three o'clock in the afternoon, when what I neglected to do suddenly dawned on me. It was a horrible moment, but I lost no time in brooding over it. I made the four o'clock boat with a machinist, and he had the car running in a few minutes.

"Mrs. Older had spent a wretched day sitting in the tonneau and wondering what had become of me."

This day he made history.

As Older came off the ferry into Market Street, he heard the morning-paper boys shouting, "Ruef Made District Attorney." The sabre-cut mouth tightened under Older's mustache as he hailed a hack. As the horses clattered over the ash-strewn Embarcadero, Older planned a sensational "extra."

That extra took the place of the old Vigilante bell that in the fifties had summoned all honest citizens. By eleven that morning twenty thousand extras were abroad. Hundreds of white-capped *Bulletin* boys ran through the streets giving the papers away.

"Good Citizens—Act!" trumpeted the *Bulletin,* and its editorial page, rimmed with an inch of black, accused, "Ruef's Illegal Act is a Confession of Guilt!"

"Nothing in the history of anarchy," raged the editorial, "parallels in cool, deliberate usurpation of authority this latest exhibition of lawlessness in San Francisco.

"Government is seized to overthrow government. Authority is exercised in defiance of authority. The office of the district attorney is seized deliberately, with malice aforethought, with strategy and cunning, and used as a fort for thieves to battle down the forces of citizenship.

"The criminals, accused of felony, after inviting investigation and pretending to assist, have shown their hypocrisy by committing an act of anarchy which, while it might be tolerated for the time being in San Francisco, would result in the execution of these men in any government of Europe."

The *Bulletin* called upon all good citizens to gather in the name of justice at the old Jewish synagogue. The public offices had been scattered over the city by the fire and there at two o'clock that afternoon Judge Graham would be forced to decide which should be recognized as district attorney—Ruef or Langdon.

By twelve the city was a-swarm. Thousands of men came tramping from every quarter through the cinder-strewn streets, answering the call of the fighting editor. By two o'clock a dense crowd milled around the old synagogue which Ruef had hastily filled with his men. Outside the doors were his followers, many wearing the mark of the underworld. Massed against them was the decent citizenry, a committee of justice many thousands strong. There were to be seen in the crowd ministers and doctors and rabbis, leading merchants and lawyers and men prominent in society.

There were men in that crowd who carried ropes.

Forty police—Ruef's police—stood guard at the doors of the tabernacle where Ruef had been wont to worship. When Older arrived with a group of his reporters, Ruef's deputy sheriffs threw the newspaper men out of the hall and handled Older as roughly as they dared.

But they were afraid of the editor. No one knew how deeply those strangely delicate hands of his were dipped in power. It was known he had visited Washington, that he was responsible for the graft prosecutors' coming to San Francisco, that he was in active correspondence with the President.

When Heney arrived, a Ruef deputy searched him for concealed weapons, to give a bad impression to the crowd.

But the people were no longer awed by Ruef. Outside the building watched the finest men of the city. They glared in windows. They fought back Reuf's hired hoodlums. They forced their way into the synagogue.

Older was magnificent in his fury. He stormed up and down with his reporters. He smiled, a dangerous smile. He was sensing the full poetry of his existence. He loved this— the danger, the imposing of his own mood on a city, the hope of justice, the sense of power!

He, Langdon, Heney, and Burns had been cheered in turn by the great crowd. His heart warmed to them. It hardened against Ruef, the curly-headed politician approaching now through the menacing crowd, attended by his special guard of police detectives. A word would have cost Ruef his life, but he seemed utterly fearless. The infuriated mob pressed around the little boss, and Ruef had to be rescued by his own police.

Judge Graham appeared in the crowded temple. He was pale. Men muttered as they made way for him.

The Judge knew, every soul in the temple knew, the mood of the maddened thousands. A word, and this would be '56 again! In the days of the Vigilantes grim-faced crowds had watched men swing at rope-ends who had betrayed their city for money. There were men in the temple who as boys had witnessed the awful scenes of primitive justice exactly half a century before.

Judge Graham, white to the lips, declared Langdon the lawful district attorney.

When that word was passed to the thousands outside, their cheering could be heard over all San Francisco.

Older pushed his giant's way through the crowded room to the judge's bench. His long arms worked like flails. The new Grand Jury would now be drawn, and by a trick Older knew.

"The names in the box had been prepared for the drawing," explained Older. "The bits of paper bearing the chosen names were folded together, so that the searching hand of the clerk could feel a thick bunch and draw from that.

"Knowing this, I had managed to force my way into the courtroom, in spite of the efforts of a big fat bailiff who tried to throw me out. When the drawing of names was about to begin I rushed up to the judge's bench and loudly demanded that the names be emptied out of the box and separated."

Through the open windows the roaring doubled in fury as the box was opened. Older had been right. Certain names were marked with rubber bands. These names were scattered among the others in the box, and there was drawn an honest jury, the Oliver Grand Jury, which within twenty-four hours was at work investigating the graft charges.

When Older stamped triumphantly back into the *Bulletin* office that afternoon, he found not one word of the great victory in the paper.

"I couldn't write it!" groaned the reporter he had assigned to the story. "It was too tremendous!"

Ordinarily Older never accepted an excuse for falling down on a story. But this time he understood. He wrote later in perfect sympathy:

"The *Bulletin* had two men there all through the proceedings, trained newspaper reporters, and neither of them telephoned a line to the paper! They decided that the situation was too big, too overwhelming, to be reported at all. They must have felt that they were at the center of the universe, that all the people in the world had gathered, that everyone knew what was happening."

It was while Fremont Older was sympathizing with his crestfallen reporters and trying to make amends to the subscribers in a late edition that he sprang from his chair with a yell, grabbed his hat, and started for the door.

He had suddenly remembered his wife, in her veils and duster, left marooned all day under broiling sun in their stalled machine across the Bay.

## Chapter XIII

### THE DYNAMITERS

NOW the graft-hunters came from under cover. Older ran large pictures of Heney and Burns on the front page, captioned, "We Are Hot After the Crowd That Has Throttled Public Decency—The Big Fellows Will Not Escape!"

The prosecution would prove, promised the *Bulletin*, that the United Railroads had paid seven thousand dollars each to Mayor Schmitz and Boss Ruef for the overhead-trolley franchise, and four thousand dollars to each of the eighteen supervisors.

"Put Ruef and Schmitz in stripes!" shouted the editorial page.

Ruef was no coward. He sneered, "Go ahead. Investigate."

But the graft-hunters had the proof, at last, on Schmitz and Ruef, on the supervisors, even, they swore, on Calhoun.

In the excitement following "Black Friday," Ruef's "municipal guillotine" had removed the head of Frank Maestretti, president of the Board of Public Works. This move puzzled the graft-hunters, for they were certain Maestretti knew all that was going on in the inner political circles.

"How dared Ruef throw him out?" they wondered.

Older sent his sharpest reporter to investigate a man named Roy who was Maestretti's partner in a skating-rink. The reporter returned with information tending to discredit Roy. Older ordered the story set up in a proof-sheet and with that lying on his desk sent for Roy.

Roy answered the summons promptly. Men always did, for Older.

"What can I do for you?" he asked as he swaggered into Older's grubby little office. He was affable and patronizing.

"Not a thing!" answered Older, and his jaws clamped. "Take a look at that. I'm sending you to the pen."

The damp ribbon of paper shook in Roy's hands. He nearly collapsed. When he looked up at Older, his eyes were desperate.

"What do you want me to do?" he almost whispered.

"Tell the truth," snapped Older.

And Roy talked. In the presence of Detective Burns and Older and a stenographer he revealed crookedness they had only guessed. He it was who first told of the money the eighteen supervisors had accepted from the railroad for the trolley franchise.

"We had reached Calhoun at last," wrote Older triumphantly.

A trap was set with Roy as bait. From a back room in Roy's skating-rink Burns and Older peered through pin holes into another room and watched Roy pay three of the supervisors money to kill a skating-rink bill. Trapped, the three confessed to everything, including the trolley steal. The other supervisors hastily followed under promise of immunity, until all but one of them had signed confessions to having taken money from the railroad owned by Calhoun.

It was the evidence Older had been hunting for six years.

"The trapping of the three supervisors," wrote Hichborn in *The System*, "led to confessions from fourteen others, which involved not only Ruef in enormous bribery transactions, but also prominent members of the bar, and leaders in the social, financial, and industrial life of California."

Upon this evidence the Grand Jury indicted the Boss and the Mayor on five counts of extortion. Bonds were fixed for each defendant at $50,000—$10,000 a charge.

While the confessions were being taken, Ruef was in hiding. The little boss had been indicted in the restaurant cases and was out on bail. His body-guard of police detectives were taken from him. He hid in an old road-house near the beach, the Trocadero. There he was trapped by Burns and his men and brought, in disgrace and a prisoner, to the Little St. Francis Hotel, a temporary timber structure built since the fire.

There Ruef was told that the supervisors had confessed and had been promised immunity. He and the Mayor were left "holding the bag."

Ruef demanded frantically to be put in jail in charge of the sheriff. The graft-hunters were in no mood to trust the sheriff. Judge Dunne appointed an elisor to guard the broken boss, and a house was rented where Ruef was kept under guard. For entertainment he was permitted to read the confessions of the supervisors he had bribed.

He refused to confess.

Two rabbis came to Ruef and begged him to confess. He would not. Then he was told that the aged mother who had been so proud of her brilliant and successful attorney son was dying. Ruef was taken under heavy guard to see her. She stretched out her withered arms to the boss who had bribed with millions and wailed, "Oh, Abraham!"

He broke then. He wept, "I'll do whatever you want me to do."

In his confession Ruef told of accepting $200,000 from General Tirey L. Ford, head attorney for the United Railroads. Of this he gave $50,000 to Schmitz, $85,000 to Gallagher for the Supervisors, and retained $50,000 himself.

He told of again giving Gallagher $169,000 of other corporation money to be distributed among the Board. Other money, it was brought out, had been paid directly to Board members by corporation representatives.

Ruef told of briberies within briberies. He repeated all on the witness-stand and pleaded guilty to extortion on May 15, 1907.

"Ruef Squeals like a Cornered Rat!" triumphed a *Bulletin* headline.

Long afterward, in prison, Ruef said to Fremont Older: "I felt in confessing I had done a worse thing than ever in my life before. I was betraying my associates."

Older would likewise regret, in a way, that confession. Heney and Langdon signed an immunity agreement promising that as a reward for confession Ruef should stand trial only in the French-restaurant cases and not on the other felony charges. Later the immunity covenant was broken, and Older came to believe that Ruef had been tricked into confessing.

The charges piled higher against Ruef and Schmitz. The owners of such famous French restaurants as the Poodle Dog, the Pup, Marchand's, Delmonico, appeared before the Grand Jury to tell of paying tribute to the grafters. Dance-hall proprietors testified to paying a percentage to Ruef and his crew of boodlers. The "Fight Trust" promoters told of paying thousands to Ruef for their prize-fight permits.

Ruef appeared before the Grand Jury and confessed to the evidence that resulted in his own indictment and that of Schmitz and several others, including the millionaire railroad president Calhoun. Ruef made possible the prosecution of those higher than himself in power.

Most powerful of all—Calhoun.

The muck-rakers had uncovered the "big fellows."

All over America and Europe were published the stories of the conditions being exposed in San Francisco. Newspapers everywhere printed excoriating editorials upon the city of graft. Older reprinted these to reveal the shame Ruef and Schmitz had brought on the city. Taxpayers read, and resented, not Ruef and Schmitz, but the fighting editor who made public the infamy.

Dirty mouths nipped at the heels of the graft-fighters.

Scurrilous attacks were made on Heney and Phelan and Older, and falsehoods whispered against them. Printed stories appeared in railroad-controlled newspapers and magazines. Older was dubbed "the Ogre." His Bohemian days as a reporter in the eighties and nineties were recalled and elaborated upon. One of the milder charges was that he beat his wife.

He clipped such items and trustingly brought them home in his pocket. Cora Older seldom shared his amusement.

"How can they!" she would wail, horrified.

"That shows they are afraid of us," he would explain, and then his rich voice would deepen. "You have to expect it, my darling. You're a reformer's wife."

Outwardly at least Cora Older remained serene under threats and scurrility.

But friend and foe alike admitted that Older was honest. He was called "the Man without a Price."

He was running, through these years of the graft crusade, an exclusive graft story every day. All the big graft "beats" were the *Bulletin's*. Older knew where the graft lay. He knew where to develop the story of the hour.

Ruef's arrest uncovered other scandals. Ruef, the *Bulletin* charged, had been protecting, through a certain judge, the "Marsicania," a notorious brothel where, it was said, women had been beaten to death, where young boys were crippled for life and children coming home from school stared in through the open doors. Through the *Bulletin's* exposures the case was taken from the protecting judge to the Supreme Court. The "Marsicania" was closed.

At last word reached San Francisco that its Mayor was turning back from Europe. The *Bulletin* dealt in bitter surmises. Would Schmitz actually return to face his looted city? Would he not hide out in Honduras?

But the musician Mayor announced that he was coming back to face all charges. When he made this decision, Older stirred the police into raiding "the Municipal Crib."

Older had bared the horror of this infamous house of prostitution in Jackson Street and given it this name. It had been built by Mayor Schmitz. It contained seventy women. Older charged that Schmitz had built it for immoral purposes and that these unfortunates paid tribute in blood-money into the City Hall. He had the house raided and the women brought before the Grand Jury.

But the women were sullen and afraid. They dared not talk. It was charged that Mayor Schmitz had been a brothel-owner since 1903, that one bagnio alone netted him $1,500 a week.

"Every street-walker that trailed her soiled skirts through the red-light district contributed her mite to the support of Eugene E. Schmitz!" stated the *Bulletin*.

The paper ran a six-column cut of Ruef wearing a great diamond "R" tie-pin given him by a grateful white slaver. It showed Schmitz in the City Hall grabbing tribute from fallen women.

But it would not be easy to bring this powerful pair to justice.

Witnesses found by the graft-hunters seemed to melt from view. One witness vanished completely. Another fled to Europe and there killed himself. Another was said to have been shanghaied. Others "forgot" the evidence they had promised to give.

At last Mayor Schmitz returned to California. Ruef, between court appearances, went to meet him at the Nevada state line. Police went along with warrants for the arrest of the Mayor of San Francisco. Older sent W. O. ("Bill") McGeehan to cover the story.

"Rather frosty home-coming," Ruef observed with a faint smile to McGeehan as they waited in deep snow at the station.

McGeehan, later one of the foremost sports writers in America, found on close acquaintance that Ruef was not unattractive.

When Older heard that McGeehan had formed this slight friendship with Ruef, he was furious. In this stage of his development a friend's enemies were his own, and Older expected the same loyalty in return. McGeehan was welcomed back to the *Bulletin* office with an explosion which nearly lifted the roof off the ice-house.

McGeehan always insisted that Older's black hair first began to turn gray during this terrific tirade.

"I am inclined to believe there were a few hairs in the 'dark-hued mane' before McGeehan came on the *Bulletin*," a softened and mellower Older wrote in a letter many years after. "McGeehan may have added a few, and this is why:

"I sent Billy over to Reno to interview Abe Ruef. I had been bitterly attacking him for a long time, and when I sent McGeehan to Reno to meet him I expected him in his article to express my own malignant attitude toward Ruef. He didn't. Instead, he treated him like a human being, as I was brought to treat him a year or two later. I was angry at the tone of his articles, and, added to this acute disappointment, I learned that Billy had several drinks at Ruef's expense, at a Reno or Truckee bar.

"That caused us to part company, but to become good friends again in later years."

It was McGeehan who gave currency to many of the expressions coined by Older during the graft prosecution. When a word failed Older, he coined one. "The higher-ups" was one of his terms. He invented it to fit Calhoun and others "higher up." Another word he coined was "gangster," derived from the gangs that terrorized San Francisco after the fire. Still another was "mutt," a diminutive of mutton, or sheep, coined by Older and popularized first by McGeehan.

Back in San Francisco, the disgraced Mayor took up the reins of government while waiting for trial. In his hands they became wires. He pulled, and they reached under the dome of the Capitol at Sacramento. The attorney for Ruef and Schmitz drafted and introduced a bill which if passed would have enabled the pair to escape trial. Edward J. Livernash, brilliant political writer of the *Bulletin,* exposed the plot.

The bill was quashed in a puff of ill-smelling smoke, but both Senate and Assembly promptly passed resolutions barring Livernash and all other representatives of the *Bulletin* from all sessions of the Legislature.

Livernash stayed on in Sacramento. He continued to send articles to the *Bulletin,* written "outside the dome," which were far more penetrating than any written within. Other newspaper men and friendly solons told Livernash all that was going on, and he wrote meat and meaning into his reports. Older ran these articles full-page with illustrations. One sketch showed the dark, ascetic-looking intellectual Livernash sitting cross-legged on a cloud above the Capitol.

"I sit me here on a big hunk of chaos, like Don Quixote upon his mountainside," wrote the irrepressible reporter.

Then, in brilliant, sizzling words, Livernash figured up the actual cost of his banning in public money. The total waste of the four days the Legislature gave to his banishment cost the Californian public $13,198.

His political sarcasms dripped like vitriol into sacred circles.

A reporter dared such things, with Older behind him.

"You knew he was with you all the way," say men who worked with Older.

Older urged on the indefatigable Livernash, knowing, and none better, how frank bribery could be in the State Capitol. When he had "covered Legislature" as a reporter, a train ticket to and from San Francisco was left every Friday morning on the desk of each assemblyman and senator. It was a tip from the railroad.

In one of his articles the reporter Older had quoted a prominent citizen as saying, "You couldn't pass the Lord's Prayer in this Legislature without money."

Immediately a special committee was appointed to investigate this statement by the brash reporter. Older was put on the witness-stand and ordered to name the "prominent citizen."

"There he is," Older answered, pointing to Mayor Glasscock of Oakland.

Glasscock was put on the stand and showed an eagerness to explain the remark. But the committee wanted no such explanation. The matter was quietly dropped.

Many threatening letters came to Older during the graft troubles. Some were from cranks. Many, he knew, were serious.

He swept them from his desk. He refused to discuss them and tried to forget them. But at times a shudder crossed his expressive features. If they did try to get him, he prayed it would be final. He sickened at visions of himself shot down, lying maimed in the street before a curiously staring crowd while men remarked:

"Oh, it's Older! Well, it was coming to him."

They would say that, he was certain. The words haunted him. To escape the strain of the exposé he drove with Mrs. Older every evening at sunset to the beach. They had a cabin there, built of an ancient trolley-car, presided over by a militant New Englander, a Mrs. Gunn—who, incidentally, would be cared for by Fremont Older for some twenty-odd years until she died.

In the curtained trolley-car the Olders changed into bathing-suits and plunged into the cold, bitter waters of the evening Pacific.

Only at the beach could they feel safe and free. Wherever they went in the city, they were followed by resentful looks. Nearly all their influential friends had fallen away. The little group of graft-fighters, Heney, Burns, Spreckels, Phelan, and Older, were a defiant and lonely company, mutually sustained only by the certainty that they were doing the right thing.

And all of them, every minute of every twenty-four hours, were in danger. They were aligned against powerful and ruthless men. Older looked forward wistfully to the pleasure of his evening swim as to his only joy.

The Kid, Older's furtive admirer in the underworld, learned of a plan to kill the editor. The King of Pickpockets was told by a professional killer—there were many such in San Francisco—that he had been hired to shoot Older. He had been paid to sit across the street from the new *Bulletin* office on Market Street and get Older with a long-range rifle while the riveters were working on a near-by building. But the gunman had decided for his own safety to follow Older to the beach and pick him off with the rifle while swimming.

It was said at this time that one could hire a man killed in San Francisco for a dollar and a half. Opium was being sold openly in Chinatown, and there were men who would risk their lives for the drug. Hand in hand with the ugly trade of drugs and death ran the business of smuggling Chinese slave girls into the city. Tiny, doll-like, mewing creatures, they were dropped over the sides of anchored ships into the arms of white smugglers and sold to slavers in Chinatown. There, in dim doorways along the narrow streets, they waited in deathly fear of the "white devils" whose trade they solicited. Men who grew rich in such traffickings hated and feared Older.

The Kid, learning of the murder plot, hurried to the *Bulletin* office. One of the six powers of the underworld, even he must be cautious. He pretended not to see Cora Older, sitting in her veils in the White Steamer before the entrance. The Kid lurked by the door until Older rushed out, then brushed past him, his face a mask.

"Keep away from the beach!" he muttered, and was gone.

Older knew the mannerisms of the Kid. He was a listener. When the Kid spoke, every word told.

"This is the real thing," thought Older instantly.

He crossed the sidewalk to the car and sat in it fuming. The daily swim was the one pleasure left in his life.

He told his wife of the warning. She sat very still, but her sympathy went over him without in the least impairing the gorgeous quality of his despair. When Fremont Older was in the mood for suffering, he wanted to suffer without interference.

This was one of the times when he grew unbearably sick of everything. He had been forced to fight bitterly for all he had set out to do. In his own office he had been forced to fight for permission to fight. He had warred with Crothers for the right to shake off the railroad subsidy. He had warred then for permission to fight the railroad. Now every hand, it seemed, was against him, the "higher-ups" whose power he undermined, the underworld whose crimes he exposed.

"I'll be damned if I let them get by with it!" he announced suddenly and savagely. "We're going to the beach!"

Older stamped into the circulation office and telephoned Police Headquarters. Within a few minutes two plain-clothes men, heavily armed, were sitting in the tonneau of the car. The Olders drove to the beach. Fighting through the breakers with the easy breast stroke he had learned as a lad in the Fox, Older forgot everything but his struggle with the sea.

Shortly after, there began arriving in the mail letters addressed to Older printed in red ink and signed with a lettered symbol and a smoking bomb. They were actual threats, he knew. They threatened to destroy him with dynamite, and they were signed "J. C."

Then the home of James Gallagher was dynamited. He was the Chairman of the Board of Supervisors and had confessed to taking orders from Ruef. He was the pivotal witness in the graft prosecution, having been granted immunity for his confession. The Gallagher family were at dinner when the explosion split the house in half, throwing a porch pillar a hundred and fifty feet but harming no one. A month later three flats belonging to Gallagher were blown up.

Gallagher was terrified by the murder attempt. He was afraid to take the witness-stand and testify against Ruef and Calhoun. Even with his confession the graft prosecutors were not certain they could make him take the stand.

"He has to testify!" stormed Older.

He promised to pay Gallagher $4,500 for the loss of his flats.

Older knew by this time that the red-ink letters were from the dynamite gang. He was risking a strange and hideous death, but he ordered into the front page a box promising one thousand dollars reward for information leading to the identification of the terrorists.

The offer brought prompt response from the dynamiters. One letter in the familiar red ink was as follows:

"Damn you! You no tak out that 1000 you God Damn paper will be blown to hell. We the RED HAND swears to do the above. If by Wednesday night it is not out you will have a prise on your head. Notice our sign."

The signature was always the same, the interwrought "J. C." and the flaring bomb.

Older continued to run the reward offer.

John Claudianos, a Greek, came to the office to see Older. He told the editor a rambling story of having heard someone tell someone else about some dynamiting, but he wanted money for his story. Older dismissed the yarn as mythical.

He told Burns of the visit. "The fellow was crazy," he said by way of conclusion.

The Secret Service chief's shrewd eyes snapped.

"That man wasn't crazy. That man is guilty. They always talk like that. Find him and we find the dynamiters."

Then an *Examiner* newsboy, selling papers on his Market Street corner, saw a man toss something into a garbage-can. Out of curiosity he fished from the can what proved to be a special-delivery letter sent to John Claudianos by his brother Peter, telling him of dynamiting the Gallagher houses. The *Examiner* found John. But Peter, guilty of the dynamiting with another Greek, Felix Padeauvaris, could not be found.

All the newspapers joined in the man-hunt. After a long chase Peter was trapped in Chicago. John turned state's evidence against his brother, and Peter was sentenced to life in San Quentin.

Claudianos confessed to Burns. Hired to get Gallagher, he said, he had first planned shooting poisoned glass into his face with a sling-shot. But that seemed dangerous, so he decided on the dynamite. That failing, he had rented an apartment next to the Gallaghers and was preparing to drop poison in the family milk-bottle when his brother carelessly exposed the plot by tossing the letter into a public garbage-can.

The dynamiters had been promised a thousand dollars for the murders, through Felix Padeauvaris.

"I thought I was working for Ruef," Claudianos explained, "as I knew Felix was a very intimate friend of his. When Felix told me to shadow Gallagher, I knew the word came from Ruef!"

The gang was caught in time to prevent the destruction of the Older car-house at the beach and probably the murder of the Olders. In the basement of the cabin next door the police found fifteen pounds of dynamite. Padeauvaris had lived there a month. Claudianos confessed that Older's name had been next on the list to be blown up.

The dynamiting case was one of dozens set spinning in the courts by the graft prosecution.

So far Older's life had been charmed. He had escaped many dangers. But there was another menace waiting which to his stern way of thinking was worse than dynamite and death.

## Chapter XIV

### THE KIDNAPPING

THE WORLD was watching San Francisco and its graft prosecution. Through all the long-drawn-out trials the London *Times* kept a special writer there who wrote a daily article on graft. The *Times* gave full credit for the prosecution to Older. *McClure's Magazine* and others referred to him as "one of the greatest living editors." During this eventful period Older found time to visit New York as a member of the International Policy-Holder's Commission, he was interviewed in newspapers and magazines, he spoke everywhere of upholding the law.

He was one of the most quoted men in America.

"Older has the Grand Jury in his pocket," newspapers commented.

Praise and condemnation followed him. A story was sent around that Older was getting a $100,000 bribe for the graft prosecution and that Chester Rowell, another editor, had accepted $25,000.

"I resent that," Rowell said with mock indignation to Older. "That implies you are worth four times as much as I am. I insist they change the scandal to say I am getting $100,000, too."

Older comforted him gustily. "You know they know it isn't true, Rowell. If they thought you'd taken that much, they would make you governor."

Just as the grafters came to trial in San Francisco, the millionaire playboy Harry K. Thaw was brought to trial in New York for the slaying of the architect Stanford White, despoiler of Thaw's flowerlike wife, Evelyn Nesbit. The sensational Eastern murder and the sensational Western exposé struggled for place on the front page of the *Bulletin*. Older presented the Thaw trial to his readers with detail as intimate as though it were taking place in San Francisco.

Newspaper photography had been perfected at last. Older splashed the pages with portraits of the lovely Evelyn, in kimono or on a rug or draped with lilies, and with the worried, clever features of Abe Ruef and the handsome but anxious countenance of Mayor Schmitz. Older ran half-page cuts of the San Francisco courtroom where the civic heads stood charged with many felonies before the bar of justice.

Never before in any court of the world had such scenes been played.

Mayor Schmitz on the stand proved an affable witness, denying, protesting, refusing to admit he had ever shared bribes with the "unsavory boss" Ruef.

Ruef felt that Schmitz had turned against him. Against the advice of his attorneys he took the stand. Tears streamed down his tragic face as he said, "I paid Schmitz!

"I gave Schmitz $2,500 and told him it was his share of money from the French restaurants," said Ruef.

The handsome Mayor of San Francisco slumped in his chair. His defense was shattered.

"If Your Honor please," Ruef went on, weeping, "I desire to withdraw my plea of not guilty and enter the contrary plea."

And then he talked with heart-breaking eloquence.

"The strain of these proceedings upon those I hold nearest and dearest of all on earth," Ruef said, "has been so grave and severe that as a result of these prosecutions their health has all been undermined, they are on the verge of immediate collapse, and their lives are indeed now actually in the balance."

Ruef's speech would have wrung the emotions of men who had fought and struggled less for a cause. But the graft-hunters had suffered much, and they could listen coldly as the little boss spoke of the family he loved.

"What is your plea?" asked Judge Dunne.

"Guilty!" answered Ruef.

A local paper commented: "Abraham Ruef should have thought of his family before he entered upon his career of crime. For Ruef himself the only sympathy possible is that which one might feel for a wolf, which, having devastated the sheepfold, has been pursued, brought to bay and, after a long fight, finally disposed of. It is not a case in which the safety of society permits leniency to be shown."

Ruef had been indicted on sixty-five charges of bribery. He had previously been sentenced to the County Jail in the French-restaurant cases. Now, charged with bribing the complete civic government, Mayor, Supervisors, and all, for the granting of franchises worth millions of dollars, he stood self-convicted.

"During the trial talk was made of money which made Al Capone and latter-day racketeers look like pikers," declared the San Francisco *Examiner* of March 1, 1936, when Ruef died at the age of seventy-one.

"Testimony was introduced that one supervisor received $10,000 for his vote on a comparatively unimportant matter.

"At one time during the proceedings Ruef was given his freedom on bail of $1,500,000! At another time he posted the 'nominal' bail of $600,000."

One week after Ruef's dramatic public confession Schmitz was tried, found guilty in the French-restaurant cases, and sentenced to serve five years in the penitentiary.

That night of June 13, 1907, the Mayor who had dined from gold plate in European capitals a few weeks before ate his dinner from a tin pan in the County Jail.

The Mayor and the boss did a great deal of complaining in jail. Ruef fussed over the lack of running water in his cell and the difficulty of bathing. Schmitz, who was a big man, disliked his cot.

"I want a longer cell," Schmitz protested. "My legs are long and I can't stretch them out. It's a beastly hole."

He was not in long. Nor did he ever serve an hour of the five-year sentence.

San Francisco had no mayor.

To the graft-hunters fell the task of finding a mayor, for the man to fill the office must be chosen by the Supervisors, and the Supervisors were now nailed by their confessions to the side of the crusaders. No one, under the circumstances, wanted to be mayor.

Schmitz, from the jail, announced his intention of running again for mayor.

"Let him amuse himself," scoffed District Attorney Langdon.

It was discovered that the mayor's seal was missing from the mayor's office and could not be found. Schmitz was said to have hidden it.

Older selected the new mayor, Dr. Edward Robeson Taylor. Respectable from his scholarly black hat to his button shoes, author of the city charter, Dean of Hastings Law College, Acting President of the Cooper Medical College, a poet and a leader of the bar for twenty-seven years—everyone agreed that Older's choice was ideal.

Taylor was sworn into office.

"I accepted this office with much reluctance," the new Mayor admitted, "and only because I believed that any man who was requested to serve the city in this capacity in the hour of her need should heed the request, no matter what the personal sacrifice might be."

Franklin K. Lane, then with the Interstate Commerce

Commission in Washington, wrote Older in congratulation:

"You made the fight! I should have liked to have been in San Francisco on the night of the election so as to lead a crowd to your office and give you some rousing cheers to offset the derisive yells of the past few years."

To Older the victory was incomplete. Ruef was trapped and would stand trial again. Schmitz would escape prison because of error. His conviction was reversed by the Supreme Court, his indictment having failed to specify that he was "Mayor of San Francisco" when he accepted a bribe.

But it was Calhoun that Older wanted.

In all the attacks, up to Calhoun, the city generally had been with Older. The *Bulletin,* he often said, might have gone on indefinitely uncovering police graft, petty graft, and political graft. The charge that Older's disclosures were giving San Francisco "a black eye" had been started by a chorus composed of an indicted mayor, an indicted police chief, seventeen supervisors who had confessed to taking bribes, and a political boss who would shortly be a convict.

But with the indictment of Calhoun the "best people" turned against Older. The fighting editor had uncovered a hornets' nest. It was one thing to expose a policeman caught rolling a cheese stolen from a warehouse down the Embarcadero. It was another matter when a great millionaire was charged with buying the people's rights with a $200,000 bribe. Now, it seemed, the presidents and the vice-presidents of corporations, the rich, the fashionable, the self-righteous, were to be haled into court like common crooks.

With a man like Older around, the powerful agreed, no one was safe.

Calhoun, indicted, calmly crushed the strike. According

to Older, he had nursed it for months in the hollow of his hand, while men suffered, went hungry, were killed and maimed. Out of the tragedy of these carmen and their families, charged Older, Calhoun built his public reputation as hero.

The "respectable people" turned to Calhoun. Older was branded an anarchist, an agitator, a disturber of the peace. More lies were circulated against him.

"They're saying Spreckels gave you $100,000 to start the graft charges," someone told him curiously.

Older liked to tease.

"You know they don't believe that. Why, if they thought I'd taken that much money, they would give me a banquet and toast me in flattering speeches."

In the midst of slander and vilification it was good to read one of the many letters President Roosevelt sent to hearten the graft-hunters:

"I want you to feel that your experience is simply the experience of all of us who are engaged in this fight. There is no form of slander and wicked falsehood which will not as a matter of course be employed against all men engaged in such a struggle, and this not only on the part of men and papers representing the lowest type of demagogy, but, I am sorry to say, also on the part of men and papers representing the interests that call themselves preëminently conservative, preëminently cultured.

"In such a struggle it is too often true that the feelings against those engaged in it become peculiarly bitter, not merely in the business houses of the great financiers who directly profit by the wrong-doing, but also in the clubs, in certain newspaper offices where business interests exercise an unhealthy control and, I regret to add, in other newspaper offices which like to be considered to a marked degree the representatives of the cultivation and high social standing of the country. . . .

"But it is, if anything, an even more evil and dreadful thing to have the merchants, the business men, the captains of industry, accessories to crime and shielders and supporters of criminals; it is an even more dreadful thing to see the power of men high in state politics, high in finance, high in the social life of the rich and fashionable, united to stifle the prosecution of offenders against civic integrity if these offenders happen to be their friends and associates; and most evil of all is it when we see crooks of a labor party in offensive and defensive dalliance with the crooks of a corporation party."

In his club, the famous Bohemian Club, men snubbed Older. He sent in his resignation. Invitations no longer came from fashionable friends. Several society women said to Mrs. Older:

"We're very fond of you, Cora, dear, but we simply cannot ask your husband to our houses any more."

"Do not ask either of us," she answered calmly.

She lifted her beautiful head higher and wrote the article, "A Reformer's Wife," that shamed many who turned on Older in those bitter days.

The city was split into two camps. The larger was with Calhoun.

Calhoun sent a message to Older.

"Name your price."

"I have no price," was the word Older sent back, "and nothing will stop me until I see you in the penitentiary."

To strengthen the case against the railroad president Older made a secret visit to Georgia. He had heard of a suit there that might discredit Calhoun. With his own money he financed the trip and paid for a copy of the transcript in the case.

When he returned to San Francisco, he found he could not leave his hotel without being followed. Two men or one trailed him at a distance. Threats poured in on him.

Calhoun's trial approached. If Older were out of the way, the graft prosecution would end. Everyone thought that. Older fanned it alive each day with the *Bulletin*. The *Bulletin* was hated and reviled as well as admired, but, most important to Older, it was read.

Many traps were laid for the editor. He was clever at scenting them. Women telephoned him in his office and told of valuable information regarding graft they would give him in some secluded place. Many seemed temptingly convincing. Then a man came to Older with the story that he was a labor leader who wanted revenge, having been hounded by Calhoun detectives.

He offered to revenge himself by procuring certain graft-revealing reports in the railroad company's safe for Older to publish.

Older was too fanatically interested to be suspicious. But he retained enough caution not to act without consulting Burns. The Secret Service chief stared at the excited editor.

"Are you crazy, Older? It's a trap. The man is a railroad dick. He would pretend to rob the safe, sell you the documents, you would print them, and the railroad would arrest you for burglarizing the safe!"

It was Older's turn to stare. He took out his large handkerchief and wiped a forehead which was growing higher with years and anxiety. A very clear picture had come to him of Fremont Older, crusader for the right, wearing stripes in San Quentin while the men he had planned to send there continued to run his city.

Older always maintained he was more grateful for that escape than for those from dynamite and rifle-fire.

"Thanks, Burns," he said humbly. "That's the narrowest squeak from the penitentiary I ever had."

He had overlooked danger in his fury to get Calhoun. That ambition dominated Older. Calhoun was the big fellow, Older felt, the man who controlled the little ones, who was responsible for the existence of men like Ruef. The very name "Calhoun" struck Older as sinister. But Calhoun wore the aura of millions. People shook their heads at the thought of punishing Calhoun.

"He saved the city," they repeated, remembering the dread days of the street-car strike that, according to Older, had been dust stirred up by Calhoun to hide the bribe discoveries.

"But don't you want to see Cauhoun convicted if he's guilty?" Older demanded of a prominent business man.

"I do not!" was the answer. "If I were on the jury I'd vote to acquit him if he were guilty as hell. He's the man who saved San Francisco."

Calhoun's power reached into many channels. In this fight he would exhaust them all.

On the afternoon of September 27, 1907, Older sat conferring with Heney's partner, Charles Cobb, in Heney's office, when the telephone rang for Older.

"How does anyone know I'm here?" was Older's first thought.

A strange voice gave a name he did not know.

"If you'll come to the Savoy Hotel, I'll give you some important information against Calhoun," it said.

"Why don't you come here?" demanded Older.

"I'm being watched. I don't dare."

Older was grasping at any straws that would help to build the pyre of Calhoun.

"I'll be right over," he promised the unknown man.

But at the door he turned back.

"Charley, this may be a trap. If I'm not back in thirty minutes, let Spreckels know."

He was off then, his long legs striding over the sidewalk toward the Savoy. As he hurried along, he noticed an automobile following him down the street. Automobiles were still rare enough to attract attention, and this one was particularly noticeable because of the heavy, brutal faces of four men sitting in the car.

He quickened his steps a little. This was idiotic, he thought resentfully, being followed in broad daylight along an open street. He glanced about anxiously. It was afternoon, and there were many people on Van Ness Avenue. As he hesitated, the car swung to the curb beside him and two men jumped out.

"Warrant for your arrest!" snapped one, flourishing a paper.

"On what grounds?"

"Libel!" snapped the man, and flashed a constable's star.

Older recalled that the day before the *Bulletin* had published a story concerning a man named Brown. The reporter who wrote the story had confused Brown with Luther Brown, a Calhoun detective. Older had caught the mistake after the first edition.

He studied the warrant. It was from Los Angeles and seemed authentic. The men, apparently Los Angeles deputies, motioned him into the car. To resist arrest would bring a more serious charge.

"I want to see my lawyer first and arrange bail," Older said warily.

"We'll take you to Judge Cook's chambers," said the leader. "You can get a bail order from him."

Older felt apprehensive as he climbed into the car. As he settled down between the two big men in the tonneau, he felt hands creep down his sides. He was being searched for a gun. But he had never carried a gun, although nearly every other male member of his staff went armed.

As the car swung from Van Ness into Golden Gate Avenue, he saw another car dart out of a side street to lead the way. In it were two men he testified later to recognizing—Calhoun's chief detective and a Calhoun attorney.

"Oh, God," he thought quickly, "they've got me!"

But he said aloud as calmly as he could, "Where are Judge Cook's chambers?"

The man by the driver turned. His lip lifted.

"We're not going there," he said.

Older felt a gun pressing painfully into his ribs.

"Make an attempt to escape," said the man on his left, "and I'll shoot you."

Older sat erect on the jolting seat. He was frightened. It was torture he dreaded most, not dying. And yet the thought of dying, of being blotted out when life was fullest and most exciting . . . Older lit a cigar, hoping they would not notice how his hand shook, but his voice trembled as he addressed the man holding the gun.

"This isn't very sportsmanlike of the railroad, is it? We've been fighting, but this part of the fight isn't fair. It's dealing the cards from under the table. Don't you think so?"

He was appealing directly to the gunman, trying to sway him. Older had practised his spellbinding powers on many men. His eyes that could dominate or be marvelously kind were hypnotic with appeal. The man's eyes wavered and lowered. The pressure of the gun lessened. With a quick gesture the man slipped it back into his pocket.

The two cars raced down the peninsula highway. It grew dark, and the drivers stepped out and struck matches to light the lamps of the machines. At Redwood City, where Fremont Older had first been a city editor on a country sheet, he was pushed aboard the Los Angeles train with a gun sunk between his ribs. Only two of the kidnappers went aboard with Older, one the attorney, the other the dark-jawed gunman whose eyes had wavered before Older's arguments in a flicker of human understanding.

A drawing-room had been reserved for the three. Older, his tongue tied by the menace of the gun, was ushered between the pair into the diner. Across the table he again fixed his expressive glance on the dark hireling.

"I don't care about myself," he pleaded, "but my wife! We were giving a dinner tonight. She'll be in a terrible state, not knowing what has happened to me. She'll be telephoning the police. She'll think I'm dead.

"It isn't fair to let her suffer. If I could only get word to her!"

The gunman laid down his fork.

"By God!" he exploded, "if you want to write a telegram to her or to anyone else, I'll send it for you when we get to San Jose."

This man later said that he had been promised $10,000 to kill Older, but the editor's friendly manner saved him.

The waiter brought a telegraph blank. But Older dreaded alarming his wife. He addressed the telegram to Rudolph Spreckels:

"I'm being spirited away on a southbound coast train. I don't know where I'm going or what is going to happen. It's a United Railroads job."

The gunman took the telegram and left the train for a few minutes when it stopped at San Jose. But the telegram was never sent. The attorney took the message and tore it up.

Older left the diner with one last despairing look. There was not a soul in the car he knew. And he had little faith in the telegram's being sent.

But though he knew no one in that car, he was recognized. At a near-by table sat a young San Francisco attorney who knew the famous editor by sight and was a keen observer. He noted that Older did not look at peace with his surroundings, that the men with him did not behave like friends.

He recognized one of them as an attorney for the interests

Older was fighting. He followed him out of the dining-car and heard him whisper to the other man:

"We'll take him off the train and give him a run through the mountains!"

The young man struggled with his conscience. This was decidedly none of his business. Besides, it was dangerous for a young attorney just starting on his career to interfere in the affairs of corporations. He had an important engagement, too, at Los Angeles the next day.

But he was certain that if he did not interfere, Fremont Older would never again be seen alive in San Francisco.

At one o'clock in the morning the train stopped at Salinas. The young man got off the train, interrupting his important journey to the south. He put through a long-distance message to the San Francisco *Morning Call*.

"Older Kidnapped," screamed the front page of the morning paper.

San Francisco broke into turmoil. Rescue parties were formed to save Older. By a coincidence Franklin K. Lane, Older's friend, was in Santa Barbara, not far above Los Angeles. A writ of habeas corpus was wired to him. The Santa Barbara papers had the story by dawn, so that a great crowd waited at the station there for the southbound Lark.

Older had spent the night tossing in the upper berth. His imagination rushed ahead of the train to his certain horrible death. He could never bear suspense. By morning he was drawn and gray.

The train slowed down at Santa Barbara. Older, between his two captors, looked out of the window. Hundreds of people swarmed around the train. Beside the station were automobiles, and women holding parasols stood on the seats looking over the crowd. People were craning, staring.

"Must be a wedding," observed the gunman beside Older.

The door of their compartment was flung open. There

## THE KIDNAPPING

stood two of Older's friends, Franklin K. Lane and Thomas ("Tom") Stork, the Santa Barbara newspaper-owner, flanked by Santa Barbara police. The train was surrounded, the entire train crew placed under arrest.

Older, stepping from the train under the blue skies of Santa Barbara, heard himself wildly cheered. Not until he was on his way to the court-house, surrounded by friendly faces, did he realize the full strain of the experience. Then, he said, every muscle seemed to collapse.

In the court the judge admitted Older to bail on the trumped-up libel charge. Lane produced the bail. The two men who had abducted Older refused to speak.

Back in San Francisco that same day, he was met with an ovation.

The two deputies who kidnapped Fremont Older turned state's evidence against the railroad men they swore had ordered the kidnapping. But the instigators of the crime were acquitted.

The story of that kidnapping went around the world.

Older was more determined than ever to convict Calhoun.

But by the time Calhoun came to trial, the various phases of the graft prosecution had been dragging for two long years through the courts, and the first jury failed to agree. Many men had been ruined, financially and in the eyes of their fellow-men. One beautiful young girl, related to one of the men involved, was so humiliated that she hid herself in a convent. Fremont Older had been ruthless in his manhunt. The country boy who couldn't kill a chicken was now breaking hearts and wrecking lives in his reforming zeal.

And the graft prosecution was no longer popular. People were sick of the continual stirring up of political sewerage. They spoke longingly of the "good old days" when graft had been condoned and undisturbed. They turned eagerly to the Thaw murder scandal, to embroidered butterflies on black silk stockings, to the Rugby game between the Stanford and California universities, to "Oh, You Kid," and "Twenty Three, Skiddoo" . . . to anything save the dreary graft revelations.

People were sick of politics. Stirring up graft, they had found, meant an end to good times. A depression was creeping over the United States. San Francisco, doubly hit, was dragging itself feebly out of the aftermath of earthquake and fire. Bubonic plague added terror to the city. Rats swarming in the débris carried the fatal germs.

Good times, nearly everyone felt, were preferable to a good reputation.

And Gallagher, the pivotal witness against Calhoun, was demanding the $4,500 Older had promised to pay for his dynamited flats.

"The case isn't over," protested Older. "I'll give you the money after Calhoun's trial."

But at the trial Gallagher did not testify against Calhoun. He disappeared. The prosecution said he had been bought off. Without him they could not convict.

The jury disagreed.

Charles Fickert appeared on the political horizon, later to play an unenviable rôle in the Mooney case. In the fall of 1909 he ran against Heney for district attorney, and won. The vote showed the revolt of the people against the graft prosecution. They wanted it to end with Ruef in prison and no more rattling of civic skeletons.

"Fickert was elected, together with Mayor P. H. McCarthy, by the railroad interests on the understanding that he would take program from the Calhoun crowd," wrote Older.

Fickert's first move after being sworn into office was to dismiss the case against Calhoun, whose second trial was pending.

# THE KIDNAPPING

So the graft prosecution ended.

Older wrote years afterward in a letter:

"The mistake I think I made in my crusade against graft was in believing that the way to stop graft was to put the grafters in the penitentiary. I now feel sure that was a mistaken policy. I no longer believe that our system of punishment is very effective in improving our social conditions. We spent months and even years in trying to convict the grafters and send them to the penitentiary. We only succeeded in one case. Abraham Ruef, the corrupt boss, was convicted and sent to prison for fourteen years. The others escaped and the graft continued. Perhaps we should have done better if, instead of trying to put those men in prison, we had persuaded them to confess and given wide publicity to their confessions. In that way at least the public would know what was being done with their government.

"In your letter you speak of my fighting for the 'right' against the 'wrong.'

"More than twenty years have passed since that graft fight and in that time my mind has undergone quite a change. I am not so cock-sure now as I was then what is 'right' and what is 'wrong.' Tolerance, kindness, and mercy are always right."

Fickert's election ended the graft-hunters' hopes of convicting the men they held most responsible for robbing San Francisco. But before the election of Fickert there was Ruef to be tried, and the prosecution fell upon him with redoubled fury.

The little boss would pay for the escape of all the others. Schmitz had outwitted sentence. Calhoun was still free. Ruef was all they had cornered after all their years of hunting.

Ruef came to trial. The jury disagreed. He was tried again. Word reached the graft-fighters that men on the new jury panel had been bribed. Certain jury-fixers were caught and sent to jail.

Hunting through the panel list for proof, the prosecution came upon a man named Haas. An ex-convict, he was having an affair with a married woman. She told her husband Haas had bragged to her that he would be on the Ruef jury and receive several thousand dollars to vote Not Guilty. The husband, to revenge himself on his rival, sent the information to District Attorney Langdon.

When Haas entered the jury-box for examination, Judge Lawlor asked the customary question, "Is there any reason why you should not serve as a juror?"

"There is not," said Haas.

Heney, questioning for the prosecution, was sorry the man had not taken advantage of the loophole. He could not afford to waste a peremptory challenge on Haas. He was obliged to expose him as having served time.

Haas brooded over his public humiliation. It became an obsession. During the course of Abe Ruef's second trial, on Friday, November 13, 1908, he edged into the courtroom, walked up behind Heney, and shot him through the head.

Older fell on his knees beside Heney, holding his friend in his arms and shouting for help. Blood gushed from the prosecutor's ears.

Ruef had been outside the courtroom when the shot was fired.

The little boss came running into the courtroom. He was wringing his hands, and his face was white.

"This is terrible!" Ruef was crying. "This is the worst thing that could have happened to me!"

## Chapter XV

### THE TIGER

HENEY, apparently dying, was carried from the courtroom. As they lifted him from the pool of his blood, he was heard to moan, "I'll get them yet!"

The little band of ostracized men fighting graft had become like brothers. Older was mad with grief. He ran after the ambulance all the way to the hospital. The surgeons said there was little hope for Heney. Older drove back to the Court House. Through the hysterical crowd he stormed, shouting Ruef's name, whipping to fury a mob already half-insane.

"Ruef! Get Ruef!" roared the crowd.

The terrified little boss was rushed back to his cell by police.

The streets flooded with extras. Every newspaper in the city cried out with horror at the attempted slaying. *Bulletin* headlines were hysterical in their demands for vengeance against Haas, the "Ruef Tool" who had shot Heney. Reporters from all papers assigned to watch outside the hospital where Heney lay called themselves "the Death Watch."

Mrs. Heney sat by her husband in the hospital. A telegram came to her from President Roosevelt, couched in the booming terms of the "Big Stick." "Inexpressibly shocked . . . fearless attempts at reform . . . all good citizens stamp out the power of men of this kind."

Washington was with the graft prosecution. So was all

the United States—except San Francisco! It had snubbed the graft-hunters for exposing the shame within.

But this night the city kept up its cry of horror. In Dreamland Rink a hastily-called mass-meeting drew great crowds. Prominent men scourged the attempted assassination. Prayers were said for Heney, "Martyr of the Graft Prosecution." Mayor Taylor presided. Among the speakers were ex-mayor Phelan, Spreckels, District Attorney Langdon, and the Reverend William Rader, who these days was writing signed editorials for Older with a revolver ready for action on his desk.

Later Phelan, Older, and Hiram Johnson, shortly to become Governor of California, sat in Older's office talking in strained tones. Under the window a mob stretched from corner to corner on Market Street. Only a word would be needed to set the waiting hundreds running to the jail to lynch the little boss crouching in his cell. The faces of the men in the street were turned up to Older's windows.

They were waiting for the word.

"I'm ready for anything that is right," said Johnson, looking down through the window. He was pale, trembling with emotion. "If it's the rope—I'm for that."

In this hour Ruef's life was in their hands. But the graft-hunters did not give the word that would have turned San Francisco back to '56 and the scarlet days of the Vigilantes.

Haas, who shot Heney, was found dead in his cell.

Where did he get the gun with which he killed himself? Why was his cell door open when he was found? Why was his dead body, the gun gripped in his hand, lying half-way across the threshold?

And whom had Haas meant when he said in his confession to Burns, "I was urged frequently to kill Heney by certain persons whose names I will not tell you."

The death of Haas was one of the many mysteries in the graft cases.

Heney was twice operated upon. Word came at last that he might live. The graft-hunters swung back into action. Hiram Johnson and Matt I. Sullivan volunteered to prosecute in Heney's place. Johnson left a handsome law practice to join a crusade for which he would receive nothing.

Ruef, trembling still, was brought back to trial. The prosecutors had a surprise for the little boss. They knew, according to Older, that part of the jury were fixed. They knew the names of every man on the jury who had taken money for the promise to set Ruef free. Johnson called each bribed juryman by name and, fixing him with a threatening eye, shouted:

"You—you dare not acquit this man!"

But it became apparent that the voice of "big money" was raised higher than Hiram's. The jury went out to decide, and stayed out. Hours passed. The prosecution grew furious, for proof of guilt was indisputable and there was no excuse for deliberation and delay.

Not one of the graft-hunters went to bed that night.

"The next morning the jury was still out," related Older. "After a sleepless night I went to the courtroom, in a very overwrought condition of mind, and insisted upon the making of an outcry in the court in case the jury came in to ask for instructions. I would demand that justice be done, and the crowded courtroom should let the jury see its temper.

"I was talked out of this foolish idea by another man no less overwrought than myself, who ended by saying that he would make the outcry himself.

"But the jury was not brought in.

"The day dragged on. The jury was still out in the afternoon. At about two o'clock Heney telephoned me that he was well enough to come down to the courtroom and pay his respects to Judge Lawlor. I thought I saw in this a chance to get a verdict.

"I telephoned Heney to wait until I came for him."

Older, inspired, telephoned the leaders of the "League of Justice," a group of "minute-men" pledged to aid the cause of the graft prosecution at a moment's notice. A hundred members rushed from every part of the city to the court. They pressed into the room, pushing out the merely curious who were waiting to see the jury come in.

Then Older drove up with the convalescent Heney. He helped the weakened "martyr of the prosecution" into the courtroom. In a room directly over the courtroom, Older knew, the jury was deliberating toward deadlock.

As Heney entered the courtroom, the "minute-men" raised a shout of welcome. Older himself trumpeted like a bull elephant. The rest of the crowd joined in. Heney was a hero to the element in the city that hated graft.

"I never heard such a roaring," recounted Older gleefully. "It lasted fully five minutes."

It was a cheer of welcome, but to the scared jury on the floor above it sounded like a bellowed demand for lynching. A few minutes later twelve good men and true filed hurriedly into the courtroom. They had hastily made up their minds. All were deathly white. Some trembled. A few were weeping. But all answered in turn:

"Guilty!"

After that there was no more cheering. All eyes were fixed on a white-faced man with a roach of black hair and a handle-bar mustache, Ruef the brilliant attorney, the ruler of a city, the little boss. Older, looking at the broken Ruef, did not at that moment see the man. He saw a treacherous villain, a betrayer of the city he loved.

This, Older knew, was his supreme moment of victory. He expected to feel as had his father and uncles when they marched away to death in the struggle to free the slaves. Had he not helped to free San Francisco from the menace of this clever-featured felon? The graft prosecution had many times narrowed down to a struggle between Ruef and

Older. Now Older held his head high with the sense of righteous triumph.

Ruef, convicted, was not without power. He summoned all that remained of his one-time authority to keep the hour for his sentence a secret from Older. Older, he knew, was his nemesis. The little boss did not want the editor towering over him when sentence was pronounced.

But Older found out the hour. He was in the courtroom when Judge Lawlor gave the man who had ruled San Francisco the utmost penalty permitted by law.

"I sentence you, Abraham Ruef, to fourteen years in San Quentin Penitentiary . . ."

When Older heard these words, the exultant fury left him. For the first time he looked upon Abraham Ruef and saw the man.

Ruef carried a million-word appeal to the higher courts, and lost.

On the day Ruef was taken to San Quentin to begin his sentence, Older in his office smoked more than his usual number of cigars. In imagination he followed the sentenced man. He knew the routine of the "big house." He could envision the broken little boss stripped of his good clothing, humiliated, dressed in the rough striped gray suit and heavy shoes. That arrogant black roach of hair would be cropped, Older thought, passing his slim hand nervously over his own head that was growing bald. He felt the utter degradation, the tears—yes, for the "curly boss" had wept, when shorn of worldly power, of human pride. Older shivered a little and went out to lunch. As he stamped to his accustomed table in the Palace Hotel, his look was thoughtful. He could not shake off the vision of Abe Ruef behind stone walls.

The *Bulletin* reporter who with other press representatives had accompanied Ruef to San Quentin was writing his narrative in the local room when Older returned from lunch. Older paused to look over his shoulder and read, a practice of his that had sent many a reporter rushing later to the corner saloon to soothe a shattered nervous system. Older had a habit of snatching a page out of a reporter's typewriter the second it was written, reading it at a glance, and champing impatiently for the next. Waiting, he gustily criticized, suggested, praised. To a nervous reporter with dead-line in five minutes and a half-column story to write, Older's volcanic presence at one's shoulder was a major catastrophe.

The reporter had written what Older called a "hell-devil" account of Ruef's trip across the Bay, triumphing in the *Bulletin's* victory and Ruef's downfall.

"We can't run this story," exploded Older. "Write it over, without showing your own feelings. Revealing your own prejudices weakens the point you are trying to make."

A terse reportorial account was then written and approved by Older. He taught all his writers the value of writing impersonally.

Ruef, in prison, had shown courage. A reporter had asked him how he liked the gray striped convict uniform.

"In many a San Francisco parade I have admired the California Grays," was Ruef's gallant retort. "The zebra is one of the most beautiful and graceful of animals. Why, therefore, should I cavil at my attire?"

Calhoun, before the Fickert election of 1909, was still left defying the graft-hunters. But with Gallagher gone his conviction was a forlorn hope. The struggle dragged on into its third year. At Calhoun's trial more than fifty defense attorneys worked in relays. In court they heckled District Attorney Langdon and the two prosecution counsel, Heney and Johnson. The tempers of the overworked graft prosecutors were worn raw.

Older was often viciously attacked in court by the corps of the defense.

"You fellows shouldn't vilify me," he once said, with his most disarming grin, to a group of them in the corridor. "If it weren't for me, you wouldn't be getting all those big fees. You should give me a banquet!"

Fourteen hundred and fifty veniremen were called before a jury of twelve were found willing to try Abe Ruef. This had been a record. But before a jury could be found to try the powerful Calhoun, twenty-three hundred and seventy talesmen were called into court and examined.

During this trial one rich San Franciscan of irreproachable reputation remarked, "I subscribed to the Graft Prosecution Fund, and before the investigation was over I had to exert myself to keep my own attorney from going to jail."

The prosecutions cost $213,391.50, raised by subscription.

The first Calhoun jury disagreed. Before a second trial could begin, Fickert was elected district attorney and dismissed the charges against Schmitz and Calhoun.

So, after all the bloodshed and heartache, there was only Ruef in prison.

"I had hoped we would be able to reach the big men," Older said with regret, "the men at the top of the whole pyramid of civic corruption. I felt they were the men responsible for the shameful conditions of the city, and I was not satisfied that we had been able to get only Ruef, one of the less important men."

Calhoun was free, Schmitz free. Only Ruef had been found guilty—of taking a Calhoun bribe!

"Is this victory?" Older asked himself. "Or is it failure?"

He tormented himself with such questions. He would interrupt his work to sit lost in volcanic thought, his cigar clamped between iron lips, his eyes narrowed.

Never before had Fremont Older looked back upon anything he had done. Life had hurried him onward, not giving him a chance at boyhood and youth and schooling, at the leisure for growth and reflection other men experienced. He had been forced to work constantly and think quickly. In newspaper work he had found a means of livelihood that gave him a sense of complete living. He loved the newspaper game. He was a hunter of dramatic passions, of large excitements.

Now, looking backward, he saw only too clearly. There was the Brown case. Why had he exposed that erring minister? Why had he ferreted so deeply into other people's lives?

It grew upon Fremont Older that his life had been selfish as Ruef's. He had sold souls into headlines. He had traded characters for a boost in circulation. He had broken hearts in his fury of building "the greatest evening paper west of Chicago."

And the thought tormented him, too, that the graft prosecution by breaking the immunity covenant with Ruef had broken faith.

"It became apparent to me that Ruef had promised to tell the truth, in return for the promise of immunity, and that later, when he refused to tell more than the truth, the immunity agreement with him was broken, and he was sent to the penitentiary," Older explained.

Ruef had refused to admit that the money given him to give the Supervisors was "bribe money." He persisted in referring to it as fees.

Out of such brooding Older came to a strange decision, the most astonishing of his life.

"I'm going across the Bay," he said to his wife. "I'm going to San Quentin to see Abe Ruef."

All the rest of his life Older would be trying to explain this impulse to his friends. To him it seemed perfectly clear.

In the dismal shadows of San Quentin the man he had

hounded for six years was brought before him, saddened, broken, in prison stripes. Older wrote of that strange and poignant meeting in the visitors' room:

"At last Ruef came in. His eyes fell upon me, and went past me, looking for someone he thought wanted to see him.

"I went over to him and held out my hand. I told him that I had come to see things differently, that I was sorry for much that I had done, and I asked him to forgive me."

They talked, hunter and quarry. In the cold light of that barred room they saw one another for the first time. Older saw a Ruef who had once been young, enthusiastic, ambitious, a brilliant young attorney fresh from college lured into politics.

There was only one sort of political game in California then. It was crooked. Ruef came of a race that could brook no failure. He played the game the only way it could successfully be played.

"He is no better, no worse, than we voters who uphold such politics," thought Older.

During the half-hour these two talked together, Fremont Older outgrew one more of his many lives—he became another sort of man. There emerged from the prison gates a philosopher who had reached the conclusion that not Ruef but "the System" was guilty.

"The System" was a new and bitter phrase he had learned during the graft crusade. His friend Lincoln Steffens, the brilliant muck-raking reporter, was pounding established order over the head with that word. Steffens had opened up a new world of thought to Older.

"I was fifty years old when Steffens woke me up to the realities of life, and it was by his guidance that I finally dragged myself out of the 'make-believe' world that I had lived in all my life," Older wrote long after. "Steffens made me face life as it is."

Older made his decision. Violently, as he did everything, he announced to the graft-fighters who had convicted Ruef, who had fought side by side with him and faced ostracism and danger with him to convict Ruef,

"I'm going to try to get Ruef out!"

He opened the amazing crusade with an editorial:

"Mercy for Abraham Ruef!"

That full-page editorial marked a crisis in Older's life.

Few would ever understand Older's change of heart. His enemies hurled the usual charge that he had been bribed. Nothing else Older ever did brought such a storm of wrath upon him.

His friends who had stood by him so long understood least of all.

During the graft prosecution he had made many bitter enemies and many devoted friends. Men had rallied around him and accepted him as a leader. In his intimate group were many professors of the two universities near San Francisco. He had developed friendships with reform leaders such as Lincoln Steffens and Clarence Darrow. Theodore Roosevelt had frequently written the Western editor that he was "delighted" and "overjoyed" with all Older had accomplished in California.

When Older changed, the faithful turned on him. Ruef in stripes was all they had to show for victory.

As a rule Older asked little of his friends. Now, of men like Heney and Burns and Hiram Johnson, he demanded everything. He asked them to give up the fruit of the bitter and dangerous years to seek freedom for Ruef. He asked Hiram Johnson to do this. By this time Johnson was Governor of California, elected by honest enthusiasm for his work in the graft crusade. He could not share Older's about-face.

Older was hurt, he was indignant, when his friends refused to fight with him for Ruef. To him it was perfectly

**THE FIGHTING EDITOR**
Older in his fifties.

simple. Ruef, the little fellow, was paying for the sins of the big fellows. Was that justice?

And if Older felt remorse, why should not his friends be remorseful as well?

So he argued, and a coolness rose, and in some cases enmity, between Older and many of his former friends.

Older himself wanted no reward for the graft crusade. He never made capital of anything he accomplished. He would sacrifice all he had won in one fight to launch out on another.

He was charged with being inconsistent. He admitted it.

"If people never changed their minds," he added resentfully, "human beings would still be living in dugouts."

Other comments were less kind. "Mad as a hatter," some were saying of him. But Older believed he was right.

"Ruef has been made a scapegoat," he insisted. "Fourteen years in a cell is too heavy a penalty to pay for another man's crime.

"It all boils down to this: Ruef is in prison because he has confessed to taking money from a corporation president many times richer than himself.

"Then why isn't the corporation head in prison for bribing Ruef? Why should a small man suffer and a big man escape? Is it less a crime to give a bribe than receive one?"

The men who had been closest with Older in the graft fight were the angriest with him now. He was sacrificing much for one small political pawn caught in the tangle of circumstance. Older suffered keenly. He could rejoice in the attacks made by those he knew favored graft and crime. But this . . . ah, this was different. The attitude of his friends made him wince with pain. Thenceforth he would heartily agree with the saying that no man has more than three friends.

In his crusade to parole Ruef he stood almost alone.

Roosevelt wrote reproaching Older for his stand.

"Roosevelt thinks I'm wrong, too," Older commented regretfully. "I suppose he thinks we should have boiled Ruef in oil."

But somewhere it was printed that Older had turned, "like a tiger, to lick the wounds of one he has wounded."

Franklin K. Lane and Lincoln Steffens understood his change of heart. Also his booted and sombreroed friend Joaquin Miller, "Poet of the Sierra," was among those who cheered Older on in the crusade for mercy.

"By all means, my dear Mr. Older," Miller wrote, "keep up your fight for the release of Abraham Ruef. Perhaps some day soon the Christian city of San Francisco will wake up to its Christian duty towards one poor, imprisoned Jew.

"What is Christianity for if it doesn't lead you to forgive your foe when you have beaten and humiliated him? The people of San Francisco first of all put him in their own prison for nearly four years and then sent him to the penitentiary—the only one punished of all those charged with the same crime. He has been punished enough.

"In the name of Christ I call upon them to follow the teachings of Christ, to apply the Golden Rule, to give Ruef a chance to go out and live a new life:

> *'In men whom men condemn as ill,*
> *I find so much of goodness still.*
> *In men whom men pronounce divine,*
> *I find so much of sin and blot,*
> *I hesitate to draw the line*
> *Between the two where God has not.'"*

Through all the remaining years of his life Older would be attempting to explain his change toward Abraham Ruef. In a letter to a group of college professors who had been his friends he showed his indignation that they had given ear to the current report that Ruef had bribed Older to aid him. Older wrote:

"I have not contended that it was wrong to put Ruef in the penitentiary. I think his being there, however, bears the same relation to our social and economic sickness as the shooting of a diseased horse would have to the curing of glanders among a band of infected animals. Nor does it seem strange to me that many should believe there was no other way to account for my plea for mercy for Ruef than by deciding in their minds that Ruef was to pay me a sum of money.

"Why should it be strange or peculiar in them to so think, when money is the only known standard of respectability and reputability that society recognizes? Here and there men have been actuated by a finer and higher motive, but the people about them would not credit it, because they could not.

"If they had stopped to think more about my case, however, they might have reasonably and logically rendered another verdict. Those who followed the graft prosecution closely, and I think most of my severest critics did, must have known that the time to sell out would have been when the largest part of San Francisco would have welcomed a changed policy, and when the largest price could have been obtained for upholding the conspicuous graft defendants. When, instead of odium attaching to such an act, the strongest and most 'respectable' part of the community would have applauded.

"To acount for my waiting until there was less money, and then taking up the most unpopular cause, excepting, of course, the cause of poverty, that anyone has ever espoused in California—my one-time friends must decide that I am at least eccentric in my depravity.

"I do not expect that my former friends can be suddenly convinced that there is a possibility that I could have had a higher motive than money."

Cora Older shared her husband's sorrow at being misunderstood. They were seeing their fellow-humans in a light that is mercifully spared the majority. Older said he never really understood people until he tried to help Ruef. He was never again to feel thoroughly at ease with the majority of his fellow-men.

But Older continued to print page editorials asking mercy for the boss. For years he kept up the disheartening fight.

This crusade, though it failed, was the greatest of his life. It revealed the change in Older the man.

He wrote in a letter:

"I have asked for mercy to Ruef because I felt that I, above all others, had done most to bring about his downfall. If you have followed the long fight the *Bulletin* has made during the past eight or nine years, you will recall that I was fighting Ruef long before the city woke up. You will also recall that I attacked him bitterly with all the invectives that I could personally command, and all that I could hire.

"I cartooned him in stripes. I described him on his way to San Quentin; told how I thought he would act en route, and what his manner would be when the barber shaved his head, and how he would feel when locked up in a cell. I was vindictive, unscrupulous, savage. . . .

"At last, after eight years of a man-hunting and man-hating debauch, Ruef crossed over and became what I wanted him to be—what I had longed and dreamed that he might be—a convict, stripped of his citizenship, stripped of everything society values except the remnant of an ill-gotten fortune.

"It is then I said to myself, 'I have got him. He is in stripes. He is in a cell. His head is shaved. He is in tears. He is helpless, beaten, chained—killed, so far as his old life is concerned. You have won. How do you like your victory? Do you enjoy the picture now that it is complete? You painted it. Every savage instinct in your nature is expressed on the canvas.'

"My soul revolted.

"I thought over my own life and the many unworthy things I had done to others, the injustice, the wrongs I had been guilty of, the human hearts I had wantonly hurt, the sorrows I had caused, the half-truths I had told, and the mitigating truths I had withheld, the lies I had allowed to go undenied.

"And then I saw myself also stripped, that is, stripped of all pretense, sham, self-righteousness, holding the key to another man's cell. I dropped the key. I never want to hold it again. Let it be taken up and held by those who feel they are justified in holding it. I want no more jail keys. For the rest of my life I want to get a little nearer to the forgiving spirit that Christ expressed.

"Isn't what I am accusing myself of true of all of us?

"Think it over. Think of your own life. Think of the lives of those around you, and see if you cannot discern that we are all guilty. And then think whether or not you believe that society will be benefited by denying Ruef a parole, which only gives him a half-liberty and still holds him under the restrictions of the prison until his term is finished."

There was small wonder Ruef had come to feel that Older, the man who had sent him to prison, was the only man on earth he could trust. He put all his money into the editor's keeping to protect it from the "friends" who offered to help him. One criminal attorney the little boss had made rich came to Older.

"I want to do something for Abe," he offered sentimentally, "dear old Abe!"

He went into court for five minutes and sent the imprisoned boss a bill for $5,000.

It was remarkable that many who hated and feared Older

would later turn to him as to an only friend. When Ruef at last came from prison, it was Older he hurried to see. When a man employed by Calhoun got into trouble, he turned for help, not to the bosses but to Older. District Attorney Fickert, who dismissed the Calhoun indictment and ended the graft prosecution and later helped send Tom Mooney to prison and once knocked Older down, would later, when ill and in need of advice, come to Older.

The long crusade for Ruef's parole was fruitless. The little boss spent ten years behind bars. He left San Quentin in 1920, and for the remainder of their lives the former boss and the fighting editor were friends.

When the graft crusade ended, there was comparative calm in the *Bulletin* offices.

"Let's not get into any more fights," pleaded Crothers.

"Of course we won't," comforted Older cheerily. "What is there left to fight about?"

He meant that.

People were saying that the stormy petrel Older owned the paper, that Crothers was only a figurehead. Such rumors annoyed the broadcloth-garbed Crothers, who had always yearned for a quiet and orderly paper, prosperity with peace.

For a time this was granted. The *Bulletin* settled down to apparent respectability.

## Chapter XVI

### THE EDITOR IN HIS OFFICE

THE SUDDEN CALM following the graft crusade brought as sudden prosperity to the crusading *Bulletin*.

"The truth is," Older once admitted in a letter, "the *Bulletin* got nowhere with circulation or advertising until I somehow acquired sense enough to stop preaching and scolding. The readers of the paper resented my attitude of superiority over them, and, I think, justly so.

"My success, if it may be called that, started when I came out in the *Bulletin* with a page editorial headed 'Mercy for Abraham Ruef.'

"With my changed attitude toward Ruef it wasn't long before my entire attitude toward life changed. Since then the old animosities have died out, or are forgotten. So you see, if I am to be taken as an example, one doesn't have to be intolerant to be successful."

While splitting the *Bulletin* pages wide with the graft stories, Older had not neglected other news. Every story was played to its uttermost limits. Features were developed. Writers and artists were finding their first chance at self-expression under Older.

A legend grew that he could discover talent at a glance.

The *Bulletin* was selling to regular subscribers for sixty-five cents a month. Older dropped the rate to twenty-five cents. Subscriptions poured in at the rate of fifteen hundred a day, until at the beginning of 1907 the paper had a subscription list of 56,000, in a city of less than 500,000.

Older's fortunes grew with the paper. Due to the offers of William Randolph Hearst, Crothers had by degrees raised his managing editor to $250 a week. Older spent every cent. The car he drove was always the latest and most powerful. Automobiles were his extravagance. The Olders lived at the Fairmont Hotel, on Nob Hill overlooking city and bay.

There was additional gray in Fremont Older's steadily receding "dark-hued mane." Little was left of the solemn, lanky country boy who had come out of Wisconsin years before. He was at the apex of his physical vigor. He smoked the finest Havana cigars. His suits were made in London, his shirts in New York. He wore expensive cravats.

But there was never an hour of the day or night that his rawest reporter could not call upon Older for advice or help on a story and not have him respond like a war-horse to battle. One night Edgar T. Gleeson and Peter Michelson of the staff rushed into his hotel with a "hot lead." The Olders had guests at dinner. Older clapped his hat down over his eyes and charged off with his reporters. All the rest of the night the fifty-year-old managing editor drove the boys around in his car, helping them track down the yarn. Physically and mentally he retained more drive than many of the young men he hired.

"Doc" Mundell, working on an assignment, telephoned Older at three in the morning.

"I've got it!" he yelled over the telephone.

Older chuckled. He could forgive anything in a reporter except lack of enthusiasm.

"Wait until I get dressed—I'll be right over!" he said.

To Older the newspaper game was truly a game, and he played it with all the resources of his boundless vitality. It would remain so to him all the days of his life. There would never come a time when he would not rise with excitement at the hint of a good story. There would never come a time when he would fail to praise the man who had scored a "beat."

"Imagine a reporter hauling the average managing editor out of bed at three in the morning!" Mundell said recently.

"Older trusted you. He knew you'd get the story, so you got it. No one ever failed him. And the minute you had the story, he wanted it written.

"Most of the stories his writers wrote were his stories. He always had most of the ideas on the paper. He never took credit for the stories—never seemed to care about credit. It was circulation he cared for."

Older watched circulation point by point. Every day he held consultation with the heads of street and country and home circulation and discussed the street sales and the net with absorbed attention. Strangely, he had a head for figures. His three years of schooling had left him ignorant of the higher mathematical processes, but by devious methods understood by no one else he always arrived at the right mathematical conclusion before anyone else.

His intensity drew around Older a group of youthful enthusiasts. They worked for less than they could earn on other papers. Older poured into them his fervor, his beliefs, his philosophies, his hopes. He never doubted their ability to do whatever he asked them to do.

"You could feel his presence through a brick wall," Ernest J. Hopkins once said of him.

Greater than editor or crusader was Older the man. Every human being who came under his influence was impressed by him. In that age of personal journalism Older fulfilled its tradition by permitting his young auxiliaries to write out their souls. He steered. He never squelched. What he could not give in salaries he compensated for in marvelously warm stimulation.

He created a Western school of journalism. Of the brilliant, highly-geared group he gathered around him, many would become famous.

John Francis Neylan, William O. McGeehan, Eustace Cullinan, Miriam Michelson, Edgar T. Gleeson, Lowell Otus Reese, Sinclair Lewis, Sophie Treadwell, Robert L. Duffus, Maxwell Anderson, Carl Hoffman, Rose Wilder Lane, Bessie Beatty, Kathleen Norris, Bayard Vieller, Ernest J. Hopkins, George West, Lemuel F. Parton, Franck Havenner, Sylvester J. McAtee, John D. Barry, Ralph E. Renaud, Bruce Bliven, John Taylor Waldorf, Howard Kreuger, John P. Coghlan, Timothy Healey, were among those who worked with Older during these years. Richard Barry wrote his first story, "Sandy of the Sierras," as a *Bulletin* serial and later dedicated the book to Older.

When they broke away from him and went to wider fields as authors, editors, attorneys, cartoonists, they continued to feel his influence. Older carried about in his pockets the letters they wrote back to him citing their small or great triumphs, the clipped reviews of their books or plays. Their triumphs were his. They were Fremont Older's children.

There are scattered here and there about the world those who refer to this period as "the golden age."

"There never was a place like the old *Bulletin* office," these say.

Its spirit was generous and creative. Pauline Jacobson said it was like a fraternity house. The staff in the main were friendly; it was difficult to be petty or jealous around a man like Older. They were a trusted group who trusted one another. After the paper went to press, the majority of the group would drift off by street-car to tea in the Japanese tea garden in Golden Gate Park.

There was no copy desk in the usual sense in the *Bulletin* office. Each writer was responsible for his own story. He wrote it and its heads, shot the copy through to the press-room in a basket on a wire, made up his own page. There never was a newspaper with better make-up or a better play of news.

"Older held the unswerving allegiance of all, from the owner of the paper to the office-boy," wrote Mrs. H. L. Brooke. "Domineering? No, it was not that. It was magnetism. It was power."

Older hired Mrs. Brooke as book-reviewer. Then, for her first assignment, he sent her to the city prison with the office-boy as body-guard to interview five murderers.

Whoever could best do the story got the story.

"Older never considered your job on the basis of your sex," commented Bessie Beatty. This pretty, fluffy, blonde girl justified Older's faith in her ability by becoming the first woman journalist to enter Russia during the revolution. She was later editor of *McCall's Magazine*. "If you could do the job, you got it.

"Another thing I appreciated about him as a boss was his willingness to permit you to stand by your own guns."

Older had no liking for "yes men." He said a man who agreed with all he suggested had no value. He hated being crossed in any way. He scowled, he stormed at those who objected to any of his ideas. But he considered the value of their arguments even as he stormed. The men and women who worked with Older were never afraid to speak all that was in their minds.

"I have sometimes worked for men who diminished one's capacities," Bessie Beatty said again. "If you went in to them with a good story or what you thought was a good idea, they sent you out diminished. The idea didn't seem so hot after all. If you wrote it, you wrote it badly. I never went into Fremont's office that I didn't come out better fitted to write the story. He made his own creative contribution to it. He helped you realize the thing you were trying to put across. He added his enthusiasm to your enthusiasm and you went away prepared to do a grand job.

"It was creative editing to a degree that no one else in my experience in the mazagine or newspaper field has ever approached.

"His tenderness; his excitement over beauty or talent; his capacity to live his life in his own individual way in a world so largely populated by sheep; his love for Cora, the dogs—everything about him seems to fit so perfectly into his pattern. He was, I think, more than anyone I have ever known, all of a piece.

"In any field he would have been a great man."

In the local room Pauline Jacobson, brilliant daughter of a rabbi, wrote full-page Saturday articles which were quoted everywhere. During the graft crusade she wrote of the evils of the city. She found her way into the back rooms of saloons, into jails, houses of evil reputation, every place a lady did not go in that age of large hats and long skirts.

Backed by generations of intellectual breeding, Pauline managed to cover such assignments with an air. She was the first woman to write sports articles in the West. Among other sporting events Pauline covered the Gans-Nelson fight in Nevada.

For Older sports had little allure, but he knew they held great interest. He recognized drama wherever he found it. He knew what men were thinking. More, he knew their dreams.

The sports page developed by Older's brother-in-law, Hiland Baggerly, was as live as any in the United States. Robert Ripley, drawing for it, had been raised to six and a half dollars a week, and "Hi" with a supreme effort persuaded the owner of the *Bulletin* to pay Ripley eight dollars. Later Ripley would earn a million a year with "Believe It or Not." "Rube" Goldberg at ten dollars weekly was doing brilliant work for the sports page as writer and cartoonist. "Tad" Dorgan's cartoons and articles delighted everyone. Herb Roth drew sparkling illustrations for the editorials.

The sports page carried such colorful serials as "Fighters I Have Seconded," by "Spider" Kelly, and "Confessions of Philadelphia Jack O'Brien."

Ralph E. Renaud, later the last managing editor of the New York *World,* was drama editor. That did not mean that he confined his talents to the theater. Older had no respect for "departmental rights." He swooped into the local room and carried off any person he felt best equipped to write the story he wanted written, so that the bewildered drama editor might find himself covering a political meeting or a four-alarm fire.

Edgar T. ("Scoop") Gleeson, later a Hearst editor, came on the *Bulletin* after the earthquake to enlist in the graft crusade. He was earning more than he could ever hope to make on the *Bulletin.* Yet for the privilege of working with Older he accepted the job of financial editor—the work he knew least about—at ten dollars a week less than he had been getting.

"He had that look about him—the cavalier look of the Virginia gentleman who fights duels in the dark," Gleeson explains his youthful admiration. "The *Bulletin* was striking bold and trenchant blows and you felt Older was always for the right.

"He made you see what he saw. He could summarize a story so that your enthusiasm was instantly kindled to the same heat as his own. You never heard him distort a fact to win a point for his side. Those who surrounded him swore by him."

Any writer, personality, or idea discovered by Older immediately became the greatest discovery of his life. Every week or so he read aloud excerpts from some new book and exclaimed with volcanic fervor:

"This is absolutely the greatest book I have ever read!"

He admitted with a resigned perplexity that he could do nothing in moderation.

"If I loved, I loved too much. If I hated, I hated too much. It was that way with everything."

No man ever read with more passion or made literary discoveries with more enthusiasm. His dramatic editor once groaned to his city editor, "What can you do with a man who has just discovered Plutarch?"

"About this time he seized upon Plato," Cora Older says of him. "He didn't read books. He ate them. They became a part of himself. He would read to anyone who happened to be near. He would have stopped a policeman in the street and read to him.

"Once he called me out of a gathering of women at the Hotel Rafael. They thought and I thought there must be something serious. It was really to read to me a passage from Plato he had just discovered. One woman said to me, 'I'd get a divorce from a man like that.'

"He had passages of Plato struck off on the press and he used to distribute them among his friends. Pauline Jacobson called them his 'Plato Tracts.'

"He read Plutarch with the same intensity."

Older read Plutarch aloud to everyone who came within his range. For a time the ancient Roman was practically a member of the staff.

"Never have I known such a man—and I'm sure there never was one—who could kick up such a thundering excitement about an idea, a fragment of poetry, a bit of human drama, a flash of ironic humor, or a dog, canary bird, or human being in distress," Lemuel F. Parton said in an interview by Edwin C. Hill.

"Back in his early fighting days, when he was a rampant Paul Bunyan of an editor, already legendary, he stormed

## THE EDITOR IN HIS OFFICE

into the copy-desk room, boiling with excitement, looking seven feet high, as he always did in these explosive moments.

" 'Rip me out two columns of the front page!' he roared. 'I've got something worth putting into this sheet. Clear a four-column head in the first edition!' "

Older was waving the first copy of Kipling's "The Vampire" to reach San Francisco.

To him a great poem was news. Among the poems he splashed over the front page were Edwin Markham's "The Man with the Hoe," "The Rubaiyat," "The Ballad of Reading Goal," and "If You Were a Tadpole and I Was a Fish."

Lem Parton tells of a typical Older incident during the graft fight:

"I remember one time, when there had been three days of heavy gun-fire in that belch of wildly intemperate journalism which prevailed in San Francisco, when it looked as if Older's entire career, and possibly his physical safety, were at stake.

"At one o'clock in the morning Older called me up at my home. 'Come down to the Poodle Dog Restaurant right away,' he commanded, with excitement in his voice. 'Camille will show you where I am—in a room on the third floor.' Of all the people I have known who were friends of Older, there has been none who ever would have thought of questioning or resisting him. I dressed and hurried to the Poodle Dog, glamorous old French restaurant of the '49 days, its name perverted by the miners from Poudre d'Or.

"As I opened the door of the private room, Older was pacing back and forth, gnawing an unlighted cigar, which he always did when greatly excited. As I entered, he reached for his hip pocket. It had seemed to me that these goings-on of the last few days might work up to gun-play.

Was Older in danger? Was that why he had summoned me?

"These thoughts flashed through my mind. But it was not a gun which Older drew from his hip pocket. It was a frazzled, battered old copy of Montaigne's essays.

"'Take a look at that!' he roared, his face ablaze with excitement as he indicated a marked passage. 'And that! And that!' Until dawn we pored over 'the wisest Frenchman that ever lived,' as Sainte-Beuve had called Montaigne. Here I was, dragged out of my bed in the middle of the night, to share a Montaigne revel in the old Poodle Dog! And the odd part of it was that Older got me all worked up over it, too.

"In thirty years of newspaper work in many different countries I have known all sorts of men. I have never known a greater human personality than Fremont Older."

During this time Older maintained a cheerful paper war against William Randolph Hearst, who was running for governor of New York. There was nothing personal in this prolonged attack. Hearst owned the San Francisco *Examiner*, he could buy all the talent Older longed for, do all the things with the paper he owned that Older longed to do. By sweeping up the entire talent-field in journalism, Older maintained, Hearst raised journalistic salaries in America fifty per cent. But Older was trying to build a great newspaper on a shoe-string, and with that shoe-string he belabored Hearst and his millions.

Older made use of any material that came to his hands. That was one element of his greatness. His very office-boys became newspaper men, attorneys, judges. Men who worked with him found roads leading upward. He was free from prejudice. He was not impressed by a writer because he was famous. Without money to buy famous names for his paper, he had to discover and build his own writers. He was not influenced by anyone else's opinion of a bit of writing. "The tag" was his sobriquet for fame. He saw the thing as it was, without the label.

This faculty of not being impressed was Older's greatest asset as an editor.

It was the same with everyone. He was never impressed by a man's standing in the community or by his wealth. People fascinated him, but a few repelled. One of the richest men on earth was an intimate friend. He made other lasting friendships with train conductors, hack-drivers, and waiters. In public dining-rooms he always talked with the waiters. A good waiter, he maintained, had unusual intelligence and a native talent for psychology. He liked to get their opinions of people and events. In later days, as his diet grew simpler, his tip was often double the cost of his meal.

At a fashionable lawn fête he might be seen in ardent conversation with the gardener. At parties the lion of the affair might strike him as an awful bore, and Older would as likely as not be found with some shy, startled soul who had never before experienced such flattering fixed attention.

With unconscious courtesy he introduced the workers on his ranch to all his guests. When Nance O'Neil, an old friend, played at a local theater, the Olders took their cook and her husband, a couple of whom they were very fond, to the theater and later to the dressing-room to meet the star.

The "hop-copy" in the office looked peaked, and Older took the little fellow home to his ranch for a month in country air.

Older resented intellectual snobbery. He had been made to feel too keenly on the *Bulletin* his lack of an academic background. He was annoyed by the conversations of two esoteric intellectuals who were wont to sit in their corner of the local room and "brill." This verb he invented to denote the act of being brilliant in a self-conscious manner.

He had scorn, too, for the modern school of prose and poetry that he termed "the school of the vague." He had an almost personal resentment of all but plain speech. The best writers, he held, wrote simply and did not use long words known by the few. Long words, said Older, were a discourtesy to the average reader and an intellectual snub.

While he talked in headlines, Older never tried to be clever. He joked, but never made wise-cracks. He loved to tease and was most amused by pomposity. He was stormily rude to people who were rude to "inferiors." He left a five-dollar tip on the table and stamped in a rage out of a hotel dining-room because a man with whom he had been dining unreasonably reprimanded the waiter. Any unkindness infuriated him.

Older was strong and protective. His gentleness hovered over the weaker and those who were fallen. Their point of view was his, and this quality had been strong in him from his earliest years.

This protective quality he extended to his staff. Only those closest to him knew how bitterly he fought to win his reporters their small salary increases.

At one time Crothers was determined to fire a certain man on the city desk. Older tried to keep him. The struggle was long. The owner lost his temper and said that either the man was fired or Older could leave the *Bulletin*.

Older was licked. The letter of dismissal he wrote reveals the tenderness he felt for those who worked with him:

"Dear ———:

"I am compelled to make a change on the city desk. What I most fear, and what most troubles me, is that you will not understand how deeply I regret it. It is the most unpleasant act I have ever had to perform. I have fought against it for a long time, but if I am to continue to hold my own position I must make this change. I am very fond of you, and I had almost as soon go myself as to have you go. But that wouldn't do you or anybody else any good. I don't know how you are situated, and that, of course, concerns me deeply, but I am powerless to help in any way that I now know. If I can be of service please believe that I will, and also please be broad enough to see the situation as it is, and don't go through life blaming me. It isn't I, it is the position I hold that does it, and this is the price I have to pay. Come in and see me when you return. Take this week and next under salary.

Sincerely yours,<br>
Fremont Older"

Though he was now rated "one of the six great editors in America," he retained the point of view of the less fortunate. Someone wrote that the motto of the *Bulletin* was "The voice of the woman accused, the man oppressed, the child exploited."

Those who knew Older knew that the *Bulletin* was sailing under a temporary calm. With his temperament there was no hope of lasting peace. In 1910 P. H. McCarthy became mayor and made a daring promise:

"I'm going to make San Francisco the Paris of America!" he said.

At that promise vice, crushed to earth by Older, rose again. Overnight the houses of vice and gambling sprouted everywhere. Again there was graft and bribery. It was an abrupt return to "the good old days."

It was a challenge to Fremont Older. He was off to a new crusade.

## Chapter XVII

### CAMPAIGN FOR JOHNSON

SIX KINGS ruled San Francisco.
They were men whose names the average respectable citizen never heard. They were the "King of the Pickpockets," the "King of the Maquereaus," the "King of the Bunco Swindlers," the "King of White Slavers," the "King of Gamblers," and the "King of the Thieves." These names were given them by the underworld they ruled. Each protected his own kind, shielded their evil trades, bribed political and police protection, and, on the rare occasions it was necessary, provided bail.

The six shared the city. It was said that if a man was killed in San Francisco, the all-powerful kings knew the name of the killer within the hour.

Fremont Older printed their photographs and life stories.

"You have to see one of the above gentlemen if you want to get on the police force," stormed the *Bulletin*. "They named most of the detectives, bailiffs and prison keepers, and when the big shift of captains, lieutenants, sergeants and corporals and patrolmen which is slated to come off any day now is made, their friends will land the fat places."

But behind the "Big Six" was powerful protection. The new Mayor McCarthy, as his first step toward making San Francisco "the Paris of America," appointed Harry P. Flannery president of the Police Commission.

Flannery was the owner of a saloon where, according to *Bulletin* charges, police and detectives and supervisors met every day to take their orders and drink with the new powers of the city, who were brothel-owners, saloonkeepers, fight-promoters, bunco-steerers, and pickpockets. Among this group, tight-lipped, their few words law, moved the six all-powerful men.

Police who showed a too great antipathy to crime were banished to the outlying districts, known as the "cabbage patches." In their place men with bad records were put back on the force by Flannery, men who had previously been dismissed from service on such charges as extortion, bribe-taking, blackmail, or permitting street-walkers to work on their beats.

This was a throwback, the *Bulletin* shouted, to the evil days of Ruef and Schmitz. Again Older ran headlines:

"Harry Flannery Dominates." "Thieves Have San Francisco by the Throat and Helpless." "Policemen with Unsavoury Records." "Mayor McCarthy and Police Chief are Mere Programmers." "Police Names on Payroll of Gamblers." "Thieves and Bunco Men under Protection."

The *Bulletin* printed the names of the transferred policemen and gave the reasons for their demotion. Usually they had made the mistake of arresting "protected" pickpockets and bunco-men. The *Bulletin* listed the new police who had bad records and cited the records.

The paper attacked the police-protected gamblers. *Bulletin* reporters patrolled Chinatown and the tenderloin with guns in their pockets and their lives in their hands. Every day a list of protected gambling-places was printed under such heads as "Police Blind as Sucker Led to Inevitable Slaughter." The exposé began with Chinatown, and one hour after the first list was printed, every lottery in Chinatown suspended at the behest of the police of the district, who dashed in and out of the places ordering the pigtailed proprietors to "close up for a few hours until this blows over."

But the *Bulletin* took its time in "blowing over." Where another editor might have made a short, sensational exposé, Older ran that printed list every day for thirty days. He raged against a city administration that took a percentage from such gambling games as craps, Klondike, stud and draw poker, and blackjack. The games, raged the *Bulletin,* weren't even on the level. One Market Street firm did nothing but manufacture the marked-card decks and round-cornered dice used in these crooked gambling games.

Police Commissioner Flannery announced in a press interview that he didn't know of a single gambling-place in San Francisco. Baited, he sent a squad into Chinatown to raid one lonely joint. The *Bulletin* hooted Flannery. It listed nearly one thousand gambling-houses running wide open in the city and invited the public to investigate.

This was personal journalism, so personal that it smoked. Mayor McCarthy was compelled to put in a new chief of police. A silly gesture, sneered the *Bulletin,* for Flannery ruled mayor and police chief too. "Chief Made Scapegoat for Administration" was the explanatory headline shouted by the newsboys.

Older determined to smash the McCarthy administration. A decent interlude had been the Taylor administration, and Older had selected Taylor for mayor and named all the supervisors. Graft had resumed office with McCarthy. Right away the Police Department, needing automobiles, omitted to advertise for bids, as they could glean $40,000 by so doing. The *Bulletin* found this out and made them advertise.

And the *Bulletin* roared and bellowed that nothing could stop this crusade, although the politicians were taking up the old Ruef-Schmitz tactics and were threatening to start a newsboys' strike and an advertisers' boycott against the paper.

"The *Bulletin* cannot be deterred from telling the truth," Older defied them in an editorial, "and as the great majority of the people of San Francisco want to know the truth, the boycotting of the truth will be a thankless task."

The politicians had the *Bulletin* boycotted. Thousands were pledged not to read the paper. But people did read it. They righteously denied it entry at their front gates, but they bought it on street-corners.

Again, under boycott, street sales went up and money was made.

When the fight against the gambling trust was at its height, a bunco-man named Joe Abbott was arrested with his gang for operating a "wire-tapping poolroom" across the Bay in Sausalito. This was a lure that promised suckers inside tips on horse-races in a far-off city. A fake race-track poolroom "board" was set up with names of imaginary horses and "dummy" telephones that led nowhere. The sucker was permitted to win until he was willing to risk his life savings on one race, whereupon the entire "poolroom" set-up disappeared with all his money. One sucker lost $125,000 in this bunco-game.

Abbott, arrested and released on bail, hurried to Flannery of the Police Commission for help. Flannery ordered him out of his house. Abbott complained to his attorney.

"Flannery has double-crossed me," he said bitterly. "And he got me to come down here in the first place!"

The attorney had a grouch against Mayor McCarthy. He sent the tip to Older.

It was all the editor needed.

Older succeeded in getting from the telegraph office a telegram written in the fine handwriting of Police Commissioner Flannery. It had been sent to the bunco-steerer Joe Abbott in Seattle the morning after McCarthy was elected Mayor of San Francisco. The President of the Police Commission wrote the bunco-man:

"Joe Abbott—Accept my sincere thanks for wire . . . the victory is grandest of the age . . . people are free once again . . . regards to Hasel, Anderson, and all our friends . . . Joe, my promise is right . . . Harry P. Flannery."

"Doc" Mundell, who did most of the investigating for the *Bulletin* in this crusade and wrote most of the stories, got Joe Abbott to confess.

Abbott agreed to testify against Commissioner Flannery. By making that promise he put his life in jeopardy. The underworld decreed vengeance against Abbott, "the stool-pigeon." The henchman of the six kings swore the "fink" would not live to go on the witness-stand. The lives of Older and Mundell were threatened.

The men who worked with Older had courage. Nerve was needed to work on the *Bulletin*. Even the women writers were daring. At the very height of the troubles with Flannery, Pauline Jacobson wrote a full-page interview with Jerome Bassity, the "white-slave dealer" who, according to *Bulletin* charges, was acting as Flannery's agent. Mayor McCarthy upon election had "tied up" with Bassity, and the *Bulletin* ran the seven-column headline:

"Maquereau Bassity's Man Named Chief of Police!"

"Look at the low-cunning lights in the small, rapacious, vulture-like eyes," Pauline wrote in describing the tenderloin king.

She spoke of his moral intelligence, "scarcely above that of the trained chimpanzee," of his love of luxury and comfort bought at the expense of women's souls. She turned the leader of the vice circle inside out for the *Bulletin* readers to view with disgust and loathing.

"After the Flannery trial was over, Bassity promised to get me," "Doc" Mundell said. "He and his gang were beating up the men that gave them their subpœnas. Well, we got him first! And that case cost Flannery $19,000 in attorney's fees."

It was always "we" with *Bulletin* reporters. The men and women who worked with Fremont Older spoke of "our paper," "our fight," "our policy," "our circulation." They might and did have their intra-office jealousies, but they presented a fighting front to the world.

Older was with them through everything. They could be sure he would stand by.

Expansive even in his hatreds, he kept the town informed as to every move made by the enemy. He ran a front-page lambast during the crusade, "Thug War Is Flannery's Threat . . . *Bulletin's* Managing Editor and Special Writer in Danger of Being Clubbed by the Police." A sensational story declared that the Police Commission, smarting under printed attacks, was planning to issue warrants on trumped-up charges against Older and Mundell and intended to send police after them and have the newspaper men beaten up on their way to prison.

"The *Bulletin* will take such precautions as it can to prevent injury to its employees," ran an editorial which was in reality a cry to the decent citizenry for protection, "but there is little that can be done against a city government in the hands of such men as now control it.

"The present situation is remindful of the dark days of the old Schmitz-Ruef régime, when R. A. Crothers, editor and proprietor of the *Bulletin,* was struck down with brass knuckles and left for dead.

"However, this paper will continue to tell the truth, regardless of what may happen."

Through all danger and threats Older refused to carry a gun. Sometimes he asked for a guard. But he was impatient of all restraint, even protective. Yet, despite his foolhardy courage, he was not free from fear.

"It's being left half-dead I can't bear thinking about," he admitted. "If they kill me outright, it won't be so hellish."

But these passing apprehensions did not serve to soften a line against the new grafters. Older could not compromise.

For the first time in his life he went into hiding, to protect, not himself, but the stool-pigeon Joe Abbott. He drove the bunco-man who was to be a witness against Flannery to the pleasant town of Healdsburg and smiled as he signed his first and only alias in the register of the country hotel. There they waited until the trial began.

On the witness-stand Joe Abbott told of receiving the telegram from Flannery. The day after McCarthy was elected mayor, the Police Commissioner had summoned the bunco-steerer to San Francisco to start operations.

Older, the last witness called, answered his questioners with dignity. He was growing accustomed to court examinations conducted with implacable bitterness. In his testimony he told of the Police Commissioner's having sent a man to his office to say that if Older would let Flannery alone, the Commissioner would "cut up the town with him."

This remark went unchallenged.

Flannery was acquitted, but he was forced to resign from the Police Commission. Within six months after Mayor McCarthy had promised to make San Francisco "the Paris of America," Older had deeply embarrassed that mayor, caused the removal of a police chief, and forced a police commissioner to retire.

He had shattered the rule of the six kings. Not again would the underworld take powerful grip on San Francisco.

Older's political strength was now tremendous. One hundred thousand people subscribed to the *Bulletin*. The editor was in great stride, and he swung into a fight that had been tempting him for forty years.

It was against the railroad.

When Older first came to California, a shy country printer of sixteen, he had been enraged by the grip the railroad held on the state. He had fought Crothers and all newspaper tradition to free the *Bulletin* from the railroad subsidy. He had broken the railroad's grip on the paper he loved. Now he wished to see it wrenched from the state he loved.

In the year Older was fighting the gambling trust and Ruef's continued imprisonment and in many other causes, his chance came to him.

Hearst had fought the railroad in California. He had shaken its power. But it remained for another man to break its grasp utterly.

That man was Hiram W. Johnson.

Johnson had given up a successful law practice to launch on the treacherous waters of the graft prosecution with Older and Spreckels and Heney and Burns. After the successful prosecution against Ruef, Johnson went on to greater fields. He was a man of determined integrity, and in 1910 he was in his mental and physical prime.

In that year Older was among the group of Progressives who organized in California to break the power of the railroad and with that ideal in mind nominated Hiram Johnson for governor.

Older liked the sound of that word "progressive." It seemed to include every meaning in the sort of politics he could believe in. From then on, whenever he registered, he termed himself a Progressive.

Sometimes, after the party was extinct, they remonstrated with him at the polls. "But there is no such party, Mr. Older."

"I can't help that," he would answer, with his disarming smile. "There should be."

It was Older who persuaded Johnson to run for governor. Just as fifteen years before he had persuaded the youthful James D. Phelan to run for mayor, he turned the powers of his oratory on Johnson. With his usual impatience he called upon Johnson so early that the attorney was still in bed. Johnson listened, and became a candidate.

"I look back upon that time as the finest in my life," Johnson wrote to Older in 1934, "and I ever hold in my heart, and ever will, you who in such great part, and those who in any measure, contributed to that glorious year."

For that year of 1910 was magnificent. It marked the emancipation of the railroad slaves.

Older put the now-powerful *Bulletin* behind Johnson. There was launched another crusade. Older gave his finest writers, his headiest editorials, his headlines, and his devotion to the Johnson campaign. He assigned his best reporter, John Francis Neylan, to accompany Johnson around the state and fill the *Bulletin* pages with his utterances.

Neylan had come to Older dramatically, as did all his star writers. He was from the East and looked rather like the young Abraham Lincoln. In his spare time he was studying law, as did many of Older's reporters. Neylan was to become publisher of the *Call* when Older became its editor, and still later chief attorney for all the Hearst interests.

Neylan had been reporting for an opposition paper, and when Older launched a big graft story, Neylan cleverly "sewed up" the pivotal witness and scooped Older on his own story. Older loved that. He could take a beating from a source he respected. He sent for Neylan that same day and with a broad smile offered him a job.

"Not until this story's over," Neylan smiled in return.

Johnson was campaigning under one slogan, short and to the point:

"Kick the Railroad out of Politics!"

He thundered that war-cry everywhere. Once Older drove with Neylan to Santa Cruz to hear him. Older's

White Steamer broke down, as was the custom of automobiles in 1910. They arrived at dusk in a village near the sea. In the evening light Johnson stood in his automobile before a grocery, talking to half a hundred villagers. In his low, powerful voice he spoke with a thrilling intimacy, as if to old friends.

"He has every man with him!" marveled Older. "If he'll talk that way all the time, he'll win."

"He does talk that way all the time," answered Neylan, "and he will win!"

Driving homeward the next morning, a tire on the White Steamer exploded near Salinas. Neylan had remained with Johnson, and Older was alone. Older's conception of machinery was as inadequate as were the automobiles of that day. His long, delicate hands were curiously inept at mechanical matters.

Changing the tire himself was not to be contemplated. He drove the limping car into town, to a garage newly converted from a livery-stable, and champed impatiently around while the mechanic changed the tire. He scowled at the heavy lugs being screwed onto the iron rim.

Would he ever be able to do that, he wondered.

He would, and always badly!

With a new tire and the damaged one on the rear seat he sped out of town. The speed increased. He was flying along at twenty miles an hour. He rejoiced in this sense of speed and power. The car flashed onto a long wooden bridge.

Under the bridge ran the Salinas River, a typical California waterway, "one mile wide and an inch deep." In the center of the long bridge there was a sound like a shot. The new tire had burst.

Older pushed the machine to the end of the bridge and after much effort wrested off the second tire. The sun broiled down on the little drama between man and machine. Older's high forehead was knotted with rage. Oaths heard in mining-camps long ago escaped between his set lips, oaths violent but never obscene.

The tire was off. Older held it at arm's length. He lifted the other tire from the seat. He marched to the center of the bridge again, and with the gesture of a man committing murder he slammed them both down into the river.

Then, looking down into the water, his face fell. Chagrin swept over him. He was like a small boy, lost in remorse.

"Of all the damn fools!" he told himself in wondering disgust. "Now I'm out two tires! I might have had them both fixed.

"Why do I do such things?"

His own rages humiliated Older. He was the first to condemn them. This passionate resentment of his own shortcomings made him loath to condemn other men.

The Johnson crusade was triumphal. Johnson was made Governor, the most popular and progressive California has ever known. Later he became United States Senator.

Hiram Johnson's election was a political revolution against the railroad. In 1912 he was one of the founders of the National Progressive Party and candidate for Vice-President with Theodore Roosevelt on the Progressive ticket. In 1914 he was reëlected Governor, the first Governor to be reëlected in California since 1853.

The power of the railroad was definitely broken by Hiram Johnson. The railroad attorney was no longer boss of California.

The victory was Older's as well. Another man would have had requests to be granted by the new Governor, wires to be pulled, jobs wanted for friends. Older asked none of these things of Johnson. The Governor offered to make Older a regent of the University of California, but Older would not accept the honor. He offered to make him a railroad commissioner. Older refused.

It was the salvation of others Older demanded. If he approached Johnson for favors, it was always in the nature of grace for someone in trouble. He asked pardon for Ruef, but Johnson, who had helped send Ruef to prison, could not see his way to granting that. He asked Johnson to parole a Chinese named Wong who had been in prison longer than any other prisoner could remember.

Johnson smiled at that request.

"I'll give him to Mrs. Older for a Christmas present," said the Governor of California.

Older bore Wong home in triumph. Wong, the Olders knew, had served his many years for homicide, but it had been a tong murder which Wong said had been justified. Cora Older made him house-boy.

Wong was a very fine house-boy. He was a meticulous duster. He liked particularly to dust a large oriental sword in a carved ivory scabbard which hung over the mantel.

"Misser Olley carried this in war?" he asked frequently.

He could not be convinced that the editor had never led an army with this curved scimitar. The weapon fascinated him. The cook, a white woman, annoyed him one day in some unknown manner, and Wong flew for the scimitar and gave chase with the naked blade. Up and down the stairs, through the garden and back, flew the stout and screaming cook pursued by the white-aproned and pig-tailed Wong.

"I cut off head!" he kept yelling, swinging the blade around his own.

After years of marriage to a crusader, Cora Older was equal to any emergency. She calmed down the vengeful Oriental. She saw him deported, a few days later, to China.

But even Wong did not diminish Fremont Older's interest in prisoners.

## Chapter XVIII

### PRISON REFORM

DURING the years he fought for Ruef's parole, Older paid many visits to the little boss in San Quentin.

His interest in prisoners matured. He never came out of the penitentiary without a story. As a young reporter his imagination had been fired by the story of Pat Sullivan, who killed the woman he loved and was hanged for it. Older wrote then what was probably the first understanding interview with a criminal.

He had met a Mexican named Moreno in prison, too, while he was a reporter on the old *Morning Call*. Older had won permission to take up a fight for Moreno's pardon, and he won the pardon. He had stood, joyful, beside Moreno when the man rejoined the wife and children he had never expected to see again.

Through his fierce crusading Older had met the corrupt, the criminal, the broken in spirit. He talked with them, talked with others more fortunate, read books, hunting for the answer: why were they what they were?

Putting Ruef in prison, putting any man in prison—did that make the man repent? Of what use punishment without true remorse? What good could be born of a man in prison that was not already in him?

"Putting men in prison is the easiest way," thought Older. "But is it the best way?"

And it occurred to him suddenly, "Why, that was Christ's doctrine! 'It hath been said an eye for an eye, and a tooth for a tooth, but I say unto you, that ye resist not evil!' " And it seemed to him he had turned back to the clear, shining faith, shorn of vengeance or dogma, that had comforted him in his lonely boyhood. He had turned back, not to dogma, but to Christianity.

He explained this attitude in a speech to clubwomen:

"What happened to Ruef would not seem to me so cruel if the community had profited by his misery. If his degradation had awakened the people to the true conditions here it might have been worth a human life. But we are still going on in the old way, believing that jails will cure our civic diseases, for which we are all equally responsible.

"But at least it has been a valuable experience to me, and has done me a great deal of good, because it has enabled me to discover myself, and to learn that we are all of us guilty, and that we can no longer absolve ourselves by putting men in prison. That falsehood can never fool me again. It will be a long time, I fear, before this view takes possession of the minds of men, but perhaps gradually we will begin to study ourselves more and learn more of the evil that is in us before we can set out after the other fellow.

"That is the way I feel and hereafter I am going to let the other fellow severely alone, and permit him, if he chooses, to work out his own salvation in his own way. I feel sure I am not fit to judge him or to hunt him or to criticize him or to put him in jail. We cannot make people good by law, by mere legislative enactment.

"Men and women must want to be good. The feeling must come from within. The Legislature can never do it. We must not want to do things that are harmful to others."

This was a new Older speaking.

He launched a campaign against hanging. "Would you

pull on the rope yourself?" he asked those who protested, with a disarming smile. In editorials he quoted the famous writers who had decried capital punishment. He believed that certain criminals were antisocial, they did not belong with their kind, they should be restrained. For such he believed in life detention in prisons that should be in reality asylums for the insane. He did not believe that the State should share common ground with the criminal by legalized murder.

"The most effective argument against killing is that it's so damned simple," he observed. "Killing is so easy when done by the Government. I'm sure the real remedy, when it comes, will be much more complicated.

"Revenge is one of the most powerful of the human emotions. I know. I've felt the desire for revenge. But I have been able to restrain myself from being stampeded over to belief in force. I do not believe the human race is ever to get anywhere by the use of force."

As early as 1907 Older ran a sensational front-page photograph of a condemned man with a gallows beam sketched in, a rope around the man's throat, and the headline in three- and six-inch type: "Young Weber Hangs!"

Again and again he carried the crusade to abolish capital punishment to the Legislature. Each time it was defeated. Older was not discouraged.

"We aren't civilized enough for it yet," he would say.

He believed that before many more generations capital punishment would be deemed as medieval as boiling in oil. But it was impossible for him to hear of a man about to be hanged and not attempt to have the sentence commuted to life imprisonment.

He framed a sensational climax to one capital-punishment campaign.

A man was to be hanged in San Quentin. As always, tickets to the hanging were sought after and highly prized.

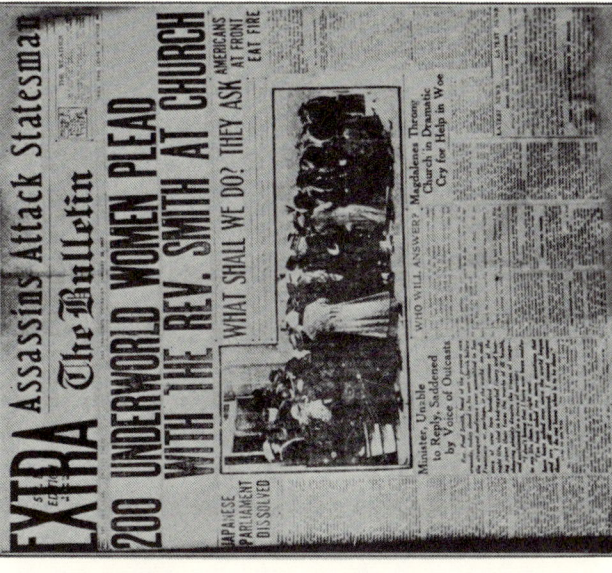

OLDER FRONT PAGES

The *Bulletin* for September 27, 1906, and January 25, 1917.

There are always far more requests to see a hanging than there are tickets. Older, to the surprise of the warden, asked for a ticket. He gave this ticket to a young man in his confidence.

The young man was admitted to the death-chamber. Around him deputies and guards and spectators talked in low voices, laughed a little, joked at times. The young man pressed as near as he dared to the trap. The door opened, and the convict was led in, eyes staring, arms bound.

The condemned man was dragged to the trap. The noose was lifted. There was not a sound in the room.

Older's young friend lifted his arm and shouted,

"I protest in the name of the Lord Jesus Christ! *Thou shalt not kill!*"

Guards grabbed him and hustled him away. The condemned man jerked to his death.

The angry prison officials tried to find a legal excuse for arresting the young man. Then they discovered that he had come to the hanging on the editor's ticket.

"It's that damn Older again!" they said.

The young man went free, Older was cursed, the story was published all over America, a play was written around the episode by John D. Barry, and capital punishment went on.

After that, to bring home to the public the full horror of hanging, Older ordered every execution covered in detail. Every horror was unveiled.

"Let the public get their fill of it," he would say grimly. "They're responsible for it. Let them have all the bloody details. Maybe some day they'll have had enough."

During one visit to Abe Ruef in San Quentin, Older met a man who would do much to revise the theory he had long held regarding prisoners—that they were men who had never been given a chance.

The warden showed Older a short story written by a prisoner.

"Why, this man has talent!" said Older. "I'd like to talk to him."

He was introduced to a slender, wistful young fellow in prison stripes, with an anemic body and look of tragedy—Donald Lowrie. Lowrie was a dipsomaniac, given to long sprees, and had committed robbery while under the influence of liquor. He could fill long periods of time with intense constructive work. Then the reaction would set in. He drank. Drinking, anything could happen to Lowrie.

Lowrie was meek, shy, easily influenced, with eyes which did not show the pupils and never revealed his thoughts. Only his mouth revealed the suffering of a man sensitive beyond the normal. His helpless quality brought out the protective instinct in Older.

In a broken voice, his head hanging with shame, Lowrie told his story. Older poured his magnificent tenderness over the man in stripes.

"Yours is a great story, Lowrie. You ought to write it. Think of the good it would do, the understanding it would create for men in trouble."

Lowrie was one of the many Older would attempt to redeem, believing they might succeed if the chance were given.

The Prison Board paroled Lowrie to Fremont Older.

One morning Lowrie showed up in the *Bulletin* office, sad-faced and sheepish.

Older welcomed him in a manner that would have stirred a dead man's pride. He called his favorite staff members into the office and joyously introduced Lowrie. They were of Older's breed, those writers, chosen for their ability to think and to perceive. They made Donald Lowrie feel that there was a place in the outside world he could fill with honor.

The almost paternal understanding Older gave to his writers he lavished over men like Lowrie. He never said to a man, "It is wrong to do thus and so." He assumed that of course he wanted to do right.

Older was enthusiastic over his find. Again and again he urged Lowrie to write his story.

"You ought to tell about it," he would plead, spreading out his expressive hands. "Not for your own sake, Lowrie! You don't count—none of us count, as individuals. But make it a story to help those who follow. . . ."

Lowrie was frightened. He had skulked too long in the shadow of his own self-disgust. But Older was building him up day by day.

Older did not know he was building a man of straw to be blown down by the first treacherous wind. He believed in Donald Lowrie as he was to believe in many men during those enthusiastic years. Lowrie had been born to walk proudly. He came of a good family.

What had happened to Lowrie that he had stumbled? Older was determined to pick him up, carry him along with his powerful understanding, until Lowrie learned to walk in pride again.

Lowrie was sensitive and intelligent. By this time he all but worshiped Older. He demurred a little, took the money Older gave him, and left the office. He brought back the beginning of a great serial, "My Life in Prison."

It was the forerunner of a school of prison literature. No feature in any newspaper had ever attracted such attention. Men and women read of life in penitentiaries where there were no rules of cleanliness or decency or justice, and were stirred with horror.

"My Life in Prison" raised the *Bulletin's* circulation by 41,000.

That serial was to reconstruct prison life in the United States. Lowrie brought facts into the open that could not bear the light of day. His story first interested Thomas Mott Osborne in prison reform, and when Osborne later made that interest concrete by becoming warden of Sing Sing, he sent for Lowrie to serve as his secretary and asked the ex-convict's advice on all matters pertaining to the penitentiary.

Lowrie, fresh from prison, was a sensation in San Francisco. He was invited to speak before the Commonwealth Club. The idea terrified him. Older forced him to write and rehearse the speech. He sat beside Lowrie at the banquet-table. When his name was called, Lowrie sat still in a cold sweat of panic. Older reached for his hand and shook it.

"Get up and do it!" he whispered.

His warm smile seemed to lift Lowrie from the chair. The thin, gray-faced young man from San Quentin rose before the representative group of citizens and made a speech no man there would ever forget.

After that Lowrie was asked everywhere. He spoke at schools, churches, universities, clubs. His name appeared in electric lights over a local theater. Older sent him to the Hall of Justice as police reporter, and the ex-prisoner did a daily column on the criminal cases. With the backing of the powerful editor Lowrie could walk freely about the courts and find welcome from judges. He was a writer born. He was sympathetic and observing and appeared to have every quality necessary for a writing career.

Older and Lowrie started in the *Bulletin* office a bureau for the aid of discharged prisoners and an ex-prisoners' fund. Men with the prison pallor came to the building to be helped to jobs and new courage by the redeemed Donald Lowrie.

"My faith in Lowrie recalled and reawakened an old interest I once had in prisoners," Older wrote. "When I came back to my interest in forsaken and suffering people, it was no new thing to me. It was rather a return to a train of thought never wholly forgotten, now brought strongly to the surface of my mind by my experience with Ruef and Lowrie.

"I became very much interested in prisoners, believing they were only men like other men, who by some accident of fate had fallen upon other lives than ours.

"The next few years were to alter considerably that point of view."

Strange characters began appearing at the bureau, among them women. It became horribly apparent to Older that Lowrie, in spite of his apparently fine instincts and upbringing, was drinking with the other ex-felons and being seen about town with women of the streets.

Drinking in public was forbidden a man on parole. If Lowrie slipped, it would reflect upon Older and all he was trying to do for imprisoned men.

Older had rescued Lowrie from prison. Now the real fight to save him began—the long and wearying task of protecting Lowrie against himself. Older learned that Lowrie went on drinking sprees with a woman of the town, an inmate of Jessie Hayman's famous house of prostitution. Older invaded that gilded den of red plush and vice and pleaded with the girl. He told her she was ruining Lowrie, and she promised Older not to drink with the ex-convict again.

Lowrie was gentle and very kind to women. He crept into their hearts, and because he was weak, he liked to be with women who were weaker still. Their attentions flattered him. He sought them out, spent his salary on them, and drank with them.

Older had a genius for forgiving. He took Lowrie into his own home and watched over him like a father.

As the years passed, Older came to believe that Lowrie's fate was fixed at birth. Lowrie would go back to degradation and despair. He would always go back. Women, drink, depression, came between Lowrie and success.

Lowrie married, he was father of a child, he fought his way upward to a good salary and a comfortable home. He became a successful publicity writer and took charge of a mayor's campaign in a Southern city.

Fifteen years after Lowrie came out of San Quentin, Older heard from him again. He had once more taken to drink, passed worthless checks, broken into a house and committed robbery. Lowrie was back in prison. A prisoner, he had made money writing under another name.

"Why?" Older asked himself starkly.

He went to Arizona to ask Lowrie that question. He found the man who had been given every chance to come back stretched out on a cot in the tubercular ward in the State Penitentiary at Florence. Lowrie was dying.

There was great courage in the frail prisoner. He knew he was doomed, but he sat before a typewriter and between coughing attacks beat out a story for Older: "Back in Prison—Why?"

Older sent me to Arizona to edit the story. Every day for four months I sat in the tubercular ward with the dying convict. Before the story was completed, Lowrie died, and I finished the story from notes taken at his bedside.

Years after his unhappy death the returns from that serial were income for the little family that had long since washed their hands of Lowrie.

Older became certain that Donald Lowrie and his kind were born doomed. Something in the man's nature and mind made him different from other men. Older no longer believed that all men in prison were there through circumstance.

How many times he had gone out to hunt Lowrie, traced him through detectives or reporters, found him at last struggling in the horrors of delirium! Older never preached to anyone. He only sat down beside the shaking, terrified man and talked to him in the low, pleading tones that were so warmly human.

"I know, Lowrie, I know all about it. Sure, drinking's a temptation. It's hell, I know—plain hell. But you can rise over it! There's so much else in life worth working for."

And Donald Lowrie would come back to life again, shaken and remorseful, and do his best to live up to the standards Older set for him, only to slip back again into hell.

He died in it.

"No power on earth could save Lowrie," said Older sadly. "Men like Donald Lowrie are different. In their making something went wrong. They are like cripples, stumbling along. Their minds are diseased.

"But we don't punish men for having smallpox! We don't blame them for being cripples! Why, then, for crime?

"Restrain them, of course. Don't let them harm others. But restraint for the sake of punishment is barbarous."

He was taken in several times by prisoners who faked stories to win his sympathy. He was disappointed in many more. He was philosophical about such failures.

"If we can save one out of a hundred," he argued, "isn't it worth while trying to help the hundred to save the one?"

Older's fight against prison conditions and for a better understanding of criminals was his longest crusade. Other crusades had been fought for God or for dominion. His were for humanity.

The years between fifty and sixty were the most absorbing to Older. The first half-century had been filled with action and the struggle to survive. Now he found time to read with deepening interest. He had found friends who meant much to him and taught him much.

Clarence Darrow was a stimulating factor in the development of the philosophical Older. They met when Darrow came west to defend the McNamara brothers, accused of having bombed the Times Building in Los Angeles. Much of the pessimism in Older's point of view came from the brilliant and cynical Darrow, who was later attorney for Loeb and Leopold, for the Massie defense, and for the scapegoat of obscurantism John T. Scopes.

Older and Darrow had much in common. Both had spent their youth in small midwestern towns. They had revolted against many things that are accepted by ordinary men. As they grew in understanding, they grew in hopelessness respecting their fellow-men.

"In a moment of sanity—he killed himself," Darrow had said in a eulogy at the funeral of his brother-in-law.

Over their innumerable cigars Darrow and Older steeped their souls in despair. What is man? they asked one another. Where is he going? And what chance of life ahead, beyond the long darkness?

"God, what can we expect of the human race?" Older would exclaim, his features twitching and his foot stamping. "A race that tortures, betrays, exploits . . . takes exquisite happiness in torture. They follow like sheep and turn like wolves! God, what a mess it all is!"

Their revulsion and despair were sincere. These shrouded, as did the cigar smoke their strong and kindly faces, their reluctant enjoyment of the world and the gregarious instinct that made them resentfully love their fellow-men.

Older summed up Darrow's bitterness by saying, "It is Darrow's sympathy for the man that goes wrong that is at the bottom of the belief that he is a pessimist. It is man's cruelty to man that causes him to despair of the human race."

Both brimmed with vitality, the reputations of both

were at their highest, while they sat together and spoke yearningly of death. Anything, they agreed cheerfully, to get out of this trap called life! Darrow congratulating Older upon his recovery from influenza, added that he was sorry Older had lived through it.

"Not that I wouldn't miss you, Older, and regret your death," the lawyer continued, "but as a friend I love, I want death to be behind you."

Older limited his friendships to fewer people as the years went by. He placed a high value on friendship; once he described a friend as one who, if you had been found guilty of the most hideous of crimes, would make the trip across the Bay to the penitentiary with you—"and carry your suitcase all the way!"

It was during this stage of his development that the Olders bought "Woodhills." As Fremont Older found need for fewer friends, there grew upon him again nostalgia for the wilderness. Land had been the greatest need of his fathers. They had wrested theirs foot by foot from the forest. He had worked half a century. He had earned the right to walk on land of his own.

With Darrow and several other close friends the Olders talked of founding a colony in the foothills within a hundred miles of San Francisco. It was to be coöperative. On a Sunday afternoon Older drove his White Steamer into the Santa Cruz foothills above Santa Clara Valley, through a wooded gulch and over the crest of a hill. Below stretched the blossoming miles of the valley and on the other side the hills of the Hamilton Range, soft in the sunlight as folded doeskin.

Fremont Older knew he had come home.

The coöperative colony never materialized, but the Olders bought the ranch—"Woodhills." To those who knew Older, such a responsibility seemed tremendous. His salary had grown with the *Bulletin's* success, but he contrived to spend every cent of it. Anyone could talk Older out of ten dollars. He kept money loose in his pockets, shoved his hands in for odd change, thrust it upon anyone with a story that touched his susceptible heart. He could not refuse anyone. He had too many times seen life wear thin when a ten-dollar bill would have made all seem secure again.

And so many needed help! People swarmed to his office—mothers with sons and daughters in trouble, girls who needed just the right word to hold them to the better way, a little boy whose mother was starving, a little girl in need of shoes to wear to school. Hungry, anxious, frightened people came timidly into the elevator at the *Bulletin* and timidly whispered the magic name, "Older."

He could not turn them away with that sick terror in their eyes. He had known it himself. He had been a lad walking homeless the wintry country roads. He had tramped hundreds of miles with broken shoes and bleeding feet, hunting shelter. He had slept in a packing-box out of the rain, and had not a dime in the world, and known the vertigo of despair.

All those he helped were that boy of long ago.

No one, not even Cora Older, knew how much the editor gave away. There were checks Older sent out faithfully every month. He was meticulous in charity as in all other matters. There were mendicants who returned again and again, doomed by some awful fate to be helpless.

Not even to possess "Woodhills" could he turn them away. Too many would stumble, fall into graver error, without him. Fremont Older plotted against himself. His attorney, Eustace Cullinan, who had been his editorial writer, arranged to have a certain amount deducted from Older's salary to be applied to payments on the ranch. Older was given an allowance. It was many years before "Woodhills" was the Olders' own.

## PRISON REFORM

Cora Older at last had the garden she had dreamed over while tending geranium slips on a hotel window-ledge for twenty years. The estate of her great-great-grandfather in Maryland had been known as "The Garden." She took over the reconstruction of the ranch and built its Western equivalent. She planned the flat-roofed, rose-draped house of silvery gray with immense windows framing the valley. She hired men, had the plowing done, and the pruning of the old prune and apricot trees. In the beginning the Olders slept in a portable house under the trees. Guests were housed in the wine-press, a circular tun without a top, canopied only by stars.

Older had no possessive sense, but all Cora Older built he appreciated and praised. It was not in his nature to understand the selection that goes into home-making. He only knew that he delighted in the finished work—the long living-room with its four large single-pane windows that framed living hills, the huge chair built for his giant frame. These he loved.

For years he had felt a growing nervousness, a restlessness, which would not permit him to be still. The ranch quieted him; it undoubtedly gave him many extra years.

In the peace of "Woodhills" he returned to the simplicity of his boyhood and to God.

The Olders had long been constricted by hotel walls. Now there were rooms for many, and Older could call his Cora from the office and tell her he was bringing a friend or two home. It might be a visiting author or scientist or editor from the East. It might be a man that day released from prison. Either would be graciously welcomed.

A little golden-haired girl, Mary d'Antonio, ward of the Olders, came to live her happy childhood at the ranch.

Many world-famous came to "Woodhills"; many unfortunates, too, who needed the almost Christlike kindliness they would find there. It was more than a country home overlooking a valley. It was a sanctuary.

They wanted, of course, a dog. Older's love for dogs was that of the country boy to whom a dog is friend and playfellow. Cora Older, city-bred, had never owned a dog.

"I think we'll get a Russian wolfhound," she decided.

In San Francisco word seeped even to the underworld that Older was looking for a dog. The Kid, Older's devoted subject in subterranea, was always eager to do anything to please the man he felt had saved him from gang vengeance.

If "the Big Fellow" wanted a dog, thought the Kid, what could be simpler? The "King of the Pickpockets" hurried to the city pound. A forlorn black puppy was rescued from the lethal chamber and delivered at the *Bulletin* office.

Older loved the puppy at first glance. He put it carefully into his pocket and caught the four-o'clock train—as he would for twenty-two years with never a miss—to the ranch.

"Oh, Jimmie," faltered Cora Older, when the smut-colored, rumple-nosed puppy was dumped gleefully in her lap by her delighted husband, "I wanted a Russian wolfhound!"

Friend, as the dog was named, was as different from a wolfhound as was possible. To complete Mrs. Older's chagrin, that evening she found the "fighting editor" on his knees before their bathtub, vigorously scrubbing his sooty treasure with her silver-backed brush.

But the foundling won his mistress' heart. She would blush and laugh when reminded that she had once wanted anything so conventional as a wolfhound. Friend, a putative shepherd, was the first of a large family of dogs of dubious pedigree and great, divine eyes that brooded lovingly after the master and mistress of "Woodhills." Never did they own a dog of pure breed. There were friends of the Olders who smiled at their choice in dogs.

But they loved dogs as they loved people: not for blue ribbons and blood, but for friendship.

Fremont Older often said angrily, "Most people don't deserve to own anything as wonderful as a dog. They don't know how to treat a dog."

He wrote in a letter to a lover of animals: "People like you keep alive my faith in the human race. Only there are not enough of you!"

Marshall Maslin wrote that Older loved animals without a shred of condescension, respecting their right to be themselves.

At "Woodhills" on Sundays, far from the roar and turbulency of life as Older lived it on week-days in the city, he walked with his dogs over the rolling hills of the ranch. He explored the gulch, the ferny ravine, discovered an old silvery olive-grove hidden and neglected in the forest, picked apples and turned the press to make cider, gathered blackberries in a tin pail for the simple Sunday-evening supper. At such times his step was youthful and his cheeks ruddy.

Under the fierce exterior "the Ogre of Western Journalism" was still a country boy.

One flaw marred the "Woodhills" sabbaths—the sound of guns as Sunday hunters prowled the foothills after rabbits and quail. At each shot Older's expressive features would twist with pain.

"The God-damn murderers!" he would mutter, wincing.

## Chapter XIX

### THE EDITOR AND THE LOST LADIES

OLDER began the commuting that was never to weary him. Every morning he was up at five, sometimes before the birds woke at "Woodhills." By six o'clock, always cheerful and smiling, he was at breakfast in the green and gray dining-room overhanging the valley. Thirty minutes later he was driving his car furiously down the gulch to "Fremont Station," named in his honor, over a mile away. He allowed himself exactly seven minutes for the drive down the twisting narrow road that rimmed the gulch. For several years he walked daily to the station. In twenty-two years a train was occasionally late, but Older never.

He gaged his movements by minutes. Like Kant, one might have set a clock by him.

Aboard the train he read the morning papers set aside for him, chatted with his friends the brakeman and conductor, watched a card game that continued day after day, and exchanged confidences and opinions with other men who chose to spend two and a half hours a day commuting.

In the beginning, he admitted, the thought of traveling ninety miles a day haunted him.

"Not once through the long years have I regretted the change," he wrote after twenty-one years of daily commuting, "nor have I been dependent upon reading and looking out of the window. There were other commuters on the train confronted with the same problem, and human companionship rescued us all."

One thing mattered greatly. He must be first off the train. Long before it pulled through the tunnels approaching the city, Older, brief-case in hand, was stampeding like an athlete through the smoker to the platform nearest the engine. Smiling, impatient, he waited for the brakeman to open the door, and he was off and sprinting for a taxicab.

One particular taxi-driver was always in wait for Older, and Older would have no other, because this man had driven him in a hack in the old days of the early *Bulletin* and the old California Hotel. Older had a genius for loyalty. At noon, in the Palace Hotel, he would delay his luncheon to wait for one particular waiter, a kindly, gentle soul who grew more inadequate with the years and maintained his position solely by reason of Older's patronage. The man had served the editor at the old Palace Hotel in the stirring days "before the fire."

But in the newspaper office the kindly, mellow ranch-owner became another person. He was again Fremont Older the fighting editor, fighting to get stories, to hold circulation, to build up writers and pages and news. The ranch gentleness and boyish simplicity vanished. He was again the tiger.

Older was getting the best from the amazing group of writers he had gathered together on the *Bulletin*. John D. Barry was writing freely on any subject he chose, for Older allowed him full play. Older gave the men and women who worked for him the limit of freedom. He could not pay them high salaries, he was not able to buy "names." He had to create his own names, and he let them write as they felt. He never wrote a line himself, or asked anyone else to write a line, in which the writer did not believe.

He inspired ambition, even greatness, yet he was constantly saying, "There are no great men." He liked to cite the smallnesses of the great. He seemed to like discovering their flaws. It was part of his passionate demand for democracy. He wanted the world shaken down to the level of fairness for all.

He despised pomposity. A woman called on him to ask publicity for a charity ball. She had known Older years before but had married a newly-made millionaire and was circling on the outer fringes of San Francisco society. She swept in, frowned at his queer little office, edged her diamonded and furred presence onto a battered chair, and rolled her *r*'s over him with patronizing magnificence.

It was not the patronizing that ired Older. He could smile at that. But he had heard her, in the outer office, arrogantly chiding the telephone operator.

Older lounged in his chair. He seldom lounged, in the office. His dark eyes twinkled as she made her throaty demands.

"Say, do you remember when you used to work the nickel dance-halls?" he interrupted suddenly with his most charming grin.

Her arrogance died in a decent human blush. Humbly she asked him for space. Kindly it was granted.

He told that at home, over the dinner-table. His gentle Cora was distressed.

"Oh, Jimmie, you didn't say that!" she wailed.

He was as defiant as a naughty small boy.

"I did say it," he insisted, gleefully stubborn.

But he was, he admitted later, ashamed. It was the climber's snub to the office girl he resented. He could never bear to see anyone humiliated.

He was a fighter for his fellow-men.

Every person Older met, it seemed, had a story. He wrung it from him. Lowrie's account of life in prison was the first of many sensational stories, written in the first person, which were the forerunners of a flood of "confession" stories, serials, books, and magazines everywhere.

## THE EDITOR AND THE LOST LADIES 259

A man dropped into the office to see Older. He was a professional gambler, of the type that had fascinated Older as a youth in the mining-camps of Virginia City and Bodie. Older asked the man to write his story. A few days later the man returned and tossed a mass of hand-written pages on the editor's desk. This was "The Gambler's Story," a revelation of life lived by the cards.

Again, Older ran "The Story of a Spotter," a spy for the street-car company who rode on cars and reported men who withheld fares from the company. Abe Ruef, the boss, wrote the story of his political career, "The Road I Traveled." Another arresting serial was "The Healing of Sam Leake," by a well-known politician who had been an habitual drunkard and cured his mind and body through Christian Science.

"A Doctor's Story," "A Trained Nurse's Story," real lives as told by real people to members of his brilliant staff, followed the Older tradition.

Then Older paralyzed the city with "A Voice from the Underworld."

Older's graft crusade had made him aware of the extent of vice in San Francisco. This serial was the life of a prostitute, Alice Smith, written exactly as it was told to Ernest J. Hopkins of the *Bulletin* staff. It began as most lives begin. It ended in the bleakness of hell. Nothing was minced or hurried over. The horrible facts of a horrible life were told.

"Do we dare?" breathed those around Older to whom he enthusiastically read the first chapters.

Older would dare anything. But he had moments of discretion. Before shocking subscribers with Alice Smith's story he showed it in confidence to several leading club-women. They were shocked, but they agreed that it was of public benefit to disclose the ulcer of vice. They promised to sponsor the story with their organizations.

It was clever of Older to have won the women's support first. Women were up in arms at the abomination, anxious to wipe the stain from the city. The men, as Older had guessed, were angry with him for printing an exposé of prostitution. Hundreds of letters condemning the story came from men. But it had the endorsement, aroused the indignation and sympathy, of many thousands of fine women.

Business men particularly were furious. They abused "A Voice from the Underworld" in clubs and organizations. Business was good once more, the panic was well over, and if certain streets were peopled with women utterly damned, that was merely indicative, they said, of better times.

While the story of Alice Smith was running, the old *Morning Call* became an afternoon paper and a *Bulletin* rival. The publisher read at the banquet celebrating the occasion the following poem:

> *Nothing dies in all creation*
> *But a paper's circulation*
> *And that expires when Alice takes a hand;*
> *As time passes we get colder,*
> *We are surely "getting Older!"*
> (*Too bad we must grow Older in this land.*)

Hundreds of women of the underworld wrote to Older or came to see him, encouraged by Alice Smith's story. Older had hoped the serial might soften public opinion toward these doomed creatures. He pitied them, he had always pitied them. He shared this sympathy with Gladstone, who took women of the streets into his home in Christlike pity.

Someone wrote of Older that, "like Gladstone, his heart was ever with the weak and miserable poor."

Those women who came to Older's office made a god of him. Many said he was the only man they had ever met who looked upon them, not as prey, but as women. Meeting them on the street, he gravely, and without self-consciousness, lifted his hat. It was not an affectation. He was by nature chivalrous.

Not of the chivalry, however, that draws a woman's chair from the table or stands with head bared in the elevator. "Monkey tricks," he termed these graces indignantly. Because he was steadily growing balder and disliked catching cold, he cursed more frequently the need of baring his head in a woman's presence, and in time he came to wear his hat clamped defiantly over his forehead in the drafty elevator, scowling, not because it was against his innate sense of courtesy, but because it was certain to be held against him. He commented that the men who paid the most elaborate courtesies to women were the men who exploited women.

How many women of the underworld Fremont Older turned from the scarlet path is unknown. He found work for some in stores and in the homes of his friends. Others he encouraged into paths that seemed less easy but were safer. Many confided in him as in a father. Every Christmastide for the rest of his life his desk would be heaped with cards and little presents from women of the underworld, from men and women in prison. One woman for years sent him elaborate striped silk shirts of many colors.

How patiently he heard their stories. Newspaper work hardens certain men. Others it makes tender. Older was tender, so easily impressed that the sorrows of others weighed on that high forehead of his like thorns.

A woman came to him, shadowy-eyed, trembling, afraid at first to speak. She was the prostitute Helen. Like every other woman of her profession in the West, she had read "A Voice from the Underworld." She was blindly reaching out for help.

Ruined at sixteen, Helen had given her fatherless child

into the care of a family and gone out to earn money for its keep. She found only one means. Now, still a young woman, she was a harlot of Bartlett Alley, which shielded the lowest, cheapest, vilest collection of "cribs" on "the Line." She had as maquereau a man named Berger, who robbed her of every sorrowfully earned dollar and beat her if he caught her sending money for the care of her little boy.

She had met another "mack" named Frank, who was kinder than Berger. She confided to him her longing to see her mother.

"Go ahead and see her," offered Frank. "Tell her you're married. You can use my name."

She was grateful, with the pathetic gratitude of lost women. She bought a ten-cent wedding-ring and appeared before her mother for a few hours in the false glow of respectability. So grateful was Helen that upon returning to "the Line" she gave her earnings, not to Berger, but to Frank.

This was violation of the maquereau code. Berger blamed Frank. He lined up the police whose beat was Bartlett Alley, who augmented their patrolmen's salaries by the dollars wrung from the "cribs." The police picked Frank up for vagrancy and beat him nearly to death.

But Frank survived. Friends carried him away to a mountain resort. Berger heard he was there and set off to finish the job of murder. He loaded his gang of fellow "macks" into an automobile and headed for the resort. Frank, lying on a cot in his tent, recognized their voices. He had a gun under his pillow, and he shot the first man who burst into the tent.

Helen hired Frank Murphy, a San Francisco criminal attorney, to defend her man. But Berger and his underworld gang were out to finish Frank, and so were certain of the police. It was all too apparent that Frank would hang. Murphy was clever. He had Helen swear out a warrant against Berger, charging him with violation of the white-slave law.

The woman from Bartlett Alley went into court to save the life of the man who had let her wear a ten-cent wedding-ring. The gang who wanted to hang Frank framed her.

"Did you visit Frank in the Napa County jail?" she was asked.

Fearing that if she admitted she had, she would weaken his case, she said she had not. At that moment the Napa County sheriff walked into the court. A trap had been laid, and Helen walked into it. The judge promised to send her to the penitentiary for perjury.

This was the trouble the friendless prostitute was in when she came to Older. Older scowled, that dreadful scowl which terrified but arose from pity. He got the judge on the telephone.

"Hasn't Helen been harmed enough?" he urged, after telling her story in a way that would have wrung a granite boulder. "Why not leave her alone?"

When he hung up the receiver, his scowl was gone. He was smiling.

"It's all right, Helen," he said gently.

But a few days later she was back again. Her man had been acquitted, she would not go to prison for turning on a "mack," but she had been boycotted in Bartlett Alley, the lowest haunt of the underworld.

She was cast out by outcasts.

Older sent for the policeman who patrolled the Alley.

"I want the boycott lifted on Helen!" he raged.

The officer became angry as Older. But he was forced by Older to see that one of the houses made room for her. Soon after, popular opinion turned the segregated district inside out, and "the Line" was closed. The inmates fled to the streets. Helen joined the street-walkers, but again she came to Older.

"The police are hounding me now," she told him. "I can't walk a block without being arrested, and I must get money to support my boy."

Older telephoned the police. Again the boycott was lifted on Helen of Bartlett Alley.

For such acts Older was vilified. It was not that he wanted Helen to continue in that life. But he had not the power to offer her another. He had found all the work he could, given all the money he could muster, to take women out of the life that was horrible to him. He talked to them frankly of disease and death and urged them to get out before they were stricken down. But an unjust world had given Helen only one trade, and her child must be cared for. Why not, then, let her go unhounded? Why stone the Magdalene?

He had read the line, "Go, and sin no more." There was a poem his friend Professor Herbert Carruth of Stanford had written around that line: "Go, sin no more . . . Ah, but whither shall she go?"

"Whither?" Older would ask, thoughtfully. "Where are we going to send them after we hound them off 'the Line'? We don't provide for them. We don't offer help. We Christians—we don't take them into our homes. They face either streets or jail—at least let them have the streets. Let them live in their hell without adding to their torment."

That was Older's point of view. Men maligned him for it.

Helen was one of the women who changed. Older was fighting the corrupt affiliation between certain police and the underworld, and because of Older's concern for her welfare she was hounded by crooked police. Thinking the street-walker had given information of graft to Older, they arrested her and hid her in the isolation ward in the prison hospital. Months passed before she was able to smuggle a letter out to Older.

Older fought stormily, was able to prove that Helen had been perfectly healthy when isolated, and had her set free. After that he did not hear from her for years.

Then she came back to him, her dark eyes burning with a wonderful happiness. She had with her the little son for whom she had entered the streets of lost women. She was through with all that. A man who loved her had taken her out of Bartlett Alley. She was reconciled to the mother who had once turned her from the door. With the rouge gone from her cheeks, with that new happiness upon her, Helen was beautiful.

"I owe it all to you, Mr. Older," she said, her eyes wet.

Tributes like that came seldom. They repaid for all the vicious and ignorant words hurled against him in his daily life.

Another woman came to Older to complain that the bills against the inmates of the "fancy house" she worked in were so high that the girls were always kept in debt. They were held like slaves. Older again lapsed into discretion. He went in person to the house, but he took with him one of the women writers of the staff that his visit should not be misinterpreted. In that gilded crib he denounced the madame, and she, red-faced and apologetic, promised the fighting editor never again to fake the laundry bills and boarding expenses.

So sensational were "A Voice from the Underworld" and the letters from other women printed in the *Bulletin* that for a time San Francisco talked of little but its own shame. Older had stimulated an interest he could not stem. Public feeling turned against the women. The demand grew to wipe out the stain.

"Drive them out!" came the cry from pulpit and press. "Close 'the Line'!"

There was panic in the underworld. The women had only the streets to run to, and there they were harried by the police. A young girl wrote to Older. She was dying of tuberculosis, but she was still pretty and living out her last days in a house on "the Line."

"Mr. Older, urge the people to leave us unfortunates alone," she wrote prayerfully. "We can't leave the life. If they didn't have the traps, could we poor rats crawl in? Mr. Older, we are done for. But try to keep others out of the life. Let the people who have the bringing up of children tell them the truth. Tell the boy. Preach to him as you would tell him not to kill. Tell him not to go near a girl only as he would his sister. Tell the girl what the life means. Don't be afraid to preach it from the housetops.

"We are the most miserable creatures on God's earth. Talk about the black slaves!—free the white slaves! If we are a necessity, then give us a crown of thorns, for we are certainly martyrs—martyrs to men."

Cora Older wept over that letter. She said, "Oh, Jimmie, you'll have to find her!"

Older succeeded in locating "Babe," as she had signed herself, through the aid of Policewoman Kate O'Connor. A kindly woman offered the dying girl a home in the country.

She did not need it long. Within a few weeks the woman who had taken Babe in wrote a heartbreaking letter to the policewoman reporting the death of "our dear child." It read in part:

"She was such a loving, lonesome little thing, never having any advantages that she should have had. . . . I am so grateful for having had the chance of knowing and loving her. . . . Mrs. O'Connor, if you know of another girl like this dear child, I would like to help another just for her dear sake."

Older rarely saved a letter. Famous signatures and their accompanying epistles he relegated to the waste-basket the moment they were answered. But this letter he begged from Mrs. O'Connor and kept for years. It served to revive his waning faith in the human race.

But still the cry went on in the city, "Close 'the Line.'" House after house was raided. Women were driven out, blinking, bruised, scantily dressed, into daylight. It was a Roman spectacle, gloated over by the hosts of the self-righteous.

Reverend Paul Smith from his fashionable pulpit was urging the closing of the segregated district. He shouted Biblical words against the myriad magdalenes of San Francisco: "Go—and sin no more!"

"Whither?" thought Older again.

Out of the word an idea was born. He summoned certain prostitutes who had answered "A Voice from the Underworld." They in turn brought friends. Older sent a reporter by night through the city cribs to tell the inmates of his plan.

The minister heard that Older was planning to send a delegation of prostitutes into his church. He telephoned the editor in dismay.

"What can I do with them," he said furiously, "in my church?"

Older was at his best. His eyes gleamed. He was Tolstoyan.

"Where else could sinners go save to a Christian church?"

There was a moment of silence.

"You are the cause of their losing their means of livelihood," explained Older.

Two hundred street-walkers marched into Reverend Paul Smith's fashionable church the day after the city government had dramatically announced its intention of closing "the Line." Not brazen, but determined, the women stood, massed below the pulpit.

One magdalene stepped forward. She was well-read and well-educated but had slipped tragically as a young girl and had never been able to escape from the life she had fallen into. She faced the minister, while behind her stood the other magdalenes with faces of stone.

"Most of us come from the poor," she cried. "You belong to the well-to-do, Reverend Smith. The average working woman in this city gets six dollars a week. We can't live on such wages. We are better off in houses of prostitution because at least we are sheltered there.

"We are driven into this life by economic conditions. You don't seem to realize that—you and your kind of people. One of the girls here asked her own brother, a minister, to help her, and he told her to trust in God.

"You can't trust in God when shoes are ten dollars a pair and wages six dollars a week!

"Which of the members of your congregation will take one of us into their homes, Dr. Smith? Which will pay us a living wage, or see that we get the care and attention we need?

"You said you didn't want our kind near your church. You want this section of the city free from our presence. That is quite different from the attitude of the Son of Mary toward the Magdalene! Jesus did not scorn the Magdalene as you have done.

"You want the city cleaned up around your churches, but where do you want the women to go? Have you made any arrangements by which they can make a living elsewhere?

"If you want to stop prostitution, stop the new girls from entering the life! They will always be coming in as long as conditions, wages, and education are as they are.

You don't do any good by attacking us. Why don't you attack these conditions?"

Older's questions, asked by a magdalene before the altar! The minister could find no answer. But Older was tormenting the godly again, said his critics. And with much publicity and bustling the city proceeded to enforce the Red Light Abatement Act and close "the Line."

An army of police drove through the segregated district, invaded the last of the houses of ill fame, drove out with their clubs trembling, cursing, or sullen women in kimonos, bundled them into the wagons, and carried them off to jail. There the magdalenes were fined and sent out to find other nightmarish havens scattered throughout the city.

Older sat in his office, wondering where these women would go, and who, if any, would help them.

Where could a woman go who sought to leave the underworld?

He called Sophie Treadwell into the office. She was a dark, slender, sensitive young woman with hair-trigger perceptions, later married to William O. McGeehan.

Sophie Treadwell had lately joined the *Bulletin* staff. She had never written a long story, and now Older was telling her he needed a serial written at once.

"I want you to go on the streets," he told her. "I want you to dress like the women you saw when 'the Line' was closed. Cheap, tawdry dresses, rouge—you'll know what to wear. Put yourself in the character of a prostitute trying to escape the life. Go out, find help, get yourself saved!"

Sophie Treadwell was a fastidious girl. As long as Older kept talking, she was as inspired as he. The whole plan seemed marvelous. But the minute he left her, she would collapse. In the local room she broke down. Closely knit as brothers and sisters were the major part of that amazing staff, and they felt keenly the sufferings of a sister writer asked to go forth in the guise of a magdalene determined to sin no more.

"I can't do it!"

Older built her courage again and again. Think what it would mean, he charged her glowingly, to the paper, to herself, to the poor women!

Reluctantly, fighting off a case of the jitters, wearing a cart-wheel hat, a blearily jaunty outfit, and far too much rouge, Sophie Treadwell knocked at the study door of a prominent minister.

She was a fallen woman, she told him in faltering tones. She wanted a hand held out! A chance at escape! At redemption!

"Sister," was his answer, "let us pray!"

Sophie Treadwell went day after day to Christian homes, Christian churches, Christian organizations, and Christian institutions. She was given a meal, advice, prayer, condemning looks, requests to depart—everything but a chance to make a living.

She returned to the *Bulletin* office and wrote "An Outcast at the Christian Door."

## Chapter XX

### PRISONERS

OVERNIGHT Sophie Treadwell became the most interesting figure in the city.

She wrote of those professing Christians who turned her from their doors. Her serial, "An Outcast at the Christian Door," was a sweeping exposé of the hypocrisy in an allegedly Christian city.

Herbert Bashford, the book editor of the *Bulletin,* saw the dramatic possibilities of the serial that Older had devised. He made of Sophie Treadwell's experiences a play which reaped him a small fortune.

The serial also marked the beginning of a brilliant writer's career. Sophie Treadwell was the first of the women serial-writers discovered and developed by Fremont Older. She would later write the play *Machinal.*

Bessie Beatty had her own page in the *Bulletin* and was known as "the most beloved woman in San Francisco." She built a summer camp for children, found homes for unwanted babies, heard the grievances of thousands, and attended to many charitable duties for Older.

Bessie Beatty brought onto the paper Rose Wilder Lane.

"My general impression was one of awe," Rose Lane says of her first day in the office. "Mr. Older dominated the whole building, the whole staff, every moment, from his invisibility in that cluttered little office on the third floor. He was a sort of permeating presence, like God in heaven."

The *Bulletin* was grinding out a steady stream of serials. Carl Hoffman, the city editor, had an idea that something romantic could be written around the jitney-buses that had just been introduced on Market Street. Rose Lane wrote her first serial, "Jitney Jane." She tried to do it lightly, writing down to her public.

"Someone told me that every servant girl in San Francisco was panting for the next instalment," explained Rose Lane. "I thought it was a great success. One day Carl Hoffman suggested that I end it as soon as convenient. He also said Mr. Older wanted to see me. So I went on into that office. Do you remember it? Shabby, dusty, with papers stacked in corners and waste-baskets overflowing, and Mr. Older behind a battered desk, in the corner.

"Mr. Older impressed me rather as a mountain does— a solitary and gigantic mountain.

"He said I could do better writing than that. I said, well, but what had that to do with it? This was a newspaper serial, wasn't it?

"From a mountain Mr. Older without the slightest warning became a volcano. He struck the desk with his fist; I all but jumped out of my skin. And he roared, a roar that lifted me right out of the chair. He roared something to the effect that the best writing in the world was none too good for *Bulletin* readers.

"I was intimidated—not for any special external reason, not because he was the boss and could fire me, nothing like that. I was intimidated because Mr. Older, personally, was overpowering. But when he roared that nonsense about good writing for newspapers, some little instinct of the cornered mouse rose up in me. I didn't believe him. I felt precisely as if J. P. Morgan should say he desired a life of poverty. And I said, 'Mr. Older, do you mean to tell me that the *Bulletin* would print . . . (I cast about hurriedly for something good that was the last thing a newspaper could use) . . . *Les Miserables?*'

"And then he really roared. He half rose out of his chair

and struck the desk a blow that all but shattered it, and roared, 'If Victor Hugo'd walk in here with the manuscript of *Les Miserables,* I'd print every word of it! I'd be damn glad to!'

"I kind of faded away. I got back to the second floor in a state of collapse. This is my first clear memory of Mr. Older."

Rose Lane would later uphold this theory of Older's with another newspaper serial she wrote for him, "The Peaks of Shala," which was brought out in book form. Many of the serials developed under Older became outstanding successes when published as books.

"He wanted good stuff," wrote Rose Lane. "He believed in the good taste and even in the average mentality, high mentality, of the mass of newspaper readers. But fundamentally, all the time, what he wanted was the readers.

"His life was the *Bulletin;* he had precisely the same attitude toward his paper that medieval kings had (and that today men like Mustapha Kemal and Ahmet Zogu and Mussolini have) toward their countries: *L'état, c'est moi.* That's real, their country *is* themselves. Cleopatra meant it when she called herself Egypt. The *Bulletin* was Mr. Older; a blow to the paper bruised his flesh. He would sacrifice to his paper everything that a man will sacrifice to himself, and more than that—everything a fanatic will sacrifice to his Cause."

Rose Lane began pouring out serials for *Bulletin* readers. They were tremendously successful. Older managed to obtain for her the magnificent wage of twenty-five dollars a week.

Rose Lane would have worked for nothing, she said, for Older. Many of his staff felt like that. She voiced the thoughts of many a writer reared by Older when she wrote in a letter to him: "I must do something really worth while some day, just in common decent gratitude to you."

To those who worked with Older he was critic, confidant, inspiration, and comforter.

The serial-writers he trained sometimes brought their chapters in "under the line." Panic smote the press-room when a next day's chapter showed symptoms of being late. Older never worried. He knew it would be there. No writer ever failed him.

The courage Older built up in his writers, the questions he asked them of life, they would remember long after they left his employ.

"The influence he has had upon journalists everywhere cannot be told," someone wrote recently.

He sent them out to find the answers to things he wanted to know—the reasons behind prostitution, strikes, exploitation and corruption, crime. When a banker absconded and Older sent a woman writer to cover the story, he told her to get, not the story of the actual theft, but the motive that had turned a respectable, comfortably situated citizen into a thief.

Older asked ministers and novelists to cover trials and write their impressions.

"He wasn't excusing criminals," Carl Hoffman explains of Older, "he was trying to find out."

In 1913, the year the Olders moved into the country, Cora Older went to the coal-fields of West Virginia to report the miners' strike at Lawrence for the *Bulletin*.

The Olders lived the year around on the ranch. Mrs. Older for twenty years had lived in hotels, pressed buttons for service, spent her evenings in theaters or some other place of social activity. Now she found herself almost reluctant to go into the city for a matinée or the opera. She disliked leaving her home in the hills, the dogs that chased the car down the gulch with beseeching barks, the garden that held her endless attention. And Older, the *bon vivant*, the man who had lived for excitement, went home every night on the four-o'clock train to lose all tension and anxiety in the hills. Relaxed in the great easy-chair—Mrs. Older had searched the furniture marts to find one large enough for him—he sat after dinner looking across the valley to Mount Hamilton, topped by its observatory domes gleaming like pearls in the sunset. And he forgot the ugliness of life, though it seemed to him to be growing ever uglier.

"I defy anyone to be unhappy here!" he said, watching the slowly reaching wistaria twining with yellow roses, feeling the trusting nose of his dog Friend nudging his hand to tease for an evening walk.

In the city ugliness began all over again. The smiles of men that hid treachery, as they struggled for jobs, for precedence, for life itself! The strain of work was joy compared with watching men. And there was always waiting for Older in the city an unending procession of those in woe.

They knew Older as a great editor, a man with power who could aid them. They knew him as a man who forgave their pasts and helped plan their futures. Seemingly Older poured out every thought to his confidants, yet he kept many secrets. He heard the stories of the hophead and the street-walker. He winced, gave them a dollar or so to "tide them over." He knew they would spend it on dope or bad liquor. But the poor devils were already in hell; why pour oil on the flame? Let them live! Let them try to forget!

A boy whose dog was in the pound came to him. There was never a tense moment in Older's life that a dog could not interrupt. He gave the youngster the two dollars for the impounding fee and waved him cheerily out of the office.

He had a dramatic way of waving people out, once he was through with them. No one ever overstayed his time in Older's office. "Well, goodby, good luck to you!" How it happened they never knew, but they were on the other side of the door.

He wrote letters to thousands of prisoners. He got jobs for hundreds. Men coming out of penitentiaries and jails came first to Older.

Older was father confessor to a city.

He never said to anyone, "It's wrong to do that!" But he said "Don't do it!" so warmingly, so gently, they could have died for him. He could be terrifying and dominant. He could be Christlike. A man of many moods was Older, and of many lives.

He could be a hurricane in shining armor, fighting corruption. He could be a gentle presence, stopping to help to his feet someone who had stumbled. There were many who did not fail his belief in them. There were more, life being as it is, who failed.

While he despised privilege, he used it constantly—to save some man from what he felt was an unfair sentence, to help some woman to another chance.

"I only use privilege to help people," he said by way of apology.

When his attempts failed, when those he tried to help slipped again, no one suffered more than Older.

Out of all these men one especially was never to fail him.

"How could I?" Jack Black always said when anyone expressed surprise at his staying straight. "Older put me in hock to him, and I had to make good!"

Older was visiting another prisoner in the Ingleside county jail. Jack Black—not more than three persons would ever know his true name, and it was one startlingly well-known—was in the cell, under conviction for highway robbery. Jack was a master burglar, keen-witted, and a genius, he always insisted, with a broad grin, in his profession. But of the thirty years he had been a law-breaker, he had spent fifteen years in prison, and he had known the strait-jacket and the torture-chamber. He was on his way to Folsom to serve twenty-five years as a second offender. But his transfer had been delayed because the records in the case had been destroyed in the fire of 1906, and Black was a forgotten prisoner in the county jail.

Something about Jack Black, his wide-open blue eyes, his large, humorous mouth, his ingenuous countenance, won Older. He went to the judge in the case, his old friend of the graft crusade, Frank Dunne.

"If you'll parole Jack Black, I'll take him to my ranch to live," offered Older.

Judge Dunne wanted time and refused to commit himself either way. Jack took this as meaning certain doom and broke out of the county jail. He was the only prisoner ever to escape from that stern building at Ingleside, on the outskirts of San Francisco. He made his way to Canada.

He was captured. Frail, weakened by years of fighting drink and prison life and opium, he was brought back to San Francisco in irons. Older went to see him again.

"Well, Jack, what can I do for you?" Jack crouched in the cell.

"Don't bother with me," he sneered. "It's all a mess. The police are sore at me, the judge is sore, the jailors are sore, and I'm sore. I'm a complete criminal and glad of it.

"Besides, I've committed the unforgivable crime! I've broken jail. You can't do anything, so forget it!"

He was surly. Ungrateful, another man might have said resentfully. Older could look beyond that to the hurt within.

"At least I can try, Jack," he said gently.

Jack was being rushed to Folsom, the Californian penitentiary for second offenders, to serve his twenty-five years, and this time there would be no delay. Older came again to the jail. He had talked with Judge Dunne. If Jack would promise the judge to make good, said Older, he might get him off with a couple of years.

"Two years!" cried Jack. "Say, I can do those standing on my head!"

Shining-faced, on the day before Christmas, Jack received his sentence. Older was in the courtroom when Judge Dunne resentenced him to serve one year in the penitentiary.

Jack Black made a speech at the bar which has been reprinted many times. It ended:

"I have promised myself, and I promise the court, that when I finish this sentence I shall look for the best instead of the worst, that I shall look for kindness instead of cruelty, and that I shall look for the good instead of the bad, and when I find them I shall return them with interest.

"I am confident when I promise the court this that I will not fail. I imagine I have enough character left as a foundation on which to build a reformed life. If I had no character, no will power, no determination, I would have been broken long ago by the years of imprisonment and punishment; and I would have been useless and harmless and helpless, a force for neither good nor bad."

Out of his one-year sentence Jack earned two months off for good behavior. In ten months he was free. He came from prison directly to Older's office and rode on the train with him down to the ranch. Every year this day would be considered by Jack his birthday, and it was celebrated as such among his friends.

Jack Black became as much a part of "Woodhills" as the oaks. Here, where he was completely trusted, where the best was expected of him, he gave his best. His attitude of suspicion and distrust, born of prison tortures and police floggings, died.

Shortly after he came to "Woodhills," a storm broke over

the valley, and a seventy-mile gale shook the newly built house on the hill. Casement windows were blown off, and the roof was in danger of being torn away. At two in the morning Jack thrust his lithe body through the opening, balanced along the pergola against the tearing wind as neatly as a cat, rescued the windows, and nailed them back into place.

When all was safe again, Cora Older laughed and said to her husband, "It's nice to have a porch-climber around the house at a time like this."

Older next morning said to Black, "You were a hero last night."

Jack's blue eyes twinkled. He said, "I do my best work at night."

For twenty years Jack Black had made his living off his fellow-men. Now he refused to be a burden to Older. He wanted work.

Older found work for the ex-burglar on the *Bulletin*. Jack Black, as Lowrie had done, went into the police courts and reported the criminal cases. Later he became a circulation head. He was a hero to the newsboys.

"If the newsboys could vote, I'd be mayor," he smiled once.

His sense of humor was constantly showering sparks. He chided the waitress in the cheap restaurant he frequented with the remark, "I believe the human race is steadily getting better, but I still prefer to open my own soft-boiled eggs."

Much newspaper money passed through Jack's hands. He was trusted by those who knew him as few men are trusted. He had spent his life either in prison or living in stolen luxury, but now he was content to make his way on a salary of twenty dollars a week. He lived on that for years.

Many of the police force were delighted by Jack's straightening out. Others were suspicious.

"Just wait!" one of them said grimly. "He'll crack! He'll be tempted and go back!"

But ten years passed . . . twenty years . . . and Jack Black, grayer, gentler, but as sardonic and witty as ever, was still hard at work. As a reconstructed yegg Jack kept in touch with men of the underworld and was able to give a hand to many who were willing to be helped. He appeared one morning in the court of the judge who had made possible his redemption.

"Judge, you have a kid on the calendar this morning. He's not a bad kid. If you'll give him probation, I'll be responsible for him!"

Judge Dunne turned the scared youngster over to Jack Black, ex-burglar. Jack was a fierce chaperon. He found work for the boy, and as he left him on the job, his eyes narrowed to blue ice.

"You make good, kid," he said threateningly. "For your sake and for 'the Big Fellow.'"

"The Big Fellow" was Jack's name for Older as well as the Kid's. The only law-breaking Jack committed after his redemption was intended to help Older. With a gun he intimidated a man who had threatened the editor.

One day Older's overcoat was stolen, and Jack, then in charge of the *Bulletin* newsboys, dropped into a certain saloon.

"Send the word around," he told the saloonkeeper grimly, "that 'the Big Fellow's' coat has been stolen and I want it back."

The word seeped through the underworld. The next morning Older's coat hung on a nail in the *Bulletin* office.

It was not the lawful way to settle the problem. But then, it was not a lawful problem. And it was Jack Black's way. He had been his own law until he met Fremont Older.

Jack Black gave Older a clarified picture of crime.

"In the beginning, before I understood as much as I do

now, I believed that men in prison were just like men out of prison, except that something had gone wrong in their affairs at some period of their lives," wrote a more experienced Older.

"It took me a long time to learn differently. I still am not sure just what it is that causes men to become professional criminals. I am convinced that they are men who are in some way different from the rest of us. They see life from a different angle. There is something peculiar, some twist in their brains.

"We cannot see what it is, because men's brains are hidden by a cap of bone. We cannot look into a man's mind and see what is happening there. We can see a clubfoot, for instance. We can see that a clubfooted man is not normal; we do not expect him to walk like other men.

"But when a man has some abnormality in his brain we cannot see that. We expect him to act like the rest of us, and when he does not, we punish him. But that is because we do not understand. We do not punish a clubfooted man because he does not walk normally."

After years of patient poverty and hard work Jack Black wrote, on the ranch, a serial for Older. It was brought out in book form under the title *You Can't Win*. It became a best seller. Jack went to New York, he toured the United States and Canada, he lectured at universities, he became a literary lion. People marveled at his well-informed mind. While in prison he had read the *Encyclopædia Britannica* through three times. Black's letters came back to Older from his successful lecture tour.

"This speaking is the softest and easiest racket in the world. Wish I had known about it years ago. Chauncey Depew made fifteen thousand speeches and never got arrested once."

Older was proud of Jack's success. He would drop casual reports such as these into the letters he wrote:

"Jack Black made an excellent talk before the New York Legislature the other day against capital punishment." "Jack Black is touring Canada as a guest of the railroad company. He once traveled on the same train in irons accompanied by a magistrate." "I hear Jack has made friends among the hard-boiled. They seem to like him."

Jack Black had become the symbol of Older's faith. Jack had every reason in the world to slip back into crime—save one, and that was Older. Something Older had seen—bruised, beaten nearly out of recognition—in the man crouched like a beast in the county jail at Ingleside had survived, knew devotion, would have died for Older. Perhaps not another man on earth would have believed in the inherent good of that hophead thief.

As Older found talent in strange places, he also found godliness. When those who failed him went back to prison, he commented sadly, "They just can't keep step with the rest of us."

Older's feeling for Jack Black was paternal. He had fathered a redeemed soul.

To Jack "Woodhills" was home. It was home also to many another. Older shared everything—an idea, an interest, a friend, a possession. He loved the ranch the more because it could be shared with others.

"I came down to spend a week-end and stayed five years," Jack Black used to say.

On the two hundred acres there were fruit-trees. These served as excuse for work for men in need of help. Older paid men fresh from prison the usual farm-hand wage. He would not have them on the ranch otherwise. He had a horror of exploitation in any form.

Attacks, as a rule, he ignored, but he was infuriated by a newspaper comment on the "convicts serving Older at the ranch."

In the valley the ranch became known as "Convict Canyon."

"Aren't you ever afraid?" people at times asked the Olders.

They were never afraid.

Older believed that every man longed to be good.

"The longing for the praise of others is strong in us," he said.

Older brought Johnny Byrne to the ranch to live. And to die. Byrne was an innocent man who had served fifteen years in San Quentin for a murder he did not commit, after having first been sentenced to hang. At the end of his time he was broken in health and spirit.

Older had done his best to save Johnny Byrne. He even ran a story naming the actual murderer. The accusation was never protested.

The day Johnny came out of prison, Older brought him to "Woodhills." A shriveled, wistful little man in too-large prison-made clothing, he sat beside the massive, genial Older in the train. He did not say much on the trip down, only stared out of the windows hungrily.

It was apparent to everyone that he was dying. He sat on the porch of the farm-house where the ranch hands lived, looking into the forest. There was a tragic enjoyment on his tired face. He was content to die.

Five days after Older brought him home, Byrne died as he had lived, without protest. Jack Black had watched over him night and day.

Every night after dinner Older had tramped down the hill to the farm-house to see the dying man.

"We're all in hell's hole, Johnny," he would say to the man stamped with prison. "It's a terrible world!"

He felt this more and more. Pity, he said, was as deeply planted in the human breast as hatred. Why didn't it come out more? Yet he believed that with the generations men would grow more kind. At least, the law no longer slit noses and branded and quartered and boiled in oil and crucified.

"Slowly, out of the darkness growing," he once said. "But God, how long the way and how cruel!"

He brought to the ranch Charley Dorsey, seventy-two years old. In prison he had been the only confidant of Black Bart, the famous Western bandit who served forty years in San Quentin for robberies of Wells, Fargo stage-coaches. Charley's fierce dignity and shaggy brows intrigued Older. He had served twenty-nine years of his life sentence for robbery when Older met him at San Quentin. In all those years not a letter, not a line, had come to old Charley in prison. Older asked Governor Johnson to parole him. Johnson gave Charley's freedom to Older.

Charley took over the interests of the ranch with a violent devotion and became ranch foreman. He loved rough, hard work and was scrupulously honest. He kept a stern eye on other ex-prisoners Older brought to the ranch. He despised most of them as petty pilferers. He would have killed anyone who double-crossed Older. He retained the speech of a Texas outlaw, salted with curses which poured innocently from his bearded lips. He referred to Cora Older, then in her charming thirties, with perfect respect as "the Old Woman."

"Some day when the Old Woman's out," he observed once, glaring at an antique Chinese gilded waste-basket in the living-room, "I'm going to give that God-damn thing a God-damn good coat of whitewash."

Charley, set free at seventy-two, saved all his wages.

"He's saving for his old age," explained Jack Black.

After a few years ranch life became too severe for old Charley. Older, through Mayor James Rolph, found the ex-stage-robber a job in Golden Gate Park. Governor John-

THE ADOBE STUDY AT "WOODHILLS"
Mr. and Mrs. Older seated before the pool.

son granted Charley full pardon and restored him to citizenship. Charley had a room overlooking the sea, where, with the beard and mien of an ancient patriarch, he welcomed his few friends with a cup of coffee and salty conversation. Charley had done his best with the bit of life given to him. When he died, at ninety years, he was able to leave several thousand unexpected dollars to some friends who cared for him in his last illness. Through his eighties Charley had raked lawns and washed dishes for this money.

Older's friendship with Dorsey was as deep as old Charley's love for him.

Men who disliked Older sneered at "Convict Canyon" and those Older brought there. Was he not "the Tiger" who had lain in wait to send Abe Ruef to prison? Now he was rescuing criminals of another order.

He was doomed to misinterpretation. His attitude toward criminals was classed with his "socialistic" tendencies. In reality, Older, who had once voted for McKinley, could never side whole-heartedly with his radical friends.

"It's all a question of money," he commented. "Take the money from the rich and give it to the poor, and the poor would be as unbearable as the rich are now."

But he was a social mediator. He bridged all chasms of distaste and fear. He talked on equal terms with the beggar and thief, the barber and Chamber of Commerce president, the bank-manager and I. W. W. leader.

The Older week-ends were epic. At "Woodhills" Older introduced the Supreme Court judge to the ex-felon, the college professor to the woman who was fighting her way back to decency, the society queen to Judy O'Grady. In that friendly atmosphere they did not condemn one another.

"If people would only talk things over!" he sighed more and more. It seemed to him that all human problems would end if people would try to understand one another.

It came to pass that his conservative friends railed at

Older's radical tendencies, while his radical friends reproached him as a conservative.

Someone had once brought Emma Goldman, the anarchist, to visit the Olders when they were living in San Francisco. Long after, an opposition newspaper ran an item:

"Miss Goldman, the anarchist, is a guest at the Fremont Older ranch."

Emma Goldman never visited them again, but for many years the rival newspaper continued to reprint the item. It was a small whip-lash they could use on Older, and they laid it on. It would do him much harm when he came to fight for Tom Mooney.

Older smiled at such pin-pricks. He knew he had many enemies among the blatantly respectable. "Stuffed shirts" was his name for these. Often, without planning it, he had his revenge on them.

One occasion was during the Panama-Pacific International Exposition in San Francisco in 1915. Leading citizens, some of whom disliked Older, stood, silk-hatted and frock-coated, on a platform in the center of a breathless crowd, waiting for the first transcontinental telephone message to come over the wire from Washington, D. C. Lord Northcliffe, the English editor, touring America, was to be the first speaker over the wire.

The voice of Northcliffe sounded out of space. Silk hats were lifted, heads bared, as the voice came squeaking from far-off Washington.

"Is my friend Fremont Older there?" were the opening words of Northcliffe's message.

The chairman grew red with chagrin. Older was not present. He invariably avoided banquets, speeches, meetings, all public functions.

"No, Mr. Older is not here," the chairman was forced to shout back.

"Well, give him my love," came the distant voice of Northcliffe, and the receiver clicked.

The sedate committee were obliged to carry the message to Older. Their silk hats were oddly out of place in his scrubby office, littered with copy and half-burnt cigars. They repeated Lord Northcliffe's message.

"Great fellow, Northcliffe," smiled Older.

He waved them chummily out of the office. It was close to deadline.

It was not the first nor the last time that men who felt themselves the superior ones of earth were forced to recognize the beliefs and capabilities that were Fremont Older. He was grandly simple. He was himself. He was, in his way, America.

Probably these, the years before the war, he most enjoyed. He loved work, he loved the hours he spent in his queer little office. He knew security and peace. After Older stopped fighting the grafters, the *Bulletin* became a financial as well as a popular success.

"Fighting wins admiration but rarely makes friends," he said. "When I stopped the fight against the powers to defend Ruef, the bitterness dulled toward me and the advertisers returned in complete trust."

It seemed to Older that his crusades were ended. The *Bulletin* with only 9,000 readers when he took charge of it reached a circulation of 111,000.

Not a share of the paper was Older's. He did not mind. It was his, it had lived up to the slogan he had adopted years before:. "The Leading Evening Paper West of Chicago." Everyone who had ever heard of the *Bulletin* knew it was Older.

His paper! He had built it with the strongest years of his life. He had poured into it all his possibilities, all his genius. His life was in its pages. He loved it with an interest and a passion money could not buy.

There seemed nothing to fight over any more. The grafters were well wiped from the city. Johnson had broken the power of the railroad in the state. Crothers, the owner, and Older got along well together. Success rested on the *Bulletin* and on Fremont Older.

Now he was sixty, and the years of storm seemed behind him.

## Chapter XXI

### MOONEY

THE YOUNG NEPHEW of the *Bulletin's* owner returned from college to take his rightful place in the office and in San Francisco's social life. Immediately Loring Pickering showed hostility to the Older policies.

In every department of the paper Older was handicapped by the interference of an inexperienced boy. His orders were rescinded; his editorials killed; his stories scrapped or changed. The sixty-year-old editor strove to maintain his dignity. But this constant process of humiliation was the most hideous of all his experiences.

Even the ranch could not assuage the despair that assailed him. Every night he left the office defeated. When he entered his country home, his features were rigid with tragedy. He brushed past his wife, went alone to his own room. There he brooded.

The old fears, lulled for a quarter of a century, came back. Where could he go if forced to leave the *Bulletin?* At sixty—to be again without a job, a newspaper, a voice!

He had always thought of himself in his great strength as immortal. He had never felt a twinge of illness or pain. It had never occurred to the titan Older that he could grow feeble and helpless and old.

Now there was no security, nothing left to trust, on the *Bulletin.*

Whose fault was that? The fault of a man who took all another had to give and then turned against him? The owner of the paper had that right. It was his journal, not Fremont Older's, although Older had saved it from ruin, built its circulation twelvefold, given it value with twenty-five years—a third of his own life! Not even the cigar-scarred desk that had so often felt the weight of Older's fist in his fighting years belonged to Older.

At dinner he could not eat. He would push his plate back and leave the house, wandering away down the hill under the giant oaks. His dogs followed, silenced by his silence. In a shadowy glen below the hill Cora Older had built for him a rustic bench under live-oak and madroña. He sat there, his dimming eyes fixed on the underbrush. He heard the trees talking to him as they had to a little lonely boy in Wisconsin long ago, like kindly mothers comforting.

"Oh, God," he groaned to himself, "if only I could stay here always—under this oak!"

Wood rats scampered from their brush nests in the trees to look down at him sharply. The dogs pressed closer to his knees, a rough-coated, tawny group. He put out his hands to them. He never failed them in tenderness.

"I wish human beings were as kind as you are," he told them.

And he thought he would like to be lying in peace under the oak—as in time he would be, by his own wish. People were terrible, life hideous, its first and last processes humiliating and ghastly. He thought he would like to be buried under an urn and have engraved upon it, "Death is eternal sleep."

"Go away," his doctor urged him, as the melancholia deepened. "You are twenty years younger than your age, but worry is getting you. Take a vacation. Forget the office for two weeks."

Older found himself tapping a nervous foot as he sat on the porch of the Del Monte Hotel near Monterey Bay.

Two days he sat there, leaping up to drive madly to the station when a train came in with newspapers from the city. On the third day he was back in his office over Market Street.

They could make life a hell for him there, but there he belonged. He had given dangerous years and sleepless nights to the *Bulletin*. To remain there he had turned down big newspaper offers and offers of political office. He would see the thing through if it meant his death.

War began in Europe. Trouble stirred the Mexican border. Talk of war was everywhere. Fremont Older could not believe in war.

As a child he had put his faith in the Civil War. He believed that if any war was ever justified, that had been. But if it had not been fought, eventually the blacks would have gone free! Evolution of thought would have brought about the emancipation of the slaves.

War talk added to his depression. Older knew many radicals. He disliked their violence as heartily as he did the violence of the militarists. He had no illusions regarding either. Human nature, he felt, remained human nature, and he had no hope of its changing.

Even in this crisis it was his destiny to defy classification.

"Why be bitter?" he asked, bitterly.

Woodrow Wilson, running again for President on a platform of peace, was the last political leader to stir the hopes of Fremont Older. Cora Older toured California speaking for Wilson.

"Peace at any price!" was lifted against the rising chant, "Let us prepare!"

In July, 1916, nine months before the United States entered the World War, San Francisco planned a great Preparedness Day parade to be held on Saturday the 22d.

On the Thursday before, a large mass-meeting in Dreamland Rink protested America's entering the war. Older promoted this meeting in the *Bulletin* in allegiance to his pro-Wilson anti-war convictions. Unfriendly newspapers reported that Mrs. Older spoke that evening. She was not at the meeting.

But one of the speakers said by way of bitter jest, "The way to end war is to shoot the war-making plutocrats in their pocket-books."

This was later misquoted to give the impression that Older and others responsible for the meeting were for violence and had guilty foreknowledge of the terrible crime soon to be committed.

The day before Preparedness Day, Older received a warning letter. Similar letters were received by other editors and by prominent citizens scheduled to be parade leaders.

Who wrote those letters?

The handwriting has never been identified. When that mystery is solved, the Mooney case will be solved.

Older often received warning letters and usually tossed them aside as the product of "nuts." But when he read the following, he realized it was written by a dangerous man:

"Our protests have been in vain in regard to this preparedness propaganda, so we are going to use a little 'direct action' on the 22nd, which will echo around the world and show that Frisco really knows how, and that militarism cannot be forced on us and our children without a violent protest.

"Things are going to happen to show that we will go to any extreme, the same as the controlling classes will do, to preserve what little democracy we still have. Don't take this as a joke or you will rudely awaken.

"WE HAVE SWORN TO DO OUR DUTY TO THE MASSES, and only send this warning to those who are wise, but are forced to march to hold their jobs, as we want to give only THE

HYPOCRITICAL PATRIOTS WHO SHOUT FOR WAR BUT NEVER GO a real taste of war.

"Kindly ask the CHAMBER OF COMMERCE to march in a solid body IF THEY ARE NOT COWARDS. A copy has been sent to all papers, our duty has been done so far.

"THE DETERMINED EXILES FROM MILITARISTIC GOVERNMENTS,

"ITALY RUSSIA RUSSIA ITALY GERMANY HOLLAND U.S."

Older immediately telephoned the chief of police, sent him the letter, and asked that police watch the I. W. W. headquarters on the following day.

There had been much dynamiting along the Pacific Coast, even in Canada. German agents were suspected. The Mexican disturbances too had led to bombings by Mexican sympathizers. Labor troubles were increasing in San Francisco, and some of the dynamitings were laid to strike sympathizers. A leader among these, listed as a dangerous agitator by the police, was a heavy-featured, black-browed Irishman, Thomas J. Mooney.

Older knew Mooney and disliked him. Mooney was a member of the Moulders' Union, described as a "left-wing agitator in the American Federation of Labor." He organized meetings at which he called on all present to strike. He had appeared at the peace meeting. Before appearing at meetings Mooney would drop into newspaper offices and tell of the trouble he planned to make. He contributed to *The Blast,* a radical sheet edited by Alexander Berkman.

As a trouble-maker Mooney was well-known in San Francisco. Press and police were against him.

He had once been tried on a charge of dynamiting electric towers during an electrical workers' strike. In this July he had tried to form a Carmen's Union, to call another car strike. The Labor Council refused to authorize Mooney's plans.

Mooney had an enemy, Martin Swanson, corporation detective for the electric-power group whose towers Mooney had been accused of dynamiting. Despite Swanson's efforts to convict him on this charge, Mooney was found not guilty. Thereafter Swanson tracked Mooney as intently as Javert followed Jean Valjean.

Older did not think the threatening letter came from Mooney. He did not think of Mooney at all . . . until later.

On the Saturday of the parade Older sat in his office with his back to the window. Four stories beneath him milled the largest crowd ever collected in San Francisco, held back by steel cables stretched the length of the business district on Market Street and by the largest force of officers and mounted police ever seen at one time in the city. Gigantic flags hung the full length of buildings. From the Ferry Building at the end of Market Street came the faint reverberation of drums. The greatest parade ever held in the city was organizing, was about to begin.

Edgar T. Gleeson and Ernest Jerome Hopkins, two of the reporters closest in Older's confidence, perched on the fire-escape outside the local room to cover the parade. They scribbled notes: "sound of drums—brasses—crowds—cheering—thin living lines approaching up the canal-like street!"

Older snorted, and squared his back to it all. The whole damn war fury, he told himself, savagely biting the end off a fresh cigar, made him sick.

As he sat there scowling through the smoke, he felt rather than heard a trembling, like that experienced the morning of the great earthquake. He felt the low, quivering detonation that was to send the humble name of Mooney around the world. His giant frame flexed with shock. He knew instantly that the threat in the letter had been fulfilled.

Older pulled himself together and rushed into the local

room. Ernest Hopkins was hauling his lengthy form in from the fire-escape. "Scoop" Gleeson was running toward the elevator. City editor Carl Hoffman was already on the telephone, his features suffused with horror.

"Bomb explosion!" he cried by way of explanation.

Older stood by the city desk. He remembered the peace meeting.

"They'll blame me for this," he muttered to Hoffman.

All that afternoon the sickening details came in. The bomb had burst on the sidewalk at Steuart and Market Streets. Whether left there in a suitcase, flung from a window, or dropped from a roof has never been definitely established. A crude thing of bullets stuffed into an iron pipe, it hurled death a hundred ways. Police marshaled the parade and kept it moving, closed in the broken ranks, fought back the curious. Ten mangled dead, fifty horribly wounded, were taken from the street. A woman was slain between her two children.

After the dead and wounded were cleared away, the scene was still revolting. The police lieutenant temporarily left in charge washed down the sidewalk with a fire-hose—washed away forever all evidence.

Details from that corner of death horrified an always excitable city.

Late that afternoon, oppressed by the tragedy, Older boarded the train for home. With him were Carl Hoffman and Robert L. Duffus, the editorial-writer. Older leaned forward on the plush seat. He whispered:

"I think Mooney did it!"

They were startled. Why?

"Process of elimination," said Older, grimly. "I know most of the 'reds' in the city, but out of all I know, Mooney is the only one rash enough to do a thing like this."

He was not surprised when Mooney was arrested. The strike-maker was vacationing at Russian River with his wife, Rena, a music-teacher whose pupils had won distinction at the Exposition of the year before. While boating on the river they read in a newspaper of the wholesale murder charge against them; returning to shore, they tied up their boat and started cityward.

Also arrested were Edward I. Nolan, head of the Machinists' Union then on strike; Israel Weinberg, a jitney-driver who had been friendly with the Mooneys and had driven them to union meetings and a labor picnic; and Warren K. Billings.

Billings was slight, red-headed, smiling, and appeared to be about eighteen. He had been connected with Mooney in the electrical workers' strike when the towers were dynamited and was arrested with Mooney on that charge. Mooney had gone free, but Billings went to prison on a charge of transporting dynamite. The Mooney defense would always claim that Billings was "framed" by Detective Swanson.

These five were charged with planting the Preparedness Day bomb.

Yet it was later proved that the entire five had been constantly shadowed for weeks before the explosion by Swanson and his fellow-detectives.

Older felt no sympathy for the five facing death. Whoever planted the bomb had made Older's peace meeting seem like a muster of anarchists, and Older himself a dangerous agitator. The parade atrocity placed the *Bulletin* in the position of advocating violence through its advocation of peace.

When Mooney was arrested, Older was certain the police had the right man.

Witnesses were brought forward. They testified that a jitney-bus driven by Weinberg, containing the Mooneys, Nolan, Billings, and an unidentified man, drove slowly down Market Street that day against the up-coming parade.

# MOONEY

Mooney leaned out of the open car. He held a suitcase on the running-board. The suitcase—said police—held the bomb.

In the horror of the tragedy no one stopped to consider what eighteen police would later testify to: Market Street had been roped off with cable that afternoon; the largest police force in the city's history patrolled the street; the chief of police had ordered that no cars should drive down Market Street that afternoon; and as a consequence no car drove down Market Street against the advancing Preparedness Day parade!

Out of all the thousands who watched that day, only one would claim to have seen Mooney, the best-known and worst-hated "red" in San Francisco, drive up to the scene of the bomb explosion in that phantom car!

Yet that man—Oxman, the "honest cattleman from Oregon"—nearly hanged Tom Mooney.

Older was certain as was all San Francisco that Mooney was "guilty as hell." Several of his reporters covering the case doubted the evidence against Mooney. Older squelched them furiously. He warned them not to write a word that would lead the public to think the *Bulletin* might suspect that Mooney could be innocent. The *Bulletin* was in enough disgrace because of its untimely peace meeting. Older was sickened by the crime, and he had always disliked Mooney. Now he loathed him.

He stepped out of character and forsook ideals. The editor who had led the fight against capital punishment for two decades waved away mention of Mooney in a revulsion of horror, saying, "Let the son of a bitch hang!"

Radical groups accused Older of selling out labor when he failed to defend Mooney. That infuriated Older. He reproached Maxwell McNutt, a friend of long standing, for acting as the Mooney group's defense attorney.

"But they are innocent!" protested McNutt.

Older turned red.

"I don't believe it!" he yelled, so angrily he was ashamed of himself a moment later. "Oh, I don't mean that you aren't convinced they are innocent. I know you are sincere. Only, I'm certain you have been misled."

He refused to hear a word in favor of Mooney, who had ruined everything the even-tempered, sane labor leaders were trying to do. Violent men like Mooney spoiled the world's chance for peace. Older believed in friendship between all classes and a slow and sober leveling that was democracy. Mooney, he felt, had made fools of them all, left them all smudged with the charge of murder. His wrath deepened against the man in jail.

He did not know that Martin Swanson, the corporation detective who had long tried to get Mooney, had rushed to the police immediately after the explosion and offered his services to them.

Billings was tried in October, 1916, found guilty, sentenced to life imprisonment. The cases against all the others save Mooney were later dismissed, after the defendants had been tried and acquitted—on the same evidence on which Mooney would be found guilty. Mooney was being tried for murder. The death penalty would be asked.

Why, many wondered, should Billings be let off with life and the others go free while Mooney hanged? If Mooney was guilty of murder, were not all?

The witnesses appeared against Mooney. They were, according to one report, "a weird procession composed of a prostitute, two syphilitics, a psychopathic liar, and a woman suffering from a spiritualistic hallucination."

One witness who attempted to swear away Mooney's life was confronted with proof that she could not have been where she claimed to be on the day of the parade. She replied, "Well, my physical body was some place else, but my astral self was there!"

On the word of such witnesses must District Attorney Fickert win a conviction.

In the meantime strong evidence was being found for the defense. On the roof of the Eilers Building, where Mrs. Mooney had her music studio, five photographers, unknown to one another, had been stationed taking long shots of the parade. Eight of these pictures, taken by three of the cameramen, showed sections of the parade taken from the roof at almost the second the bomb exploded . . . and, leaning over the parapet of the roof, the unmistakable figures of Tom and Rena Mooney!

A street clock in the photographs pointed to 2:01, a few minutes before the bomb exploded, and the positions of parade sections showed that this time was correct.

During Mooney's first trial the defense was denied the original films. The prosecution produced blurred prints which did not show the hands of the clock. It did not occur to anyone to check the positions of the parade groups to prove the time.

Thirty witnesses, all of good reputation, in staggering contrast to the "weird procession" produced by the prosecution, would testify to having seen both the Mooneys on the roof at that time.

The photographs and witnesses were convincing proof of innocence.

Yet all their proof was offset by one witness—Frank Oxman, "the honest cattleman from Oregon."

He was a surprise witness. Sunburned, expansive, sixty-odd, this perfect embodiment of an honest Westerner was introduced unexpectedly into the bomb case by Charles Fickert, the district attorney who had come into office on a railroad program and nullified the efforts of the graft prosecution by dismissing the charges against Schmitz and Calhoun.

Apparently simple, kindly in appearance, and unruffled

by the gun-fire questioning, Oxman told his story. A stranger in town, he had stood by chance on that very corner where the bomb exploded that Saturday. He had seen the "phantom car" drive to the curb. He had seen the Mooneys, Billings, Weinberg, Nolan, and a "dark, heavy-set man" in the car. This last was evidently intended to be a description of the anarchist Alexander Berkman.

And the honest cattleman had watched curiously while Mooney and Billings placed on the sidewalk the suitcase holding the bomb.

"Did you note the license of the car?" he was asked in court.

"Why, yes, I took it down, because the men acted funny and I thought the suitcase might be stolen," drawled the cattleman, and he drew a telegram from his pocket.

On it was written the license number of the Weinberg car. Frank Oxman, the first and only witness to see the "phantom car" near the scene of the bomb explosion, clinched the case against Mooney.

In February, 1917, Tom Mooney was sentenced to hang by Judge Franklin Griffin, though no date was set for many months.

The testimony of Oxman removed any doubts Older may have retained that Mooney planted the bomb. The case was perfect.

"It's too perfect," a criminal lawyer who had heard Oxman's testimony said to Older. "Oxman's testimony was without a flaw. An honest witness always skips a few beats. When I tell a witness what to say, he talks as Oxman talked. That 'honest cattleman' is a perjurer!"

Older smiled indulgently. Mooney would soon be hanged and the ghastly bomb cases ended.

Then Andrew Furuseth dropped in to see Older.

There were few men Older respected as he did Furuseth. His love for this stern, tragic labor leader amounted almost to reverence. Furuseth was like a crag jutting from watery wastes. He had lived the hard sailor's life and had founded in 1885 the Coast Seamen's Union. He was honest, he was hopelessly poor, he lived in a five-dollar-a-month room, he had given up everything most men desire in his struggle to make living less horrible for men at sea. In Older's mind Andy Furuseth stood close to the Apostles.

During a labor disturbance the editor had been anxious for his older friend.

"Will they put you in jail, Andy?"

"I don't know and I don't care," Furuseth had answered. "They can't put me in any smaller room than I have always lived in. They can't feed me any plainer food than I have always eaten."

And he had added, his tired old eyes filling with tears, "They can't make me any lonelier than I have always been!"

So when Furuseth spoke of Mooney, Older listened as no other man could have made him listen. He had sealed his mind to Mooney, who would hang.

"Mooney didn't plant that bomb, Older."

Older frowned and waved his cigar helplessly.

"Let's not go into that, Andy. Why be foolish? Mooney's as guilty as hell!"

"He was framed!" said Furuseth.

He told of letters he had read in the East—the Oxman letters.

Oxman, "the honest cattleman," the star witness who had sworn to seeing Mooney plant the bomb, had felt the need of another witness to bolster his testimony. He wrote Ed Rigall, a poolroom owner at Grayville, Illinois, inviting him to come west and be a witness. And Rigall, it was proved later, did come west and was coached by Oxman and entertained by Fickert, but he developed "cold feet" and returned to Illinois. Oxman was forced to testify alone, and he did it so effectively that Mooney was condemned to death.

These letters were in the hands of "Big Ed" Nockels, Chicago labor leader. It is said that labor raised several thousand dollars to buy them from Rigall.

Older read the first letter. Instantly he knew that Oxman was a liar and Mooney had been framed.

"DEAR ED: has been a long time since I hurd from you. I have a chance for you to cum to San fruco as expurt wittness in a very important case. You only hafto answer 3 & 4 questions and I will post you one them. You will get mileage and all that a witness can draw. Probably 100 in clears so if you will come ans me quick, in care of this Hotel and I will mange the Balance. It is all ok but I need a witnes. Let me know if you can come Jan 3 is the dait set for trile. Pleas keep this confident al.
"Ans hear.
Yours truly
F. C. OXMAN"

And in another letter "the honest cattleman" wrote: "I thought you can make the trip and see California and save a little money.—You will only have to say you seen me on July 22 in SF, and that will be easy done. I will try and meet you on the way out and talk it over. . . . You know that the silent road is the one and say nothing to anybody. The fewer people know of it the better. . . . When you arrived register as Evansville, Ind: little more mileage."

He wrote also to Mrs. Rigall, saying he would probably be able to use an extra witness and asking her to come and "see California."

When Furuseth showed Older the letters, he knew they would be published. Not another editor in the West would have dared to publish them. The hue and cry was up for

Mooney, and it was not safe to speak his name with anything but a curse.

Older read the letters in indignation and sorrow, knowing that justice demanded their publication, and knowing too that publishing them would mean a heavier load for his already anxious heart. It would mean that in his declining years he would engage in the most hopeless of crusades. It would probably mean his ruin.

But he had to go through with it. Just as the Older men of other generations were compelled to march away to wars they felt were just, so was he driven. Older ordered the letters set up.

He was keeping faith with his ideals of justice. It was his destiny to cleave to truth. He had closed his eyes to Mooney the man. He knew little of the real story behind the Mooney case. But he was convinced by these letters that Mooney had been framed and denied a chance to prove his innocence.

In a *Bulletin* extra on April 12, 1917, Older launched the fight for a fair trial for Mooney under a gigantic headline, "Fickert Framed the Mooney Case!"

He published the letters revealing Oxman a liar.

That headline cast panic and fury over San Francisco.

Older was cursed as a dangerous "red," the defender of murderers.

He accepted the brand. He had known this would happen. Against his self-interested judgment he was undertaking the Mooney defense.

It was his greatest and last and most fruitless crusade.

"I think the thing that made it so difficult for so many people to understand him," Bessie Beatty said of Older, "was this ability to change his course of action when he got new light on a question. You remember how incomprehensible he seemed to the old graft prosecutors when he took what was for him an absolutely logical stand on the Ruef situation.

"In a world where most of us ossify very early, he kept on growing to the end."

Cora Older, who had endured so bravely and so long, experienced with him the full penalty of trying to be just. Returning on the train from a matinée in the city, she found herself sitting in front of two wealthy commuters who spoke of her husband.

"Someone ought to shoot Older," one growled.

She turned, her face flaming. "Oh, you believe in perjury!"

All the West was screaming for Mooney's blood. The world was a-scream for war.

Older took the full brunt of war hatred. By nature militant, he remained a pacifist even after America entered the World War. He was branded pro-German for believing in peace. During those harrowing years Older found consolation in the friendship of Jane Addams of Hull House and David Starr Jordan, the beloved president of Stanford University who in the face of virulent criticism refused to believe in war.

Yet even among pacifists Older was resented. He was not bitter enough and not violent enough to please the majority. It was his fate to be rated too mild by the few, too extreme by the many. He was by nature an extremist, but his ideals were temperate. He could not believe in violence, not even for the sake of peace.

So he earned the wrath of both the righteous and the unjust. It was his destiny to walk in loneliness.

He did what he could to help the conscientious objectors in prison. It took more courage to resist, he felt, than to face war.

Always fierce in his defense of the under dog, his sympathy went out to the Germans left as aliens in the United

States. He took to work on the ranch a German professor and his wife whose campus home had been stoned by rabid students.

For some reason he was never to discover, his name was put on the lists of dangerous radicals in Washington. Nothing ever hurt him more.

"We are in the back yard of Napa," he said in despair, referring to the asylum for the insane.

He was not pro-German. He was for humanity.

"The youth of this country can best contribute to durable peace by ceasing to hate foreigners," he wrote again.

But society girls pinned yellow feathers on young men seen out of uniform. Espionage was in the air. This was no time to write of peace, no time to speak a fair word for Thomas Mooney.

Older, after publishing the Oxman letters, found himself ground between his employers, the employing class generally, and the laborites.

It was the last that wounded. He was amazed to find the labor leaders furious with him for publishing the letters.

"Why didn't you let them hang Mooney first and then publish the letters?" some of them raged at him.

Mooney, hanged, would have been a martyr, a symbol of labor crucified.

Older had known most of this would happen. Such clairvoyance was his doom. He was nearly shattered. He was going through torment only a man of his indomitable strength could have survived.

In the *Bulletin* office he was being crucified. The Mooney crusade was too unfashionable to suit the nephew of the owner. He humiliated Older daily in petty ways.

He gave Older orders to stop the fight for Mooney.

But the aging war-horse was again in the thick of battle. Older was wildly interested now. Certain trusted reporters, like "Scoop" Gleeson and Hopkins, were scouting day and night, sifting evidence, turning up indisputable bits of perjury, flaunting the hidden sins of a district attorney's office, of a city, a state, a system.

And these men working with Older were beginning to ask the question: What if Oxman had not been in the city at all, that Preparedness Day?

No, Older could not give way. He had to go on with the fight, even if it meant destruction of the life he had been building for half a century.

But every night he left for the ranch with death in his heart.

It was not Older alone who refused to quit the Mooney fight. His trusted staff members were so infuriated by the frame-up that they would have marched to death with Older to give Mooney a chance for a fair trial. Encouraged by them, he went ahead exposing the truth they uncovered behind the sensational bomb case.

"I followed the Oxman story with other evidences of perjury," he explained in a letter, "until the Law and Order Committee of the Chamber of Commerce sent for the owners of the *Bulletin* and exacted a promise from them that they would not permit me to further pursue the fight to establish the innocence of Mooney and Billings."

Before that body Crothers and his nephew throw the blame of the exposé upon Older. He was impetuous, they explained, easily misled. They promised that never again should another word in favor of Tom Mooney creep into the columns of the paper.

They repeated this to Older, firmly. They said in effect what he had said before he became certain that Mooney was innocent: "Nobody cares about that agitator. Let him hang!"

Every night he reached home in ghastly weariness. He went to his room without speaking, without food, and sat with his head sunk in his sensitive hands. This was death he was facing. Death to every hope. Sometimes he feared he was losing his mind. Dickens was piled beside his bed, the beloved worn green volumes with dog-eared pages he knew by heart. He could not even read Dickens.

After sixty years, nearly all spent in intense labor, he could call nothing his own. The ranch he had developed and loved was not completely paid for. The paper he had built was not his. He had no security.

At sixty, in that wind-swept room where the acacia thrust its golden head over the window-sill, Older felt himself without a future. The "greatest editor in the West" was facing extinction.

"Oh, God," he groaned, "what is this damnable thing called hope that makes us want to live on and on?"

Cora Older suffered with him. Whatever happened, they were together. She prayed for Older to retain the right to help Mooney as once she had prayed for defense against the enemies who sought to kill him. He had been protected against bullets and stones and dynamite, through the bitterest fighting.

Now there was no fighting. Older's hands were tied. He tried to keep the shame of it from being known.

"I was living the darkest hours of my entire life," he wrote long after. "Only my most intimate friends knew I had been stopped. I kept it secret, hoping that I might yet find some way to continue the fight."

Living in this hope, he struggled along on the *Bulletin*, a bound Prometheus, for two years. Every hour was torment. Deep lines cut into the features that had scarcely before shown age. Fighting against orders, he continued to uncover many facts in favor of Mooney.

Franklin K. Lane, in 1918, asked Older to take charge of the work of Americanization. Older refused. His life was bitter, but he could not leave.

There was not a moment when he could not have thrown

over the Mooney case and returned to security and peace. He was being attacked from within and without the office. Advertising was taken from the *Bulletin*. Lies were circulated and printed against Older. But he could not turn back. He could not stand by while an innocent man was hanged. He could not hold with a saying prevalent then and now: "Better let an innocent man hang for the bomb horror than have nobody hang."

If Mooney had not planted the bomb, added many, well, he was a radical and capable of it, so hang him anyway!

More and more often during this time Older broke out in the cold sweat of the terror that should have been long forgotten—the dread of again being jobless. He could face that, or give up trying to help Tom Mooney.

He groaned at night, and tears rolled down his cheeks as he slept. Cora Older shared his unvoiced misery. It was her own.

One day, like a man in a nightmare, he stood beside Crothers, who a quarter of a century before had asked him to try to save the dying *Bulletin*. He had revived the perishing sheet for Crothers. While he had remained poor, he had made rich men of both Crothers and the nephew to whom Crothers was speaking over the long-distance telephone.

All Older was asking now after twenty-four years of service was a promise that he would not be thrown on the ash-heap. It seemed little to ask of them.

"Ask him," Older urged Crothers, his voice husky with pain, "ask him if he will guarantee me a job for life on the *Bulletin*."

Older heard the damning answer. After twenty-four years of service he would be promised nothing.

Instead, the order came, sharp and final like an inescapable blade, that the fight for Mooney must definitely stop. Older must betray Mooney, and that was to be his ultimate humiliation. Older felt doomed. In his misery a powerful hand reached out to his. The hand of a man he had been fighting many years—Hearst's.

## Chapter XXII

### A NEWSPAPER TRAGEDY

IN MANY WAYS Fremont Older was not unlike William Randolph Hearst. Both were giants—cut from a matrix that was America. To one the building of a great newspaper, to the other the building of many great newspapers, had been supreme drama.

For years, furiously yet with respect, they had fought one another.

Some years before the crisis on the *Bulletin,* Hearst sent for Older and offered to make him managing editor of the New York *American.* Older had turned down the offer. He was having far too much fun with his precarious sheet, struggling, crusading, trying to make the *Bulletin* pay. And he liked defying with his shoe-string paper the powerful publisher Hearst.

He fought Hearst because Hearst had every means for making a paper successful and he so few. But he had sided with Hearst in many battles. They had combated the railroad monopoly and opposed the war. Both had been maligned and misinterpreted. Both had been branded proGerman for wishing to see America kept out of war.

Older went east when Hearst offered him the New York editorship. But he saw clearly that he could not leave his dogs, his ranch, his West. He refused, too, an offer from Edward W. Scripps, to be managing editor and part owner of one of his newspapers.

The order to drop the Mooney case was virtually an order to let Mooney hang. No other editor would fight for the man convicted of bombing the Preparedness Day parade. It was this knowledge that plunged Older into a deathly depression which would never completely leave him.

Hearst heard of his crisis. Hearst sent another message, shrewd and businesslike, but friendly with understanding:

"Come to the *Call*. Bring the Mooney case with you."

Many years of Hearst's career had been spent defending the underprivileged and exploited. He had lost many fights and won many more. One more hopeless cause like that for Mooney meant little to Hearst.

Older would never have left the *Bulletin* under other circumstances. To the paper he had built with half his working life he had given the finest that was in him, something that had taken millions of years to evolve. Now he met the jeers of his enemies who said he was defeated. He faced the disappointment of his radical friends who considered he had "sold out" to Hearst. He accepted these for a man who meant nothing to him, who was less a man than a meaning—Tom Mooney.

In his own eyes Older maintained his integrity. Only a Hearst paper would give him the right to carry on that crusade. Only on a Hearst paper could he be free.

But he suffered, making his decision. It was with a deep sense of severance and tragedy, nearly two years to a day after the Preparedness Day parade, that Older sat at his scarred desk before the wall plaster his head had battered, and wrote slowly and carefully on *Bulletin* stationery:

"July 16th, 1918.

"Mr. R. A. Crothers,
   Editor and Publisher, *The Bulletin,*
      San Francisco, California.

"Dear Mr. Crothers:

"I wish to resign my position as Managing Editor of *The Bulletin,* and I should like the resignation to take effect immediately, as my temporary continuance, as representative of policies with which you are less and less in sympathy, would be of no real value to the paper.

"More than two years ago you began to show hostility to nearly all of my activities as Managing Editor, and the feeling grew upon me, from day to day and week to week, that there was very little left that I could do to hold the paper to the course it had pursued for many years. In arbitrarily altering the policies that I believe have been the heart and soul of *The Bulletin* since the graft prosecutions, you have, in my judgment, made it impossible for a big newspaper to hold the confidence of the people. Thought throughout the world is rapidly changing. Democracy may soon cease to be the comfortable, meaningless, and empty phrase it has been in the past. It may come to have a real meaning; it may gather force and power, and rather quickly bring about a readjustment of the economic inequalities which now exist all over the world. In that event, even the advanced policies of *The Bulletin* of a few years ago, which are now forbidden by you, would be regarded as mere commonplaces by a world awakened to the realities of life and to the injustices that all through the centuries have been the lot of the common man.

"Intellectually and emotionally, I have been deeply interested in the old policies of *The Bulletin*. While they may have been crude and faltering, and still clouded by misunderstanding—the parent of hate and intolerance—I believe they contain something of the message that should go out to all mankind. But, even though I had chosen them as a matter of economic expediency, and had held the same views on labor and capital that you do, my newspaper judgment would still have compelled me to hold the paper firmly in the path it had been traveling for so many years. But you willed that there should be no further advocacy of, or sympathy with, the causes that had grown so dear to me. You had a legal property right to make this decision. I have at all times recognized that right; but, while recognizing, I continued for a long time to hope that I might be able to persuade you at least to let a dim light burn in *The Bulletin* window—not to snuff it out as you have done, and leave us in utter darkness. Even though I have thus far failed to convince you that you should be more in accord with my views, I feel that our close personal relations, extending through so many years, might have inclined you, though unconvinced, to yield somewhat to my views, and I might go on with the struggle, if I had you alone to deal with. But the influence of your nephew is growing upon the conduct of *The Bulletin*. He now owns a one-quarter interest, and will ultimately own it all. As you well know, he is hostile to me and to everything that I represent. If you were in full agreement with me as to policies, I doubt if you would have the strength to control him, much less when your views are so nearly in accord with his. He will eventually have his way. Thus my usefulness to you is at an end.

"I do not blame you for your attitude of mind. No doubt you are honestly convinced that you are right, and you are by no means alone in your belief. Most of those who are comfortably placed in life agree with you. I cannot. It may be that the old policies of the paper, which are so dear to me, were only dreams, but they have taken such a firm hold upon my imagination that I must cling to them to the end. I have gone too far now to turn back. I should get lost on the way.

"Parting from you and *The Bulletin* after twenty-four years of intimate association is a tragedy, but I see no other course.

Sincerely yours,<br>
Fremont Older"

Someone who was with Crothers when the publisher received that letter has told of his crushing it in his hand, staring out of his office window with unseeing eyes. He was like a man stunned.

"How could he!" Crothers kept repeating, forgetting the many times he might have made life a little more bearable for his managing editor, forgetting that he had refused to promise Older a permanent job after twenty-four years in his service. "Why, we've been like brothers!"

Then he brightened a little. "Well, anyhow, I'll save ten thousand dollars a year on his salary."

The *Bulletin* before many years would be losing $125,000 a month.

Older prepared to leave the *Bulletin*. He plunged into the litter of his historic scarred desk with the cigar burns rimming it like bullet marks from battle. Twenty-four years of litter! Old letters. Old dreams. The secrets of a great city. He found a letter from Arthur Brisbane, Hearst's great editor.

"Talking to you as a newspaper man, I shall say what I wrote to Henry Watterson long ago," wrote Brisbane. "The newspaper worker who belittles the earnestness, sincerity, or usefulness of Hearst will regret it one day—especially if he happens to outlive Hearst.

"A sincere man—a courageous man."

Older had quoted that letter many times. Hearst was responsible for his own good salary on the *Bulletin*. He was responsible for lifting the salaries of newspaper people fifty per cent in the United States through his competitive purchasing of talent.

Older put a few such prized letters in his pockets, lit a fresh cigar, pulled his slouch-hat low over his eyes, and walked out of the office.

"Half my life I left behind me in that office," he was able to write long after.

## A NEWSPAPER TRAGEDY

"I was happy to go, but sad memories clustered around that old desk of mine where I had suffered through the defeats of many fights. While I had no financial interest in the *Bulletin*, I had been directing its course for twenty-four years and the paper seemed like my own child. But this child had suddenly died just when it was most interesting and at a time when I foolishly thought it was on the threshold of a glorious achievement.

"I gathered up my personal possessions and said goodbye forever to the old newspaper that had become very dear to me."

In August, 1918, a few days before his sixty-second birthday, Fremont Older entered the office of the *Call* on Montgomery Street as its editor.

From everywhere came telegrams of shocked condolence or sympathetic congratulation. The men who had served under Older knew the price he had paid for ideals. Newspapers and magazines reflected varying points of view. Many reëchoed the cry that Older had "sold out." The critical barrage of the graft prosecution had left him curiously immune to the attacks of enemies.

George P. West, who had worked with Older, wrote, "Mr. Older's resignation from the *Bulletin* is the greatest newspaper tragedy of the day." Lord Northcliffe telegraphed from England his congratulations to the *Call*.

All over America Older was flayed for going over to Hearst, the man he had fought for a quarter-century. It was one of many crosses Older must bear. The larger salary had not tempted him. He had several times refused the salary. But when he passed into the Hearst fold, he became, for the first time since he had been an editor, *free*.

As free, he always added, as any editor can be free.

"If I had my own paper," he remarked, "I could not publish what I'd like to publish. They nearly lynched us on the old *Bulletin* because we exposed things the public thought best kept hidden. They smashed our windows and beat up our men because we attacked some of their 'sacred cows' in print.

"The business men and advertisers boycott the paper that prints the truth. My opinions are nearly always unpopular. I don't believe in graft, in letting corporations rob a city, in letting a bank president go free for taking a million while a man goes to prison for stealing a loaf of bread. But most people believe in these things, whether they know it or not, and a newspaper is at the mercy of its readers.

"I am as free on the *Call* as I could be on any newspaper in this world."

The year 1856 that marked the birth of Fremont Older had also given birth to the San Francisco *Morning Call*. The *Bulletin* had begun the preceding year. When Older became editor, the paper was known as the *Evening Call-Post,* having bought the paper founded by the economist Henry George.

Of the many papers born of San Francisco's gold era, only these two, the *Call* and the *Bulletin* survived. They had fought through memorable battles, the *Bulletin* in the tradition of its crusading founder, James King of William, the *Call* under the stirring leadership of the aggressive publisher and forty-niner, George K. Fitch. Both newspapers were fitting vehicles for the crusader Fremont Older.

In the new office Older met new men. But as he shook hands and talked and listened, he was remembering, vividly as if the youngster stood at his elbow, a lanky, burning-eyed idealist of a country boy—the Fremont Older of sixteen. He had been a printer on this very *Call* exactly forty-six years before. How high his hopes had been then!

# A NEWSPAPER TRAGEDY

How fierce his ideals, fired by the life story of Greeley, the writings of Dickens and Mark Twain!

That was his first newspaper job in San Francisco.

"Somehow, through all the years that were to follow," Older wrote, "I was drawn, as if by an invisible influence, back to the *Call*.

"I was a reporter on its local staff in 1886. In a year or two I again drifted away. In 1894 I was back as city editor. In a year I shifted to the *Bulletin*, to remain twenty-three years. Then I became editor of the *Call*.

"It was my first San Francisco newspaper; it will be my last."

Older had bridged the pioneer age and the new. He was part of them both.

"I found he was the best-loved and the most bitterly denounced of any citizen of San Francisco," wrote F. W. Kellogg, the publisher of the *Call*, upon Older's arrival on the paper, "but friend or foe alike always stated or admitted that Fremont Older was honest in his beliefs, courageous in advocating them, and was the friend of the downtrodden, the outcast and the unfortunate in general."

Panic struck the *Bulletin* offices when Older left. The paper had then 100,000 net paid circulation, and in certain years it reached 111,000. This he had built from 9,000, and this he would presently outstrip on the *Call*.

He took a large slice of this circulation with him, and yet Older's name had never appeared on the *Bulletin* pages as editor, and the *Bulletin* never, in any manner, admitted publicly that Older had left.

The *Call* had a circulation of 99,000. Older's arrival brought it immediately up to 103,000. Six months later, from having been 3,000 behind the *Bulletin*, it was 9,000 in advance. At the end of Older's first year as editor the *Call* had the lead by 12,000.

Of its character as a newpaper Older wrote:

"The policies for which the *Bulletin* stood under my editorship and which have since been transferred to the *Call* include:

"Municipal ownership.

"Investigation of municipal corruption and the connection between special privilege and corrupt policies, as the result of lessons learned in the 'graft prosecution.'

"For minimum wage and eight-hour day for women.

"For initiative, referendum and recall.

"The Johnson policies of political and economic reform incorporated in California law during his terms as governor.

"The abolition of capital punishment.

"Prison reform and a better understanding of the causes of crime, so that scientific methods may eventually be substituted for stupidity and brutality.

"Understanding of the problem of prostitution and similar problems in the light of the latest sociological research.

"Equality before the law for rich and poor.

"Fair trial for Mooney and the other bomb defendants in order to remove the stain of a legal frame-up from the courts of California.

"A square deal for the workers and frank discussion of their problems and aims."

For the public he printed a pamphlet, "Why I Left the *Bulletin* and Have Come to the *Call*." In it Older explained:

"Had I stayed, I would have been obliged to betray them [the *Bulletin* readers] in little things day by day. I could not do this. I could not sit pretending that the *Bulletin* was what it had been when I knew it was not. Just as strongly as I felt that I had work to do, I recognized that I could not do it on the *Bulletin*.

"On leaving the *Bulletin* I was called to New York, but I felt that my work was here, not there. I have returned to a smaller field, but it is one where I have spent the best years of my life, the land of my hopes and dreams, and where I shall continue to hope and to dream."

Invariably in his writings Older gave the honest reactions of his honest mind. He wrote in his foreword to the biography of William Randolph Hearst written by Mrs. Older:

"After I came to work for him [Hearst], and got rid of the biased point of view that a competing editor invariably has, I became aware that my earlier impressions of the *Examiner's* policies were rather vague and undefined.

"As I realized the deeper meaning of them, I was enthusiastic over the gallant, lonely fight he had made for more than thirty years. I saw him as the most misunderstood man in America. As familiar as I had been with his newspaper crusades, I had failed to realize what a colossal job he had done in America."

Gratitude to Hearst, personal pride in himself as an editor, and the chance of proving the innocence of Tom Mooney plunged Older into work on the *Call* with recharged enthusiasm. He was like a whirlwind gathering its forces. The *Bulletin* had ordered him to change his policy. Instead, he brought that policy to the *Call*.

Older would be grateful to William Randolph Hearst for many things, but chiefly for the right to go on with the Mooney case.

"As the columns of the *Bulletin* closed in the Mooney case, they opened in the *Call*," wrote Older. "Mr. Hearst, in his long years of battling for justice for the helpless, had become familiar with 'lost causes' and 'forlorn hopes,' and another one added to the long list did not disturb him.

"In his many crusades he has changed some seemingly

lost causes into living issues, that now are recognized as vital to the future of America."

Of the enthusiastic school of writers he had gathered about him on the *Bulletin*, a few followed Older. Maxwell Anderson, Robert L. Duffus, Rose Wilder Lane, Bessie Beatty, and others left for New York. They had outgrown his sheltering wings, but the partings brought mutual sorrow.

"After I left Older," one of his writers confessed, "it was a shock to me to discover how much a part of him I had become, and how difficult it was to think and act without him. It seemed for a time I couldn't have an idea or reaction without suddenly thinking: That's Older!"

From that unforgettable *Bulletin* staff Older brought a chosen few to the *Call*. With these around him, with the zeal of a man in his twenties, the sixty-two-year-old editor charged on with the Mooney fight.

## Chapter XXIII

### MOONEY AGAIN

THE DANGER of supporting a cause like Mooney's was the branding of a newspaper as a "class paper."

"I agree with you that if such classification were to be fixed upon the paper," Older wrote William Randolph Hearst early in 1919, "there would at once be a limitation of its objects and ideals and a lessening of its power for public service. . . .

"I am trying my utmost to reach, as nearly as it is humanly possible, a policy that is broad, liberal and tolerant. . . . It is extremely difficult to convey that impression while advocating justice for a cause that is as unpopular with the powerful people as the Mooney case.

"It is impossible for us to make them understand that it is the integrity of our legal procedure that we are trying to uphold, rather than a personal concern for a man like Mooney.

"Misunderstanding is certain to manifest itself, and the policy declared a radical one, when in point of fact it is quite the reverse. If the conservatives had real understanding and penetration, they would be making every effort to bring about a rehearing of the case, for the reason that at a critical time like this it might be the cause of serious trouble."

For himself, Older cared for the praise of neither radical nor liberal nor conservative, but for justice. Again and again, in print and to his intimates, he stressed this point.

"I took up the Mooney case not because Mooney was a good man or a bad man," he repeated, "but because he did not have an honest trial."

With the exception of the Oxman letters, all the important disclosures of the Mooney case were made in the Hearst-owned *Call*.

These revelations represented years of effort on the part of Older and his trusted group. In secret he sent his reporters on lead after lead. Dogged as bloodhounds, they spent months tracking down a single clue.

Who planted the Preparedness Day bomb?

After years of sleuthing and sifting Fremont Older came to the firm conclusion that it was the work of a German spy. Many facts that could not be substantiated in print pointed to this. Years afterward a German in the East confessed, when dying, to having dynamited certain boats along the San Francisco water-front and planted the bomb during the parade. The names of the boats he listed were verified: such explosions had occurred.

This dying confession, articulating with other facts, convinced Older that the German spy was the murderer.

But the men who tracked down Mooney appeared to be hunting Mooney the radical, not the truth of the bomb outrage.

A rumor came to Older—out of the air, it seemed. It reached him in his new office at the *Call*, which had a carpet and a desk that shone, for at last he had succumbed to mahogany. He resented the mahogany, for he could not bring himself to lay his burning cigar-butts along the edges, as he had been wont to do. But no tray was ever found large enough to catch his cigar ashes, which continued to strew the floor together with a litter of proof, newspapers, and discarded letters. The sun poured into this new office, it fairly blazed on his head which was steadily growing balder; but it never occurred to Older, so lost was he in the ferment of office life, to pull the shades against the most furious sun. Surrounded by his new dignity, he was passive but amused. Sometimes he tilted his neat new chair backward, put his feet on the desk, and spoke wistfully of his shabby little littered hole of an office at the old *Bulletin*.

He didn't see, he said, how a man could work surrounded by folderols. Men who needed magnificence to work in, he felt, were on a par with those dubious beings who had studios and were too important to be disturbed. He scoffed at the demands of "genius."

"If genius is in you, it will come out in spite of all interruptions and handicaps," he often said. "Genius that has to be nursed and surrounded with reverence isn't worth the nursing."

In this tidier office, then, a rumor of suspicion reached the new editor of the *Call:*

"Had Oxman, the honest cattleman, been in San Francisco at the time the bomb exploded?"

Oxman, the surprise witness, on whose testimony Tom Mooney was to hang, had sworn that he stood on the Market Street corner at two o'clock that July 22, 1916, and watched Mooney plant a suitcase containing the bomb that killed ten persons and wounded fifty more.

He had just arrived in the city, he testified, from Woodland, a charming leafy town north of San Francisco.

Older sent "Scoop" Gleeson and Charles Brennan to Woodland. Brennan was a former reporter who had studied law and was now with the Mooney defense counsel. Gleeson telephoned Older from Woodland.

"Mr. Older, Oxman wasn't in San Francisco when the bomb exploded!" he said in excited tones.

The men had talked with a Mr. and Mrs. Hatcher, hosts of Oxman while in Woodland. The Hatchers were reluctant to enter so sensational and horrible a case. Gleeson made some twenty dogged trips to Woodland before he persuaded them to appear before the San Francisco Grand Jury and testify that Oxman could not have arrived in San Francisco in time to witness the parade.

Oxman had taken the afternoon train, not the morning train, out of Woodland. There were only two southbound trains a day. On the day of the bomb outrage he had written his name in the hotel register at Woodland and at noon signed for a telegram. Not only the Rigall letters but the Hatcher testimony proved that the "honest cattleman" had committed perjury.

The testimony of the Hatchers broke the ice in the Mooney case. People who had been afraid to talk before came forward. Reputable citizens who had watched the parade from the Eilers Building roof told of seeing Mr. and Mrs. Mooney there. Through the pink and white sheets of the *Call* marched the recantations of many who had helped to convict Mooney. Witness after witness was impeached. The policeman who had "framed" Mooney confessed to the frame-up in Fremont Older's office in the presence of Mayor Rolph and other city officials.

Despite these disclosures, the officials who had ensnared Mooney remained adamant. A trouble-maker was trapped at last, and one charge was as good as another.

Tom Mooney was at last sentenced to hang in October, 1918.

The imminent execution was protested by rioting in every part of the world. In revolution-torn Russia there were demonstrations in behalf of "Muni." The simple Irish name became a symbol like that of Dreyfus in France. In the United States the protests drew the attention of Washington.

President Woodrow Wilson appointed a Mediation Commission, headed by Secretary of Labor William B. Wilson, to investigate San Francisco's Mooney case and report on its effects on labor. The Commission moved into San Francisco in secret, as once the graft investigators had come.

While the government men began their clandestine work, Woodrow Wilson wrote urgently to the Governor of California:

"Would it be possible to postpone the execution of sentence of Mooney until he can be tried upon one of the other indictments against him, in order to give full weight and consideration to the important changes which I understand have taken place in the evidence against him?

"I urge this very respectfully indeed, but very earnestly, because the case has assumed international importance."

The request from the President of the United States could not be ignored. Mooney was reprieved.

In the meantime, under secret orders from Secretary Wilson, government agents disguised as telephone repair men had placed dictaphones in various offices used by District Attorney Fickert. From several places in the city they picked up the expletive-riddled voice of Fickert, violently discussing with intimates the secret processes of the Mooney case.

The conversations seeping over the secret wires fitted together. The completed picture was one of ruthless intrigue against a man condemned to die. Government men took down the conversations to form an imperishable record, the Densmore Report.

"My first knowledge that the Government was making an investigation into the Mooney case came from Captain Charles Goff of the Police Department," related Older.

"Goff had originally been connected with the preparation of evidence in the bomb cases. But after the Oxman exposure he seemingly became convinced that the prosecution had made a terrible blunder. He had Captain of Detectives Mathewson write letters to the Governor favoring a pardon. Goff was so sure he had been mistaken that he accepted employment from the Government and was assigned to the job of shadowing District Attorney Fickert."

Goff introduced the editor to George Parson, chief aide of J. B. Densmore, director General of the United States Employment Service and author of the report that embodied the findings of the secret investigation in San Francisco.

Older was permitted to listen in an office near his own. Over the dictaphone there came into the room the unmistakable voice of Fickert, profanely discussing with an assistant the Mooney case.

"If it weren't for that blankety blank judge, we would have had Mooney shoved off right at the end of the trial."

"We need another witness. I think I can get a witness."

"If you can get a witness who will put Mrs. Mooney at Steuart and Market Streets, I don't give a damn if you put her there in a balloon."

On and on ran such evidence, to become part of the Densmore Report. It was lurid in patches with details of the voluminous love-life of the District Attorney, who, to judge by the solemn report now part of the *Congressional Record,* devoted a great deal of his private and official hours to frail women in astonishing numbers. Not only was the plot to clinch the case against Mooney without fair trial exposed in this investigation, but many cases of court "fixings" and evidence of the bribing of a judge of the Supreme Court.

After the Densmore Report was written and sent to Secretary Wilson, a copy of it was brought to the *Call* office by George Parson. Older grew white with excitement as he read it. The inner secrets of the district attorney's office, the complete frame of the Mooney case, was in its pages.

"Why have you brought me this?" Older asked, looking up.

"Because," said Parson, "it should be published. The American people ought to know what's going on in this town. I thought you might print it."

He added that not another editor in the West would dare to print it.

When Older printed the Oxman letters, he brought wrath on his head by exposing as a perjurer the sole witness to convict Mooney. The Densmore Report was even more shocking an exposé.

He ordered it set in type, every word. It filled nine complete pages. All that morning the *Call* office was under guard. The press-room doors were watched. The Densmore Report would be released at 12:15 in the "Final Home Edition."

Shortly before noon a telephone message came from Washington. Secretary of Labor Wilson had received Older's message that he was printing the Densmore Report.

"Don't publish it until I have time to think things over," telephoned Wilson.

"You can't stop it now—it's on the press," Older yelled back.

The first paper off the press was rushed to him. He shoved the warm sheet under his coat and left the building by way of the stairs. At the door a taxi waited. It shot him to the station. He left like a fugitive with the Densmore Report in hiding, fearing that at any moment he might be enjoined and its publication stopped.

Only when safe in the train did Older unfold his newspaper and gloat through every word of the nine small-type pages.

The publication of the Densmore Report was the greatest scoop of his career.

"It was without doubt one of the most sensational documents that had ever appeared in an American newspaper," commented Older. "It involved men in high places and revealed conversations held in the office of the District Attorney that could leave no doubt in anyone's mind that the courts had been used to convict and hang innocent men.

"It made a deep impression not only upon the people of San Francisco, but it aroused the indignation of the entire nation.

"Subsequently it was read in Congress and made a part of the *Congressional Record*. It can now be found on file in the Congressional Library in Washington."

One amazing bit of chicanery revealed in the Densmore Report was the bribery of a Supreme Court judge who had received a small fortune for a decision on a deed of trust established by one of the great multimillionaires of the early West, James G. Fair. Older had uncovered the plot years before, but the judge had promised to resign from the bench if Older did not expose him. Older agreed out of pity.

Now, in the Densmore Report, this judge was heard again, having broken his pledge to Older, conspiring with the District Attorney to introduce a new witness into the Mooney case. Older hauled from his desk the long-suppressed story of the Fair bribery. It was incorporated in the Densmore Report, and it likewise eventually entered the Library of Congress.

Many declared that not another editor on earth would have dared to print such an attack on a justice of the Supreme Court. The result was a sensational litigation, "The Breaking of the Fair Will," by the breaking of which deed of trust the heirs came into their legal rights.

The Densmore Report saved the life of Tom Mooney. His death sentence was commuted to life imprisonment.

Older then commenced the fight to set him free. He maintained that crusade for eighteen years, all the remaining years of his life. It outlived him. Tom Mooney is still in the penitentiary.

Where once Older had urged a fair trial, he now urged unconditional freedom. Mooney's imprisonment, he protested, was not for Mooney's crime, but for California's.

District Attorney Fickert blamed the exposure of the Densmore Report upon Older. He was an immense, iron-handed man with heavy features, who in college had been noted for his football prowess, not for scholarship. He was drinking in the bar of the Palace Hotel one day when Older entered.

Older was nearing seventy yet erect as a redwood tree. Much of the grimness was gone from his dignified features. All that remained of that "dark-hued mane" was a silver rim. The once-powerful shoulders sloped ever so little in the well-tailored coat.

The youthful ex-footballer lunged for the editor. His iron fist shot for the tired and kindly face.

Older, falling, showed only astonishment. Even in his prime he had hated physical combat. Once an angry reporter had struck him, and the giant editor had scorned to strike back. Now he was carried to a room in the Palace, and the report reached his home and his office that he was dead. The blow had been murderous.

Years afterward an impoverished and jobless Fickert, the shadow of the powerful District Attorney who convicted Mooney, came into Older's office at the *Call*. Something about Fremont Older brought his enemies to him when they in turn needed help. Many, among them Abraham Ruef, when broken in spirit, turned for help, not to the "higher-ups" whose tools they had been, but to Older.

Fickert came to Older to ask his aid. It was given.

Never a word of reproach came from Older. His face glowed as he told of the visit.

"Fickert came to see me today."

"You let him in?"

"Of course. Why should I be vicious because he was vicious? I'm writing a letter to ——, trying to give Fickert a boost."

"But he nearly killed you!"

Older's seraphic look shifted to a scowl.

"You're behaving as badly as Fickert did! Can't you ever forgive anyone? I've forgotten it, and so has Fickert."

Sometimes his friends found it difficult to forgive Fremont Older his capacity for forgiveness.

He met with other blows in his crusade for Mooney, not physical, but far more hard to bear.

Witness after witness, official after official, who had helped convict Mooney came forward with statements that they believed him entitled to a new trial. Among these were the judge who had sentenced him to hang; the Attorney General of California; the Federal commission appointed by President Wilson; Patrolman Draper Hand, a member of the bomb squad, who confessed to Older that he had arranged the evidence that convicted Mooney; and every living member of the jury that had voted Mooney guilty.

The *Call* published the affidavit of John McDonald, narcotic addict, that he had lied against Mooney. Older sleuthed witnesses, tried for years at a time to persuade them to tell the truth. It took him five years to get McDonald's affidavit.

But Mooney, a thorn in the flesh of public placidity for many years, was in prison. Public opinion held that he was better there. Governor after Governor refused to set him free. Politicians stood solidly against Mooney.

"Nor do I blame them," confessed Older. "The governor

takes office as a representative of the people. The average person wants Mooney in prison, not because they think he planted the bomb, but because they know he is an agitator."

Yet hope sprang up often for Mooney's release. Many times he seemed on the verge of being set free. Many promises were made, and many broken. Men whose lives Older had helped to build turned upon him for siding with Mooney.

There was one man he had saved from financial ruin and later helped to find refuge in a political office. Older's letter-files swarmed with letters from this man protesting gratitude and devoted friendship. Yet in one hearing he took the witness-stand and with downcast eyes, avoiding Older's kindly and reproachful gaze, testified that he considered Fremont Older a dangerous radical.

The staff in the *Call* office raged against the ingratitude.

"But you don't understand," Older protested sorrowfully. "He thinks I'm a wicked man!"

"He thinks I'm siding with Mooney. He thinks Mooney is dangerous."

And he added, softly, of his tormenters: "They want to punish me for having discredited the courts. They don't hold the courts at fault, but the man who exposed the chicanery of certain court officials. We want to think our system is perfect. We hate finding out anything crooked of the men we have put in office. It's an awful exposure of our own bad judgment, and most people can't stand for that."

They put Older on the stand in the first Billings pardon hearing. They crucified him, he said later. One would have thought, hearing the questions asked in that solemn room, that Fremont Older was accused of planting a bomb, framing witnesses, seeking to undermine courts and government and destroy human life.

"Well, human nature has improved a little," he said after this ordeal. "Once they would have boiled me in oil for daring to say I thought Mooney innocent."

There were occasions when he grew resentful of the continued attacks.

An Attorney General of California, in his brief on the Mooney case, stated: "We are reliably informed that all or nearly all of the jurors were persistently importuned by Mr. Older in oral and written communications to sign such petitions."

Older wrote him in his own defense:

"I never wrote a letter to any of the Mooney jurors, and with the exception of Neustadter and William McNevin, I never met or spoke to any juror.

"Unsolicited, Neustadter and McNevin called on me, told me they were convinced a great injustice had been done Mooney, and asked me what course they should pursue. I replied that if they thought Mooney was innocent they should write to the Governor to that effect. They left my office saying they would write the Governor and I believe they did.

"Your statement about me is wholly untrue. I am sorry that you thought it necessary so flagrantly to misrepresent me."

A woman of the city's night life, who had served as a witness for Fickert and later changed her testimony in behalf of Mooney, took the stand and coyly admitted having received "a string of pearls" from the seventy-year-old editor. Rival editors made much of the gift and the implications it entailed. Mrs. Older held herself responsible with some annoyance.

"A friend who was importing these artificial pearls from Japan sent me a dozen strings," she said. "I didn't care for them, and told Fremont to take them to the office and give them to the office girls. He kept them on the desk, and offered a string to any of the secretaries and telephone girls who happened in to the office.

"Not all the strings had been disposed of when this woman dropped in to see him, as she often did. She admired them, and he waved his hand at them and said, 'Help yourself.' That is the romantic history of the string of pearls."

All the old whispered accusations born of the graft crusades were dragged out against the aging editor. One evening he arrived at the dinner-table chuckling with amusement.

"Well, Cora, they've started something new about us at last. They're saying that you and I take dope! They've started the report that we're hopheads!"

She was horrified. "Oh, Jimmie, they couldn't!"

He grinned back like a boy over his pink bowl of crackers and milk. He ate with increasing care as the years went by. The strong Havanas he had been wont to smoke were also discarded with the foods he loved, and now he smoked the mildest of five-cent cigars. These were his only vice. He had not touched a drop of liquor in many years.

"Yes, they have, Cora. They say we're hopheads!"

She pondered over her salad. Cora Older was beautiful and queenly, her cheeks roselike with shining health. She wore a linen dress of delicate pink. In that sun-swept dining-room draped with living roses she looked like a modern Flora.

"I know what it's based upon!" she announced triumphantly. "Someone has heard I sometimes take a second cup of coffee at breakfast."

Both the Olders were now vegetarians. Occasionally, with guilty haste, he would take a slice of chicken breast from the platter, but Cora Older never. The men and women of the ranch who gathered at their kitchen table fared better than this simple-living pair.

The chickens on the farm knew their kindness of heart. It was the law that nothing could be killed at "Woodhills." At one time forty cats, all uninvited, found refuge in the barn. The fifty hens scorned egg-laying and went unpunished. They became hens of legendary age, living out their years in the runs beside the kitchen garden while the chickens for Sunday dinners were bought in town.

"We know it's illogical," Older would explain cheerfully, "but we don't care if it is."

Once, driving a Mooney sympathizer to see Billings in Folsom, Older struck a chicken on the highway. His strong features winced at the slaughter.

"Anyway, I hope some poor tramp finds it," he said, by way of consoling his conscience.

During nearly two decades, all through the remainder of his days, he kept the agitation for Mooney alive from one end of the continent to the other. He piled up a Mooney correspondence many feet deep.

He wrote to his friend the motion-picture director Paul Bern, who was taking an active interest in the Mooney case: "It looks now as if you had cast your lot with a lost cause, but you and I know that lost causes are the only ones worth while."

Over the radio, before men's clubs and women's organizations, he discussed the Mooney case. In 1932 he was asked to talk on Mooney before a communistic organization. His refusal revealed his attitude toward the extreme radicals, who, he felt, had constantly conspired with unseasonable demonstrations to keep Mooney in prison.

After nearly twenty years of unremitting struggle Mooney and Billings were still in prison. The crusade was arduous and fruitless, but being permitted to carry it on had been necessary to Older as life. For that privilege he continued to swallow the attacks of those who hated

Mooney and, so perverse is human nature, of some who were for Mooney.

He would not live to see an end to the crusade for which he had abandoned a paper he had built and loved for twenty-four years.

"To me the most interesting thing about the Mooney case is the Supreme Court's attempt to link me with those who believe in violence," he wrote.

"I have never entertained that doctrine, and my experiences of the last twenty-five years have confirmed my belief that hatred and violence never permanently solve any problem. Hatred poisons the blood and unbalances the mind. It hurts both the one who uses it and the one it is used against. It never has worked and it never can work. It is a force that wastes itself in wanton futility.

"Growth and understanding, on the other hand, nearly always come from kindness and tolerance. I was told by an experienced physician in one of our hospitals for the insane that kindness frequently calms raving maniacs.

"Gentle words have a far greater force than bullets and bayonets and machine-guns, greater than steel-barred prisons and the murderous gallows. This is no new philosophy. It was expressed by Christ nearly two thousand years ago. The doctrine set forth in His imperishable message is extremely hard for us to follow. But, possibly, as time passes, its influence upon our behavior will increase, and Christianity will be recognized as the only influence that can bring about a real civilization.

"I have long been convinced that if the human race is ever saved, it will be by loving kindness and tolerance and not by force and violence."

During the years on the *Call* had grown his admiration, his whole-souled loyalty, and his deep friendship for Hearst. Those two understood one another.

Older was able to write gratefully:

"The Mooney case would have died years ago if it hadn't been for William Randolph Hearst."

Such statements did not prevent certain radical publications from printing comments like this:

"Older was forced to spend his declining years working for Hearst, a man he despised."

Older wrote and sent to that magazine a wrathful answer. It was never published.

CHAPTER XXIV

THE PESSIMIST

DURING the years of fighting for Tom Mooney, Older changed. He was no longer violently partisan. He saw both sides. George West wrote of his "Olympian humorous tolerance."

The editor became Tolstoyan.

"If I hated, I hated too much," he had once said of himself. "If I loved, I loved too deeply. I could never do anything in moderation."

But he had fought long enough for independence. His battles had been as great as any waged by his grandsires. Now he was content to watch the efforts of others, pityingly, and with a growing despair.

He maintained his physical exuberance. One of the attorneys in the Mooney case tells of Older, at the end of a grueling day that had left the young men exhausted, running his hands over his face and yawning, "I'm losing my pep."

The slag of the city continued to visit his office. He could be patient and endlessly forgiving of human frailty. He could accept with philosophy the news that a man he had tried to help was again in jail.

The police reporters conspired with him against the city editor to help people in trouble. Often the boys "on police" were hard put to it to explain to the city editor how they had been spending their time when in reality they had been on some secret errand of rescue for the editor-in-chief. But Older would not help any man caught with a gun. He waved one such out of his office with horror:

"How can you expect me to help you? You were carrying a gun!"

Even to possess a gun, he said, implied the wish to kill. Older hoped to see the sale of firearms regulated by law.

"Either manufacturers of firearms should be stopped, or every decent citizen should be allowed to arm himself," he wrote in a letter. "If I had my way no pistol or revolver would be in existence. If their manufacture were stopped, ninety per cent of our crime would disappear."

He wrote to a man he had tried to help:

"Of course I was terribly disappointed when I learned that you were caught with a gun on you. I did not judge you or condemn you. But you made it impossible for me to boost you any further with the courts. You know that as well as I do.

"But I am just as anxious as I have ever been to see you keep out of jail and go along with the rest of us to the end.

"While I can't intercede for you, I do hope you will get another chance from the court."

As a rule his patience with human beings seemed inexhaustible. But his moods could be inexplicable. One could never be certain of his reactions. At times he did not feel able to see a caller he usually greeted rapturously. Then he waved his secretary away furiously.

"I can't see him! Get him out of here! Tell him I've gone to Australia! Tell him I just died! Tell him anything, but for God's sake get him out of here!"

Men and women sat on the bench in the hall outside his office, hoping for a chance to tell their troubles to Older. His departures at the end of the day became escapes. He pulled his hat low, grabbed his brief-case, and bolted for the elevator.

Most of his kindnesses never became known.

He kept inviolate many confessions, persuaded wives to forgive husbands and husbands to forgive wives, urged drunkards to keep off liquor and drug addicts to withstand their curse. He stopped attempts at blackmail. Open and frank in every way, Older could yet be astonishingly discreet. He had many friends on rival newspapers. At times these confided to him plans for some stunt or story they were about to spring and asked his advice. They could trust Older not to betray their schemes.

In his files were locked away the secrets of many tragedies that never made their way into print.

He seemed to live for everything and everyone, for all that happened and existed, save himself. People fascinated Older. Many he actively disliked and was ashamed of that dislike. Events still stirred him. He was the complete extravert. He lived as thoroughly outside himself as a sea-urchin turned inside out, and when at times he paused to look at his innate self, it seemed to astonish and bewilder him.

Only to a few intimate friends could he give himself freely. The shy, hurt boy he had been survived long after Fremont Older had grown to man's estate. Without resentment, without even recognizing his attitude, he would always feel himself betrayed of youth and the security that should belong with youth. So Older had turned outward, lived for others.

At heart he remained the homeless country boy wandering along alien roads.

"We are all just men going home," he quoted at times.

And he wrote indignantly to an adoring subscriber: "I am not a 'great big saintly person!' I am just a red ant like all the rest of the race."

He was utterly without personal vanity. Someone wrote asking him for a personal description. He wrote back briefly:

"6 feet 2 in height; weight 220; erect but old looking, mustache; bald; dark grey-green suit; green tie; light green soft hat."

"How you must enjoy being so big! Looking right over other people's heads!" a woman said admiringly.

"So much the more carcass to carry around," he answered.

At a dinner-table he sat beside a woman who told him with languishing regret that her husband did not understand her.

"Great God, what does she want to practise on me for?" he complained later to his wife. And he added, with a sudden comprehensive grin, "Well, I've never had to complain about your not understanding me."

Mrs. Older held her peace. She was above petty jealousies and petty remarks.

Usually women talking to Older forgot they were women. He liked women markedly, finding them of more sentient quality and far kindlier than men.

He was universally kind. If he struck out, it was against a hurt done someone else, never to himself.

A maid at "Woodhills" went on a trip to the city with one of the ranch workers. She was obviously a good girl and the jaunt innocent, but it wounded the feelings of the houseman, who was in love with the girl. Older was furious with her for grieving the houseman. He insisted she be sent away.

Through her tears the girl coined one of the classics of "Woodhills." She had been reading of his kindness toward the girls of the underworld.

"Maybe if I was one of those fallen women Mr. Older writes about, he'd forgive me," she sobbed.

This was reported to Older, who became penitent. His philosophy had become part of him, but it would desert him in moments of strain, and this oppressed him.

"Human beings!" he would groan, condemning himself along with the entire race, "God, we're awful!"

He was getting weary of human beings. Sometimes, riding between office and station in a taxi, it struck him that the faces of those he passed bore an unpleasant resemblance to certain animals. He did not like this mood in himself. He loved a very few people with an almost tragic tenderness.

He lavished affection on the dogs. He wrote many stories about animals. Any story of cruelty to animals sickened him.

And yet he remained ageless in his enthusiasms—as quick to praise, as excited over new discoveries, new poems, books, people. His eyes, which had once flashed darkly and were now a mellow hazel, scanned every line in his new newspaper. As he stampeded through the *Call* local room, jangling the money and keys in his pockets, he was quick to note and appraise a new face bending over one of the many typewriters.

He was watching for talent. On the *Call* Older developed new writers, new stories, new crusades. In the beginning he faced not only the task of building the circulation of the *Call*, he was faced with the need of putting together a new staff.

Many of his literary fledglings trekked eastward when he left the old *Bulletin*. Robert L. Duffus went to the New York *Times* and novel-writing. Rose Lane was in Albania, Bessie Beatty editor of *McCall's*. Maxwell Anderson was brooding over poetry that would beget the dramatic classics *What Price Glory* (written with Lawrence Stallings), *Winterset, Mary of Scotland*.

Older's strong features gleamed when he told of their successes. They were his own.

Of that splendid self-sufficient school of writers on the old *Bulletin* there remained to him Carl Hoffman, Warren

Brown, the sports editor, and Edgar T. Gleeson. Gleeson had supported Older in his most daring journalistic escapades. He had urged on the fight for Mooney, and on the *Call* he encouraged him to publish the sensational Densmore Report. He tossed aside many a good Eastern offer to remain with Older. Older glanced anxiously at "Scoop's" personal appearance whenever he hove in sight.

"I can tell if Ed has a good story by the angle he wears his hat," he commented fondly.

William Randolph Hearst purchased another paper across the Bay, the Oakland *Post-Enquirer,* and Carl Hoffman reluctantly left Older to become its editor. Warren Brown became sports editor of the Chicago *American.*

John Francis Neylan, who as political reporter on the *Bulletin* had been with Hiram Johnson through the triumphant gubernatorial campaign, had studied law, become a prominent and powerful attorney, and was made publisher of the *Call.* "Jack Neylan was the best reporter I ever had," Older commented at the very end of his life. Older was the *Call's* president. Neylan, with his sound and conservative theories, served as a perfect balance in the public mind to an Older tarred by the Mooney and antigraft crusades. Theirs was a happy relationship.

If Older's personality was perhaps overshadowed on the *Call* by the Hearstian majesty of his position, it was also bolstered and upheld by that same majesty. For the first time he had free choice of policy and personnel, and he could at last pay the salaries he had always longed to pay.

His search for new writers was unending.

There came back from the war—for war at last was over—an eager new crop of writing youngsters. Older grabbed them, sorted them over, and set them in their special fields. Marshall Maslin, editorialist and columnist, John Medbury, humorist, were among the first students of his new school.

## THE PESSIMIST

The reporters in the local room did not dream how he searched their most fragmentary items for a spark of genius. He found it in a news story once—the flash! He sent into the local room for the writer. He came exultantly home that evening.

"Cora, I've found it—someone who can write!"

When he said *write* like that, it was in capital letters.

He had discovered a slim little red-headed person with the boiling intensity of lava in motion—Elenore Meherin.

A few days later he called her into his office. A little red-headed man was there—Al Jennings, the ex-desperado, who had been in prison with the great writer known as "O. Henry."

"Sit down!" Older told Elenore Meherin, waving her to a seat, "I want you to listen."

For three hours, lunchless, she listened. At the end of that time she was rich in material. Jennings left.

"Go out and write it," boomed Older, and then, with a sudden look at her, he added, "Have you had your lunch?"

She told him she didn't want any lunch. That seemed to please him. It was that glowing intensity of hers he believed he had recognized, and he was delighted to find he had not been wrong. She went into the local room and began writing the story, as a news feature for one day's run. Older came up behind her, picked the story sheet by sheet from her typewriter, and told her to stop.

"This is too good to waste in one story," he said. "We'll make a serial of this."

So he stood watching at her typewriter as she wrote the foreword to a great newspaper serial, "Through the Shadows with O. Henry."

Having discovered in Elenore Meherin a great serial-writer, Older set her genius to the music of circulation. Together they talked, planned, flamed, all but wept, as they worked upon romantic plots to enchant San Francisco. In the beginning she followed his lead, then soared on to unprecedented heights. She wrote record-breaking serials, setting an all-time high for serial popularity with the immortal "Chickie."

Years later, "Chickie," rerun in a Chicago paper, lifted its circulation by thirty thousand.

Older developed serial-writing to one of the fine arts of journalistic work. Never before his innovation had a continued serial been a daily feature of a newspaper. Older kept serials overlapping, so that the circulation one gave, another held. In time the newspaper world would be flooded with the serials he, more than any other editor, made popular.

Manuscripts poured into his office. Thousands wrote him of their desire to write. He glanced over manuscripts and people quickly for "the spark." Either it was there or it was not. He recognized it instantly. He saw it in manuscripts written on wrapping-paper, and he scanned many thousands of pages of neatly typed "copy" without glimpsing it at all.

"Not a gleam!" he would sigh, tossing another sheaf aside. "Mechanical. You can hear the wheels go around, grinding it out. Writing with a rubber stamp."

Such accepted phrases as "a sea of upturned faces," "it's a far cry," "youth must be served," he pounced upon in newspaper copy and noisily damned. He preferred spontaneous writing to too-careful grammatical construction.

"Never believe a man who punctuates a love-letter properly," he said once.

He was as irritated by literary snobs as by worldly snobs. He flayed what he termed "mystical writing" by his young writers. "Little sister of the vague," he dubbed me mockingly, for my dabbling in modern verse. And he would say testily:

"Don't write things the average person can't understand. Don't insult people with fine long words. That's just showing off—it's smart-aleck stuff—and people resent it."

He cited the Bible, Stevenson, Hugo, Dickens, all the simple and tremendous literature, to offset what he termed the "grand."

He liked poetry that held meaning as well as song—"The Ballad of Reading Gaol," "The Man with the Hoe," Emerson's "Goodbye, Proud World." He liked simple things that sang. He ran over and over again in the *Call* "Let Me Live in a House by the Side of the Road, and Be a Friend to Man." He was tickled by the sardonic "The Righteous Man" from *The Note Books of Samuel Butler* and ordered copies typed for his friends:

*The righteous man will rob none but the defenseless,*
*Whatsoever will reckon with him he will neither plunder nor*
   *kill;*
*He will steal an egg from a hen or a lamb from an ewe,*
*For his sheep and his hens cannot reckon with him hereafter—*
*Therefore right is with the righteous men, and he taketh*
   *advantage righteously,*
*Praising God and plundering.*

This was bitter, but it was man as Older had known him. He had been named "the Crusader of Righteousness," but it was the self-righteous who had betrayed him. In the graft prosecutions those who should have been the protectors of the inarticulate had failed to support him. The heads of Christianity, with a few exceptions, had turned the pretended magdalene he sent them from their doors. The self-righteous had kept Ruef in prison for ten years.

Marshall Maslin, whose office was next to his, wrote: "I know how he stiffens up when the high-hats and fakers come in. How gentle he is with the poor devil who is in a jam and can't find his way out. I know how he hates cruelty and arrogance. I've heard him mourn for the race of which he is a part and despair of its upward progress, but I've seen him constantly stirred to pity and comfort by the sufferings of the obscure."

As many writers as Older encouraged, he discouraged more. He answered a young man who wrote of his desire to be a journalist:

"I would not advise a young man to choose this career for the reason that unless one has very exceptional ability it is not a well-paid business. There are only comparatively few who ever rise to a point where they receive a worth-while salary. Big salaries are only paid to executives, editors, and special writers.

"Reporters are not very well paid, and unless they have very remarkable talent they remain reporters. There is no promotion."

He wrote to a professor who had asked his advice upon launching a course in journalism:

"I would be very careful to restrict those who take the course to youngsters who have demonstrated some natural talent for writing and who have a good 'word sense.' Test them by having them write articles for news stories. In my experience I have found it utterly hopeless to try to develop writers who haven't considerable natural ability.

"Nearly everyone thinks he can write, but very few can."

The fascination he had found in California history since as a boy of sixteen he first entered the state became productive now. He developed in serial form what were advertised as "fascinating and romantic" stories of early California. One of the first of these was the life of Vasquez the bandit, written for the *Call* by Mrs. Older. He had taken her as a bride on a tour of the California missions.

She had looked unmoved upon the dirt-colored ruins of adobe buildings that were God's rosary, strung along the California coast by Father Serra.

Then she too caught the historical fever and became an ardent Californiac.

"Cora's become a nut," Older would remark fondly as she pored over ancient legends.

But he loved her enthusiasm. They shared this passion for the historical, and from this hobby developed many stories.

Older had Elenore Meherin write the historical romance "The Story of the Sanchez Treasure." Shortly after, and during an anxious fight for country circulation, I joined the staff. He sent me to counties where circulation was sluggish, to write "fascinating and romantic" historical serials of those regions, along with present-day descriptions.

"No wonder you're cleaning up," the country circulation manager of the rival *Bulletin* remarked resentfully. "You billboard the towns like a circus."

We followed up and developed this historical interest through succeeding years with such serials based upon dramatic events in Western history as "The Tragedy of Donnor Lake," "I Am Joaquin," a study of Murieta the bandit, and "Loves of Lola Montez in California." All these serials and many more were thoroughly discussed chapter by chapter, if not inspired, by Fremont Older, and what was true in my case was also true, I know, of every serial-writer who worked for him.

A serial or a sustained feature tied readers to a paper, Older believed. Even if they had not "pulling power" as quick circulation-getters, they had "holding power." Through sustained interest they made readers feel the paper was their own.

"Fremont Older developed more people than any other

editor in the United States," William O. McGeehan said of him.

Frequently one read in published articles after mention of his name, "one of the two great American editors." The other was Arthur Brisbane. These two had corresponded for many years, but they did not meet until Older became editor of the *Call*. Brisbane smiled and appeared astonished.

"Why, you ought to be a little man!" he protested. "The little fellows are the fighters."

In his hunt for new writers Older discovered himself. Someone suggested that his own story would be a circulation-getter. No other excuse for a personal narrative would have convinced him it was worth the writing. The minute he made up his mind, he called in a stenographer and proceeded to dictate the story.

For many years Older had not written. The editorials he inspired were written by his editorial-writers, the stories, by his reporters. But now, in his early struggle to defeat the *Bulletin* he had himself developed, he agreed to write of himself.

Since he left the *Bulletin*, it had made no sign of his withdrawal. With this serial Older would force his new position on the city.

He was sixty-three when he wrote "My Own Story" and began his literary career.

"It is difficult, it is almost impossible, for anyone to talk about himself and his actions without unconsciously trying to excuse wrong-doing or to exaggerate his better motives," Older said of this story.

Having begun the story, he was in a fury of excitement until he had finished it. He could patiently edit and reëdit the work of others, but he shied from the rereading and reëditing of his own copy.

"In an almost incredibly short time he had dictated

most of the narrative to a stenographer," wrote John D. Barry in a foreword. "He had gone at the job like a whirlwind, as he usually did when he became interested in any job. His newspaper sense made him feel that he must keep it moving and moving fast."

The story was a swift recording of Older's many crusades. Someone said it should be called "a romance of righteousness." In it he showed with appalling honesty all that had been going on in San Francisco and in Fremont Older in the past half-century. Into it he poured his philosophies. He gave in it what he said was his "innermost belief":

"Losing my faith in the ability of man to change has not made me cynical.

"His helplessness and his inability to do any better than he does incline me toward a greater pity and compassion for all mankind. From being a savage fighter against wrong and injustice as I saw them in the old days, I have gone clear over to the point where I do not blame anybody for anything."

Writing this he sighed, knowing there were few living who would agree with him.

His old friend Charles Edward Russell wrote Older that his story was "the most tremendous piece of protesting literature these times have brought out. It is the indictment of existing conditions to which there is no answer and from which there is no escape.

"It is the greatest Socialist tract ever penned.

"You gather up the whole of the Capitalist System, looking carefully about to see that you miss nothing—the corrupting of men's lives and souls, the hatreds bred by competition, the darkened and circumscribed horizons, the ruin of all civic virtue, the straits that men are put to that they may get daily bread, the incitement of class against class.

"Then you scrupulously place it all upon the anvil, lift your sledge-hammer and batter it to fragments, then to bits and then to powder, finishing by sweeping up the débris and casting it into the sewer. I think there has never been a job better done."

But by Older the story had not been intended as socialism. He no longer raged against the capitalist, but against us all—the viciousness, the greed, the cruelty, in us all. He did not think much could be done with the human race.

"I have never pretended to be an idealist," he said once. "I frankly confess to having all the sins of the human race. I wish I were an idealist, but my feet of clay forbid."

He wrote to Lillian Symes, who had written about him in *Harper's*:

"Of course I don't mind what you said about me in *Harper's*. It is true. I am disillusioned, and perhaps tired, too. But that would naturally come with age. But disillusioned—

"Strangely enough I knew nothing about the human race until I was in the fifties. I stubbornly held to the belief that something could be accomplished by political action. But long before I left the *Bulletin* I learned that politics were hopeless. Nothing could be done. I stopped scolding and beating the empty air with my fists. All that I got out of that was high blood-pressure. The same old corrupt system continued.

"I am disillusioned only in the sense that I have, by long experience, learned the futility of crusading. Did you stop to think what the chief aim was of that fiery old *Bulletin?* It was out to cure civic corruption by putting boodling officials in the penitentiary. When I found at the end of that seven-year fight that we had only 'bagged' Ruef, the boss, I quit, and began trying to get Ruef out. It was then I became disillusioned. But even though I was disillusioned I sailed into the Mooney case only to be stopped by the owners of the *Bulletin*. It was then Hearst asked me to bring the case to the *Call*. All of the exposures have come since the change, and the *News*, that you say 'carries on the liberal tradition,' never touched the case until about three years ago. I played a lone hand for twelve years."

Older in his seventies was dropping ever more heavily into the depression and pessimism that had followed the World War. This world was a terrible place, he often groaned in his intimate circle, and human beings—save for the special few he loved—were pretty terrible. He remembered crowds wherein every face was dehumanized with hatred. Such memories oppressed him with a spiritual nausea.

Any human being, he growled, who could find happiness in such a world was either callous or feeble-minded.

"I am sincerely glad you are getting such a kick out of living," he wrote reproachfully to Rose Lane, "because I am very fond of you and I want you to be happy. But I really believe one must be half-mad to be happy in this world.

"The happiest person I think I ever met was in Napa some years ago. He was confined in what is known in the insane asylum as the 'back yard.' He was dressed in an old faded uniform and his face was beaming.

"'I'm Edward the Seventh,' he said, holding out his hand.

"I shook it cordially and thanked him for the honor of his acquaintance. I met several other great personages in the 'back yard,' all just as happy as Edward."

Older invariably did the unexpected, and not because he liked doing it. At some pleasant gathering on the ranch, when the sun poured down over acres of roses and friends sat under colored umbrellas around the swimming-pool, he would suddenly growl cheerfully:

"Good God, what have we to be cheerful about? We are all living in the 'back yard' at Napa."

He was Savonarola and Socrates. He was Peck's Bad Boy.

## Chapter XXV

### THE EDITOR WRITES

BITTERNESS was most real to Older when he looked back to his last days on the old *Bulletin*. He recalled himself towering over the owner, a humiliated giant, learning he had nothing to look forward to after his years of magnificent work.

He would again feel himself standing there, and his world falling away.

Without desiring it, for he was above pettiness, Older had his revenge.

From his office at the *Call* he watched the old *Bulletin* that he had loved and built slowly dying. He himself, with the *Call*, was draining the life-blood from his own creation.

When Older left the *Bulletin*, its owner had consoled himself with the thought that he would save $10,000 a year on Older's salary.

After he left, the *Bulletin*, lately a powerful journal with 111,000 readers, sank to a bare 55,000. It began losing $30,000 a month, and then more, until in 1927 it reached the magnificent debacle of a loss of $125,000 in a single month.

The *Bulletin* had been a paper with a soul. That soul had been Older.

No private fortune could sustain such losses as these. When the *Bulletin* could struggle no longer, Hearst bought it and joined it to the *Call*. The *Call* by this time had a circulation of 111,000, the peak once reached by the old *Bulletin*.

Older at seventy-three became editor-in-chief of the *Call-Bulletin*.

He had them both now. His newspapers, reared on the pap of blood and tears, sentiment and belief and bravery. He had used them as flails and fiery crosses.

The merging of the *Call* and the *Bulletin* was perhaps the greatest triumph of Older's life. It was also his saddest. The death of his estranged paper was like watching a part of himself die.

"The merging of the *Bulletin* with the *Call* was not only a surprise but a startling coincidence," he wrote. "When we held a conference in my office over the bones of the old *Bulletin*, I felt as if I were sitting alongside my own ghost."

The first paper he had worked on in San Francisco was the *Call*. He had first seen his name in print as a reporter on the *Call*. He had first been a managing editor on the *Bulletin*.

He had dreaded old age because he dreaded being helpless. He had never provided against the feeble years. Nor would he experience any. Hearst did not give his editor an opportunity to think of age. One strong man understood the other, and Hearst, who never spared himself, gave new work and opportunity to the seventy-three-year-old giant, knowing it was work and responsibility Older needed.

Hearst before long was suggesting that Older, as the oldest San Francisco newspaper man living, add a column to his other editorial duties.

Older shied from the column. It was long since he had written at all, and "My Own Story" had been dictated at lightning speed. He wrote by way of excuse:

THE EDITOR AT HIS DESK
In the *Call-Bulletin* office, 1929.

"I would be delighted to do it if I thought I could make a success of it. But for more than twenty years I have directed editorial, feature, and serial-story writing, suggesting subjects and treatment rather than doing the writing myself. To prepare a daily column of the character you suggest would require the selection of a number of subjects daily, treated in an interesting way. I have a feeling that if I tried it I should disappoint both you and the readers of the *Call-Bulletin*.

"At present I am directing the tone and quality of the editorials, reading a vast number of fiction serials, attending to quite a large correspondence, and meeting a great many callers. But lately in addition to this work I have been writing occasional signed articles on subjects that seem to me as being interesting. I had a page a few days ago on 'The Romance of San Francisco Journalism.' I have a signed article on the editorial page tomorrow. I shall do others frequently.

"It distresses me more than I can tell you that I don't feel able to do this particular thing that you suggest. I want to expend every particle of energy and talent I possess to help you, but I have an intuitive feeling that I wouldn't be able to hold a daily column up to a high standard. But I shall certainly write as many signed articles as I can make interesting and readable."

He wrote Mr. Hearst, too, that no one could possibly compete with Arthur Brisbane. The publisher would not be denied. Hearst wrote:

"Nobody can do a Brisbane column like Brisbane; and I believe that nobody can do a Fremont Older column like Fremont Older.

"If I were you, I would not decide in advance what kind of a column I ought to write. I would write the kind of a column I wanted to write.

"You have the ability to write, you have the ideas, you have the sentiments, you have the knowledge, and you have had the experience.

"In fact, you have everything that will make the column interesting.

"You are producing the ingredients of the column now in your short editorials. Perhaps you would rather produce that way. I do not mind if that is your preference; but I think a combination of two or three editorials as short or a little bit shorter would make a perfect column.

"There are daily occurrences to write about; and then there are reminiscences to include in the column. And there are visions of the future.

"You have ideals. Incorporate them in the column. Make it the expression of your personality, of your thoughts and beliefs."

Older was in reality delighted.

"Well, I see I'll have to make a bluff at writing," he said cheerfully.

These articles became the keenest interest in his life. He had always shared his reactions with everyone who would listen. Now he had a wider audience. He broadcast his thoughts on men and events, economics, religion, crime, history, dogs, colds, medicine, waiters, police—everything that occurred to his mind. If he stayed in the city to dine, met a new personality, went to the theater, or read a new book, he acquired material for an article. He found stories everywhere.

He wrote so many articles that he kept months ahead in his work. Ever on his desk were the yellow sheets written in pencil in his large, generous handwriting. He wrote at home, in the office, on the train. He wrote in a letter:

"My early years as a reporter were spent in chasing news stories and trying to 'scoop' my competitors. In those days writing ability was secondary to what the city editors called 'the news sense.' If one lacked that quality, he wouldn't get very far even though he wrote fairly well. But even news stories must be written interestingly and in fairly good English or they would be turned over to a rewrite man to be whipped into shape and polished. When this occurred too often, one would soon find himself shunted into the ranks of what were known as 'leg men.'

"After I became an editor, I wrote less and less. My time was taken up in directing writers and keeping track of the news.

"Now, in my old age, I am leaving the active work to younger men and have taken up writing short articles for the editorial page. I read a great many books, mostly biographical or philosophical. I don't skim them. If I get hold of a book that doesn't interest me, I drop it instantly.

"I live on a fruit ranch in the foothills of the Santa Cruz Mountains fifty miles south of San Francisco. I commute to and from the city every day but Saturday and Sunday. But I do most of my writing at my home in the hills. I have a little studio built of adobe bricks that came from one of the early California houses built a hundred years ago. My studio is on the edge of a swimming-pool and close to a forest and a rose-garden. I have a large library at hand, a fireplace for cold weather, and an easy-chair. There with a pencil I write a little, think a little, and wonder much about the meaning of life."

He followed the story of his crusades with the poignant serial of his boyhood, "Growing Up." He said with a far-away look in his eyes, "That little boy is very real to me."

All through the years the Mooney case, like an ugly dream, dragged its way through the pages of the *Call*. Older toyed with the thought of writing the history of the case. He waited in the hope that Mooney would go free.

He continued to write in favor of the abolition of capital punishment.

"The futility of hanging as a deterrent is so obviously futile that it leaves revenge as the only possible motive," he wrote at one time. "It is a relic, a hang-over, of barbarism. The state kills a man in cold blood, in the guise of justice. In other words, the state commits the same crime that the man who is executed committed."

Hanging, he said, was legalized lynching.

When three men were lynched at Santa Rosa, he ran photographs of the dangling bodies on the front page. A storm of protest followed. An Eastern magazine published an indignant criticism of the "playing-up" of the lynching story. Older wrote the editor as follows:

"Had I followed my personal inclinations, I should have handled the story in such a way that only one thing could have happened—the building in which the *Call* is published would have been wrecked, and the further publication of the paper would have been made impossible. As I am only an employed editor, I had no right to throw away another man's property.

"The town was insane over the occurrence, and the undercurrent of criticism was directed at me for having, as it was expressed, 'pampered criminals,' and this was the result. I heard this remark from many sources: 'We'll wait and see what that son of a bitch Older says. He ought to be taken out and hanged.'

"If one is a visitor to a dangerous ward in an asylum for the insane, one doesn't try to convince a maniac who thinks he is Edward VII that he isn't. If he is wise, he keeps quiet. It would have been foolhardy for me to have commented editorially on the lynching. It was just what rival newspapers hoped I would do. An editor of a daily newspaper relying upon popular support to pay expenses can do very little for the common good, as you and I see it. I do what little I can. It isn't much, but it is enough to keep this town pretty well stirred up.

"Recently when I obtained the confession of Policeman Hand about the frame-up in the Mooney case and published it, the paper lost two big advertisers. Years ago when I published the Oxman letters, some of our big financiers met in a prominent bank and considered whether or not I should be run out of town. When I left the *Bulletin* to come to the *Call,* there was a meeting of the advertisers, and but for the negative vote of one firm every advertiser would have withdrawn from the *Call.*

"Please don't think I am trying to glorify myself or extenuate any of my shortcomings. I am too indifferent to criticism and too near the end of the road for that. I wonder if you had been in my place how much farther you would have gone. If I had fulfilled your expectations, I should have been compelled to step out of the editorial chair of a daily newspaper and give up my only means of a livelihood. Would that have helped the cause of humanity? Don't you think you editors of liberal magazines ought to keep in mind fellows situated as I am, and not forget that the things you do cannot be done by an editor of a daily newspaper who has to meet all his expenses by public patronage?

"What I have here written is entirely for you personally, and I ask you not to publish a line of it."

His kindness toward individuals seemed to increase as his love for the race weakened. He continued to bring to the ranch people he felt needed a touch of happiness or beauty. He himself would have died years before without the solace of country life. Summer and winter he remained faithful to it. He was restless and nervous and never able to be still very long. The ranch gave him peace.

"I defy anyone to be unhappy here," he would say, his gentle hazel eyes, softened by the decades, turned on the far-off hills beyond the valley.

One summer he brought a colony of Russian refugees to the ranch. Year after year they returned, filling the gulch with their songs of a vanished world. They helped pick the prunes, they put on lively entertainments and gave picnics. They were impoverished and very happy, and Older loved them for their gay and gallant ways.

Some were aristocrats and some were peasants; a few were "Reds," and many were "Whites," but all were friends.

"How wonderful they are!" Older would say, listening to their songs at evening. "How tolerant with one another. They don't hate one another because of opposite political views.

"You couldn't mix a Chamber of Commerce bunch in with a party of I. W. W.'s and have them behave as civilly as these Russians."

More and more he sighed for tolerance in his fellowmen. Punishment had been practised long, and had failed.

"Why not get away from the old assumptions, and try kindness, tolerance, and understanding?" he asked. And, again, he said thoughtfully, "I am certain if mankind is ever saved, it will be by following the doctrine of Jesus Christ."

This was not religion. It was a sociological tenet. To Fremont Older, Jesus Christ was the greatest of world leaders, the kindliest man the world had ever known.

Curiously he inquired of a minister, "Why don't you preach Christianity?"

"I do!" snapped the indignant divine.

"If you did," Older answered solemnly, "we would have reporters and cameramen out covering your church, because the congregation would be outside stoning it."

He brought to the ranch one evening a white-faced, broken man, a member of the clergy who had turned drunkard and been suspended from his church. This strange and miserable guest lived on at "Woodhills," trying to make up his bewildered mind to undergo the penance that would reinstate him. Occasionally he solicited a ride into town and would be found later in rags and delirium.

Each time Older brought him home.

This continued for three years. Everyone else turned against the unhappy man. Many begged Older to cast him adrift.

At last came a scene that was particularly hideous. Word came that he was in jail, charged with drunkenness and disturbing the peace. Older brought the staggering creature into the house, bathed him in his own bathtub, put him into his own bed. Patiently through the hours of delirium he watched beside him.

A few days later Older drove away from the ranch with him. The contrite man had determined to make one last effort at redemption for the sake of Fremont Older. The editor stood in the shadowy doors of a sanctuary waving goodby to him hopefully. There were people there that day who said later that Fremont Older resembled one of the military saints. A few months later the redeemed one preached in a great church. Among those who listened was Fremont Older. He could not thrill to pomp, but he could to the appearance of this man officiating before an altar. He watched a man transfigured.

"That is two years ago, and he has never fallen since," Older wrote later. "In fact, he has become a very prominent and highly influential member of the clergy."

The redeemed one wrote a sermon upon the forgiving spirit of Fremont Older, whose loving understanding had saved him after three years of horror. He did not use real names, but the sermon was so popular that he gave it many times, and it was later published in book form.

Older had many friends in many churches.

"He was not a Roman Catholic, but certainly he reflected the spirit of Jesus Christ in his mercy and compassion for sinners," Father Murray of the Paulist Fathers said of him.

Older had no leaning toward any set religion. He took retreat with the priests at Los Altos. It was a happy experience. He had intimates who were rabbis, having many friendships among Jews. He never failed to resent an attack upon their race.

"What is happening to the Jewish people in Germany is beyond belief," he wrote indignantly in a letter. "I get the feeling at times that the entire human race is drifting back to the dark ages—that the great struggle of the centuries for a world civilization and culture may be altogether blotted out. While this may be a pessimistic view, it is in a measure justified when the German people, so far advanced in science, literature, art, and music, suddenly turn backward a thousand years and resort to cruelties that I hoped had disappeared from the world forever.

"But I am not prepared to blame the German people too much as a nation for this sudden reversion to medievalism.

"It was that infamous Versailles treaty that burned into the hearts and souls of the Germans. That treaty bound them hand and foot, enslaved them and left them at the mercy of their enemies. In their rage and despair they turned to Hitler.

"As you well know, I have always been a great admirer of the Jewish people, some of my most intimate and dearest friends being of that race.

"How much we owe to the Jews for what civilization we have will not, I fear, in our time at least, be fully acknowledged.

"Personally, I feel that all of our moral laws we owe to the Jewish race, and that Jesus Christ, a Jew, gave us in the Sermon on the Mount the only social program that will ever save mankind—the doctrine of love."

Through all his bitterness and despair he continued to love living.

He seemed happiest in the rainy season. Every wet morning he was heard stamping over the flat roof to the rain-gage. At the breakfast-table he would announce the night's rainfall by fractions with never-failing triumph. One morning he appeared at the table exhausted and pale.

"I had a terrible dream," he groaned. "I dreamed the well went dry!"

The water-supply was a constant source of worry for many years. Once, when it failed, Older was obliged to shave at the fountain. He went so far as to investigate, so open was his mind, the source of supply with a "water witch," a split willow twig offered him by a near-by farmer who claimed its certain ability to locate water. The giant editor tramped wherever the pointed twig seemed to point, up and over hills, holding the "water witch" far out in his long arms.

"Look, look, its beginning to bend!" he shouted in pure astonishment.

Eventually a well-borer went down 145 feet at the ranch and struck an artesian supply. The awful dreams of drought ended.

"I'd rather have it than a million-dollar oil-well," Older said jubilantly.

Every Christmas there was a party at "Woodhills." The fire blazed, the long room was wreathed in California toyon, the Christmas tree of berry-studded toyon swept the ceiling with lighted stars. Simple folk from the surrounding farms gathered about the friendly tree.

Older sat back in his specially-built chair, tossing cigar ash about in circles as he watched the festive scene.

"Christ's birthday!" he would proclaim suddenly during the noël rejoicings. "What is it all about, anyway? Who remembers Christ? Who tries to live in his steps? Why, if anyone tried to live like Christ today, he'd be locked up in jail!"

So he gloomed, so he beamed, brandishing his cigar.

Cora Older set her pretty chin against such demonstrations. Fremont, she reflected, was in one of his naughty-boy moods. She loved the sound of bells outside the long windows, the startled shouts of excited children, and Santa Claus—for three hundred sixty-four other days of the year the hired man—bursting through the French window in scarlet suit and cotton snow. She wanted to lose herself utterly in the remembered bliss of childhood.

Fremont Older refused to be lured into make-believe.

"What is man?" he might be heard demanding, over the jingle of bells, of one of his relatives or a ranch worker he had fixed with his twinkling eyes. He had a way of selecting one person, talking to him only. "Ah, old Mark Twain had us all spotted! He was on to us! And Carlyle. Bifurcated radishes, Carlyle called mankind. This damn world wouldn't be such a bad place if it weren't for the people. But these awful human beings . . ."

So he philosophized, while Mrs. Older helped Santa Claus distribute the gifts. At least, she reflected, Fremont was sitting up for the party. Usually he went to bed at six or six-thirty, stamping away with a volume of his beloved Dickens under his arm.

So he despaired over the human race, while he happily unwrapped the tie set of a particular green shade he liked that Mary had found for him, or the woolly slippers that were our annual joke.

Later Cora Older, clearing away a small sierra of paper and ribbon in the glowing, friendly room, would find comfort in the knowledge that her pessimistic spouse had spent a very happy Christmas.

"The Tiger" purred beside his hearth.

## Chapter XXVI

### THE DEPRESSION

THE DEPRESSION was at its worst in 1932. Fremont Older's desk was heaped with letters of tragedy. His telephone rang with cries for aid. In the anteroom waited men and women with despairing eyes who sought him for help.

All newspapers, barometers of public feeling, were forced to retrench. The Hearst newspaper employees were given a general cut. As he was an editor under contract, Older's salary was not subject to the reduction. But he insisted upon taking the cut too. He wrote to William Randolph Hearst:

"When you assumed control of the San Francisco *Examiner* more than forty years ago, newspaper men in this city were wretchedly paid. City editors received $30 and $35 a week, and managing editors $40. Only two reporters in the entire city received as high as $30 a week. . . . Twenty-five dollars was high. Most of the men received $18 or $20 at the most. I had $25 as assistant city editor of the *Morning Call*.

"Soon after you came, salaries began to go up on all of the papers because you forced them up. The same thing happened in New York when you took charge of the *Journal*. Later a similar situation occurred in Chicago.

"All through the succeeding years every newspaper man in America with any talent at all has enjoyed a heavily increased income, amounting in the aggregate to millions of dollars a year.

"The newer generations of newspaper men may be unaware of what you did for them, but I am not because I have lived through those years and personally know what every working newspaper man in America owes to you.

"Now that hard times have come and you find it necessary to retrench, I am happy for the opportunity of showing, very inadequately, my appreciation for what you have done not only for newspaper men, but for the great masses of the American people."

The effect of the depression on the people he met daily made him ponder.

"Perhaps it will do us all good," he said thoughtfully. "Perhaps it will make us realize the futility of money in its relationship to happiness."

But as the cries of need grew louder, his sense of suffering grew. His sensitivity had increased until he identified himself with every living thing. He winced at every blow received by another. He continued, with his cut resources, to help all he could.

"I've never learned to spend money wisely," Older observed almost defiantly, "and I'm glad I haven't. I've spent it impulsively instead of thoughtfully."

It grieved Older that as the depression deepened he could help progressively fewer. He could no longer provide aid for many. He could no longer find jobs for men in need. He wrote to an ex-prisoner he had tried to save, who was again in prison:

"I was of course sorry to learn that you were back in the big house, but I knew from your previous letter that you were on the way.

"If you had to go, it was well that it was at this time when the entire world is flat on its back and millions are starving. At least you don't have to worry about a bed and food.

"Business is very bad here, but I still hold forth and

commute to and from the ranch, which just now is very beautiful. The depression has not affected the beauty of the roses."

Older that August was seventy-six. A few days before his birthday he was driving with Mrs. Older to San Simeon. Suddenly the car pitched forward and flew.

"What are you doing?" cried his startled wife.

"Celebrating my seventy-sixth birthday!" he yelled back. "Driving seventy-six miles an hour!"

She told this story at his birthday party at "Woodhills." There were gathered together on the picnic-ground in the hills the most amazing group of people ever to meet on equal and friendly terms. There was a bank president, a former governor, editors, novelists, stenographers and telephone girls and reporters from the newspaper office, poets, a priest, a rabbi, several ministers, a communist out on bail for conspiracy, and an ex-burglar.

"Everyone got on beautifully, didn't they?" Older remarked afterward, beaming. "All the hatreds were forgotten, at least for the time being."

Cora Older had built the swimming-pool, ready for this occasion. All the rest of this summer the Olders were up at five and swimming in its warm waters. Not another soul was awake on the ranch, and they took the additional enjoyment of swimming naked in the pool. The dogs swam with them, plunging and barking.

The nudist craze was on, delighting and amusing Older.

"Why do they call it a cult?" he snorted. "Why don't they admit it's plain damn curiosity to see how everyone else looks without clothes?"

He was not like an old man at all. He was never to become peevish, suspicious, self-centered, or heartless, as too often the old grow heartless. He never would know a twinge of rheumatism. For years he had often swung off down the hill mornings, walking the two miles to the station. Now he always drove to the train. But he continued to take long walks on Saturdays with the dogs. Physically he remained unconquered.

"If only the old noodle holds up," he remarked nervously at times.

He dreaded having his memory fail. He recalled with anxiety Emerson's saying at the bier of his lifelong friend Longfellow, "He has a nice face. Who is he?"

"Emerson died at the top," Older commented.

His memory, however, remained phenomenal. The reporter who covered an interview with Older present underwent an ordeal. Older remembered every word and furiously corrected any mistake.

He often said that if he had his life to live over again, his editorial methods would be different. He was weary of dashing his head against the stone wall of average thought.

"I used to think if we tried hard enough we could reform the world by next Wednesday at exactly four o'clock," he sighed. "Now I know it will take many millions of Wednesdays to make things any better.

"Nothing can matter. Nothing can change anything."

His friend John Dewey, the educator, held to the theory that if children were correctly trained, a truly fine civilization might be produced.

"I don't believe it," Older would answer, shaking his fine old head. "Perhaps a few could be made gentle and kind. But cruelty is deeply ingrained in the majority of humans.

"I no longer bubble with joy when a baby is born into this world, knowing life as I do."

Yet he loved children as individuals and was pleased when they clambered trustingly over him. He was interested in the new methods of child-rearing.

"I think this new freedom for youth is desirable," he said. "When I was a child, my brother and I weren't allowed to talk before our elders. These modern children are being encouraged to think."

Then he frowned when a small namesake declared against carrots at dinner.

"I wonder what would have happened to me," he stated impressively, "if I had told my grandmother I didn't like carrots. Why, when I was a little boy . . ."

Suddenly he interrupted himself and burst into laughter.

"Bounderby!" he exploded merrily, referring to the Dickens character who boasts of his humble origin. "I'm getting to be just like old Bounderby—boasting about my lowly beginnings."

He chuckled over that for the rest of the meal. He loved to discover human pretentiousness, even in himself.

Older's love for Dickens increased.

"He seemed to feel that Dickens was almost the beginning and end of all novel-writing," Cora Older said of him. "I don't think he thought that any writer since has done much more than imitate Dickens. He probably read some books of Dickens a hundred times. His set of Dickens he literally wore into tatters during the last twenty years.

"He used to read himself to sleep every night with Dickens, and often woke me up in the middle of the night when he had insomnia to read me some passage of Dickens that, although he had read many times, charmed him as if he were reading it for the first time.

"Among fiction-writers Anatole France alone approached Dickens in his affections. Then of course there was Mark Twain. He loved Emerson and Thoreau, and through Emerson he was led back to Montaigne, who was his great love among essayists. Fremont adored his honesty and naked frankness. They were his own qualities, and he recognized them and admired them in Montaigne."

Older never read a book as a matter of duty. Best seller

after best seller he threw across the room, refusing to finish it. He took advantage of his years by refusing to do many things, usually of a social nature, that were expected of him.

There were lonely moods that came upon him, when he felt himself doomed.

"I have reached an age when I feel exceedingly temporary," he wrote. And again, "I feel I am nearing the end of the road."

And he told of rising mornings and facing himself in the mirror to shave and groaning, "Oh, Lord, this old map again!"

He had broken every rule of health for sixty years.

He seemed astonished and hurt by physical change. At times his heart beat rapidly, and he developed "dizzy spells." Then everyone he talked with, even the telephone operators on the board upstairs, heard of his sufferings. Older shared his disturbances with everyone as he had shared everything, all his life.

Medicines began appearing on his office desk and bedside table. He dieted faithfully, ate but little, smoked less.

He refused to attend any more funerals. The death of every old friend was a part of himself dying.

He grew less willing to spend a night away from his home. Even the opera and theater did not tempt him any more. He had seen the best, he said—Calvé as Carmen, Caruso as Canio, Clara Morris as Camille. Each evening he rushed to the hills, but he seemed nearly as eager to leave them every morning.

He was still, at seventy-six, the first man off the train each morning. Only when he felt "dizzy," as he expressed it, did he drop to second place, or even third.

When a big story broke in the office, Older was still the human dynamo. He was jubilant when one morning on the train he heard the truth of a story all the reporters had been trying to get and failed. He "scooped" the town that day and was as thrilled as a cub.

Once a tactless reporter rushed in to praise him for a "beat."

"I knew it was still in you," the man yelled. "They were saying you were dead—but you showed them!"

Older was thoughtful after the enthusiast left.

"If you're not beating someone over the head every minute, they say you are dead," he said.

He had no more interest in politics. Nothing could be done about politics, he argued, and he had not voted for many years. This lack of interest, he maintained, had nothing to do with the condition of his arteries. Not old age but disgust had made him wary of politics. He had hoped that women might be a good influence in politics, but after observing a few in office he decided they were no improvement over the men.

"It seems incredible that it should have taken me so long to lose my enthusiasm for politics," he commented. "But it came many years ago, and I have been much happier since. I have not expected anything from politicians, so whenever one of them does a decent thing it is all to the good."

When referred to as "the Tiger," Older smiled sheepishly. He often wondered how he had been able to care so greatly about so many things.

He had been so many men, held so many ideals, lost so many battles and hopes and points of view. He had known few personal dreams.

The depression growing over him now would never be wholly lifted.

"It was not until I passed sixty that I fully realized I was mortal," he wrote in a letter. "I think most people never fully face mortality. I know no one does who is under forty.

"I can't help resenting the dust heap I am heading for. I wouldn't mind bitter effacement if I could definitely get hold of any purpose back of life. But I can't, and as a result I bitterly resent ever having been brought into this conscious world."

And of his crusades he added: "I also resent that impulse planted in us all to have aspirations, and to plunge headlong into 'causes' for the 'betterment' of mankind. I suppose it is the ego in us. Well, then I resent having an ego!"

Clarence Darrow in one of his letters to Older asked if his will to live were not weakening. Friends of nearly the same age, they exchanged messages of affectionate gloom.

"Have you read G. Stanley Hall's book on *Senescence?*" Darrow inquired of Older. "If you haven't, get it. I am sure you will find it worth while. I did.

"Of course it is none too funny for us old fellows, I tell you. I have a habit of looking things in the face, and somehow this didn't hurt me. Do you think your will to live grows stronger or weaker as you grow older? I believe mine weakens, but am not quite certain.

"I trust you are better and will be able to fairly enjoy the ten or twelve years which are probably still to come. I am not sure that I hope for any more for you."

The editor replied to the lawyer:

"You ask me if my will to live has grown weaker. I think it has a little. But, like you, I am not at all times sure it has. It must be one's infernal egotism that makes it so hard for me to face death contentedly. I don't know what else it can be. I haven't any doubt whatever that death is complete annihilation, that in my case it is merely closing the gap between the 30th of August, 1856, and the time of my death.

"In other words, it is the resumption of unconsciousness, which was interrupted when I was born. We had millions of years of it and there was nothing unpleasant about it. . . .

"I am feeling quite well these days, and I get quite a good deal of old dog comfort out of sitting around in the sun and looking at the hills."

Yet he was gratified when given honorary membership in the newspaper men's fraternity, Sigma Delta Chi, and when chapters of that and of the Quill and Scroll were named in his honor.

The editor who had had three years of schooling was initiated in Sigma Delta Chi with lads a fourth of his years and received with pleasure the gold pin of the national order. It was not in him to wear that pin, although he liked it and carried it for a time in his pocket. All the personal jewelry possessed by Fremont Older was his large linked silver watch-chain, his gold watch, a pair of gold cuff-links, and one pearl stud remaining of a set given him by his wife many years before. These he wore only because they were necessary.

Hearst made Older president of his Fiction Board. In addition to his editorial work and his own writing, Older selected serials for the Hearst papers. He read many thousands of stories, accepting this additional work with intense interest and pride. Work was a drug that made him forget that "temporary" feeling.

He collaborated with Mrs. Older in gathering the material and edited the life of Senator Hearst—*George Hearst, California Pioneer*. Hearst seemed to sense that to give work to Older was to give him vigor. He asked his editor to write the life of his pioneer father. Then Hearst authorized his own biography, *William Randolph Hearst, American*, written by Mrs. Older. Older wrote the foreword.

The Olders went east to gather material for the life of Hearst. In November, 1932, Older addressed in New York the American Civil Liberties Union, of which he was vice-president, on the subject of Mooney. All through these years, since 1918, he had continued to fight for Mooney in the *Call*.

In an interview for *Editor and Publisher* Older said on that trip:

"Facts win crusades. If I were doing it [the graft crusade] over, I would remain cool. I would let the facts talk for themselves. But in those days I didn't know as much about human nature as I do now."

He was asked whether, had he his life to live over, he would be a newspaper man?

"Yes, I would," he answered. "It is an interesting life. And something interesting is about all you can get out of life. Newspaper work keeps you continually occupied, and keeps your mind off yourself."

On this, his last trip out of California, Older undertook what he wrote about later as "My Sentimental Journey." This was a return to the scenes of his Wisconsin boyhood.

Exactly sixty years before, the lanky printer lad of many dreams and ideals had wandered out of Wisconsin.

"I had crossed the continent many times during those intervening years, and although always longing to revisit my childhood home, I was never able to spare the time," he wrote. "But this time I determined, no matter what happened, to visit the old places I knew in my boyhood.

"The tenderest memories cluster around my childhood days passed in the little village of Omro."

Often in his dreams, he said, he had found himself swimming again in the Fox River, or making "snow men" at recess with his playmates of over half a century before.

This visit was to be a reaching backward. More and more his thoughts turned backward, as if eternity lay in the past.

He rented a car at Milwaukee and drove with Mrs. Older toward Oshkosh.

"As I drove along the highway, past the strange-looking farm-houses, red barns, and silos, I suddenly seemed to have entered a foreign country. But, with head whirling, I set my mind on Oshkosh, the river, the lake, and the old wharf where I used to land as a cabin-boy on a river steamer."

The old wharf where as a printer's devil he had joined the *Berlin City* for life as a cabin-boy—the old wharf, the river steamer, were as lost in eternity as that little boy. Fremont Older stood in a park that once had marked the landing-place of the river steamers that had lured him with their mystery.

"How long since the river steamers stopped running?" he asked a man walking in the park.

The man stared at him.

"There haven't been any steamers here in my time," he answered.

Older felt like a man from Mars.

"I felt like the last man left alive in a changed world," he said.

But he drove on toward Omro, his boyhood home. Speeding over the new highway, he felt strangely, psychically, to be in part the little boy whose grandfather had driven him along that road in a buggy, hawking him off as a harvest hand. Out of the twelve hundred souls who had lived in Omro when Fremont Older was a boy, his cousin May Augur was the last one alive, living in the house his grandfather had built seventy years before.

Nothing remained of his boy's world. He left Wisconsin, and leaving, he said, something within him that had endured these many years died, this time forever.

Home was "Woodhills." Home was the office in the *Call* building. He was glad to return to them.

His interest in prisoners had not lessened, although it held less of hope. He no longer in aiding a man expected to redeem him. His belief in the great majority of them "turning straight" was badly shaken. Jack Black remained like a living banner of his lingering faith. Jack and old Dorsey had "squared out" and had never failed Older.

"Jack would die for a friend without a moment's hesitation," Older often said, and this was true. More difficult still for Jack's nature, he had changed his life for a friend. Once Jack tracked a desperate man who had betrayed Older, shoved a gun into his ribs, and made him promise never to go near the editor again. By this act Jack put himself in jeopardy, for certain police were anxious to pick him up on any charge, and for an ex-convict to be found with a gun meant return to prison.

Patiently through the years these police watched Jack Black.

"Just wait," a few of them were still saying at the end of twenty years, "sooner or later he'll slip! An ex-con always goes back."

But Older's faith in Jack Black was sublime. Jack did not go back, but upward. The one-time burglar and fugitive had become famous as the author of *You Can't Win*. Writing articles, plays, and making speeches, he continued to reinforce Older's belief in his fellow-men. Jack returned from one lecture trip in the East in time to celebrate Older's birthday, riding through Canada, where he had once been tracked as a criminal, as an honored guest of the Canadian Pacific.

The ranch was Jack Black's home. He returned to it gratefully. Fremont Older realized with anxiety that Jack's health was failing—he had developed tuberculosis. The thought of attempting to write another book in his weakened condition made him feel ill. He had written a best seller. He was too weary to try again.

The royalties dwindled. Jack returned to New York to work on a play. The depression closed down on his speaking engagements. Older wrote anxiously begging him to return to "Woodhills."

"It is your home as long as I am on this earth," he wrote the man he had taken from a convict's cell. "The adobe is waiting for you."

Jack wrote back whimsically, with mock courage.

"I am now reduced to taking money from churches—for lectures," he wrote.

But he said nothing about returning to the ranch. Older's brow creased over that letter. Jack did not mention that the play had failed and he had no money to come to California. He knew that Older, who never failed anyone, would spring to the chance to help him. Jack would not borrow.

"I'm not borrowing money," he said grimly to a friend in New York. "I'm afraid I'll never be able to pay it back."

Jack Black had his own way out of despair. He vanished.

They found his watch in a pawnshop. He had pledged it for eight dollars. Then Older knew Jack Black was dead, for that watch was his dearest possession. It had been given him by an ex-prisoner he had helped.

Jack had remarked several times to intimates that if life became too merciless, he would not be a burden to his friends. He would tie weights to his feet, row out over New York Harbor, and drop overboard.

Beyond any doubt he did this thing.

Fremont Older was terribly moved by Jack's extinction. Jack had been loyal as few are loyal. He had followed as a human shield down Montgomery Street as Older hurried along the sidewalk expecting any moment a shot in the back. A gunman was stationed across the street. Whenever Older was threatened in any way, somehow, soft-footed as a savage, Jack Black was there as if called by telepathy. The presence of this gaunt, gray, blue-eyed man, feared and respected by the underworld, was a shield against its malevolence.

"Darrow would say Jack is better off than we are, with death behind him," Older wrote sadly to a friend. "No doubt that is true, but it is difficult for me to be philosophical about the loss of such a rare friend as Jack."

Jack's death left life less interesting to Fremont Older. Things that happened to those he loved crucified Older. For himself, he had faced death many times; he did not fear death so much as the humiliation of death, the being felled by it, blotted out forever.

There were times when that awful cosmic perception was upon him that he saw men and himself among them as animals walking down a gangway to protested death. This perception amounted almost to vision. It was too clear to permit of happiness.

Driving toward the ranch one afternoon, his car was struck by the Santa Cruz train and carried an eighth of a mile. The automobile was hurled in pieces down the embankment. A dazed giant sat amongst the wreckage gripping in his thin hands a broken circle that had been a wheel.

The train stopped. A horrified crowd swarmed down the slope to Older. He rose, talked, smiled pleasantly for an *Examiner* cameraman who happened to be aboard, and calmly lit a cigar. But an hour later, sitting under the rose-shaded lamp in his large living-room, looking across at his wife, in a dreamlike unreality he suddenly knew he was going . . . was gone.

"Why . . . there is life after death!" he thought dreamily. "Cora wouldn't be smiling if I were dead! We are going on—just as always."

In that moment, fully conscious, he experienced the

aftermath of death. After that he was less certain of the permanent blotting-out he had dreaded.

"No one knows what to expect," he concluded, a little more hopefully.

And he would never again harbor a shocked memory of what had been a nearly fatal accident. He could meet calmly the major accidents in life, while he stormed and fretted over petty incidents.

"I dread only pain, and being helpless," he said.

Then the very foundation of his life was shaken. Cora Older, who had always been so strong, so comforting in her invincible appreciation of life, was stricken suddenly at the ranch and taken to a hospital near San Jose. An emergency operation was performed at midnight.

Older waited in a little room across the hall. On the wall—the hospital was Catholic—was a chromo of Christ sitting on the Mount of Olives looking down over Jerusalem. Christ, too, alone at midnight, facing Gethsemane.

One could not speak with Fremont Older then, no human being could reach his consciousness. The hours passed while he stared at that sad and glorified countenance on the hospital wall. Suddenly he spoke out of his blind agony:

"He looks as if he were sorrowing for the entire human race!"

He had never turned from God. Ritual, mummery, greed in God's name, he hated. Christ remained his ideal of mankind. In those hours he was with Him, alone in the darkness above the world awaiting crucifixion, and Fremont Older was never to be the same again, never again to be ruthlessly strong.

When Cora Older came from the operating-room, her pulse was 102, his 104.

"That shows how closely knit we have become," he said.

It was after this that the heart attacks came upon him with their menace of approaching doom.

He wrote to a friend after his wife's illness, "What we have been through in the past three weeks is convincing proof that hell is here on this earth."

## Chapter XXVII

### "THIRTY"

"I AM STILL hanging onto life," Older wrote to a friend early in 1934. "I am surprised every morning when I wake up. I am fortunate to be working for Hearst. Any other boss would have retired me long ago."

He discounted the fact that he ranked everywhere as one of the two great editors in America, that his mind and memory were far more active than the average young man's, that he was the soul of the *Call* as he had been of the *Bulletin*, and that Hearst, choosing him out of all his editors, had put the preparation of his father's biography and his own in Older's hands.

Cora Older did nearly all the work on the Hearst biography. Older suggested, criticized, and edited. He wrote his own daily articles in the meantime, preferring to write in the "adobe" by the swimming-pool which Mrs. Older had fashioned for him of old adobe from a historic *casa* in San Jose. There, with his pencil and sheaf of yellow paper, he sat in complete serenity, lifting hazel eyes to look over the pool and the pillared roses to Mount Hamilton on the other side of the valley. He loved these things she had built, this house and pool and garden. She had fashioned them around Fremont Older as she had her life.

He wrote of her beautifully, seeing in her all womankind:

"She has a fine spiritual nature, great tolerance and understanding. She has slipped a 'firm foundation' under my feet and without her I would probably have failed utterly. I hope there are many like her. I don't happen to know very many."

After her illness his tenderness seemed to deepen toward all life. One midnight they heard a coyote give its lost, quavering puppy-cry in the hills.

"I'd like to take him in my arms and comfort him," whispered the man the world still knew as "the Tiger."

The growing misery of mankind seemed to weigh heavily upon Older's deepening sensibilities. The depression grew worse, there seemed no hope of its lifting. Visitors put many burdens upon his weary heart—people on the verge of suicide; people wanting to get jobs, money, food, clothing, to be put on relief. Every day he was racked. So many leaned on him, not guessing his secret frailty. He seemed so strong—that thrusting jaw still indomitable, the large head held so proudly. He was still like a redwood tree towering. Few guessed how weary he had grown.

The general strike of 1934 spread from the water-front over San Francisco. Armed troops patrolled the water-front, trucks were overturned, tear-gas bombs thrown in angry crowds. Older was met mornings at the train by police and guarded to his taxi. The restaurants were closed, and at noon sandwiches and coffee were served to the newspaper people in the office. From the near-by water-front came the screaming of police sirens and the occasional sound of gun-fire.

During those sinister days Older recalled his pioneer boyhood. How different life had been then! If a man's crop failed, he never went hungry. Neighbors borrowed and loaned. He who had gave to his neighbor, and there was peace at the day's end and at life's end. There had been struggle then; now there was turmoil.

What had happened to Fremont Older's America? And those words his uncles and father had met death for—what were they? "The Republic Forever!" Now, commuting, he stared out of the window at men in automobiles blocking the highway, waiting to overturn trucks bringing produce into the beleaguered city. Citizens were storing away tinned foods and burying cans of gasoline in their yards.

The situation aroused all his pity. The workers who struck for higher wages had always been the worse for it, he believed, and this strike was more bitterly fought because of its Communistic tinge. Older's written opinions as voiced in letters were impersonal:

"I am not specially interested in whether Capitalism is dead or not, or whether or not Communism is coming. Maybe it matters to those who have reasonable hopes of a stretch of years ahead.

"But to me, merely a week-ender, the question fails to disturb me."

And he wrote again: "I might become more excited about the situation if I hadn't learned through experience that power is never intelligently used, no matter who acquires it. . . .

"I am trying not to become emotionally stirred over something that is beyond human power to change. Meanwhile I sit on the porch and watch the birds and squirrels with my favorite dog at my feet. Human beings are too much for me. To think about them, even, sends my blood pressure up."

Communistic agitators were arrested in San Francisco. Friends wrote Older protesting the treatment being given a woman agitator in jail. Older wrote:

"Of course, the Capitalists, who are reasonably secure financially, are not going to accept Communism complacently and philosophically. You know as well as I do that the human race has not yet arrived at that point and I doubt very much that it ever will.

"If I were to enlist in a world-wide bloody revolution,

I should expect to get even worse than a prison sentence. One oughtn't to attempt to upset a government and not expect the worst to happen. As for trying to help her with the Sacramento authorities, one might as well attempt to placate the wild lunatics in the 'back yard' at Napa. Everyone seems to have the rabies these days. The people are behaving as badly as they did before and after we went into the World War. It is the same old story. I shall try to keep from being again deeply stirred emotionally over any cause whatsoever, I think I am entitled at seventy-eight to sit on the porch and watch the squirrels and the birds and play with the dogs. No more human-race battles for me. So far as I know no one has yet been born who is capable of using power intelligently."

He wrote to a friend in New York:

"I have delayed answering your letter mainly because I am so deluged with hard-luck letters, appeals for help, and callers on the verge of suicide, that my nerves are all upset. Even a week-end at the ranch doesn't straighten me out as it once did.

"The gardens were all frozen stiff during those two months of cold weather. There is desolation all around us. My beautiful bushy-tailed tree squirrels are going blind and dying of some contagion or squirrel depression. Everyone around me is jerky and nervous, and it is infectious. I suppose this condition is general all over the world.

"I know there isn't anything the matter with the world. It is just as beautiful as ever. It is the behavior of the people that is wrong. If we would all be just good neighbors for a week, our troubles would be over. But of course that is too much to expect of the human race."

As he turned from man, he rejoiced more than ever in the sun rising behind Mount Hamilton, a dip in the pool at morning, the light of evening on the summer roses. More and more he walked down the hill to the shadowy glade where the dogs lay buried. The little row under the live-oaks was growing in length. The gentle golden Bessie lay there, and honey-eyed Brownie, and the darkly passionate, fierce and gentle Friend, so like his master in temperament that he had been beyond all the others Fremont Older's dog. Now other dogs pressed to the editor's knees as he sat on the rustic bench before the graves. Peace dropped over him from the trees. This was his land, his earth. Someday he would be even more a part of it.

"I'd like to curl up under an oak for the few days left to me," he said, and out of the peace of that lovely place he exclaimed thoughtfully, "I cannot doubt that some great power is behind all this! This universe couldn't have just happened."

After a heart attack in San Francisco the doctor put Older to bed. He rose after the doctor left, dressed, and drove to the ranch. In the morning he returned to the office. He would not rest.

"What are the days, weeks, or even months that one squeezes out of life worth at that sacrifice?" he wrote indignantly to Lincoln Steffens.

"I'd rather go on with my office routine and let the end come where and when it may."

Even five minutes of complete rest a day, the doctor assured him, would quiet that excitable heart. In the various rest-rooms of the *Call* were several couches. Attempts to have one of these placed in his office were met with resentment.

"Put it in your own office," he stormed. "Rest in the middle of the day . . . I'll be damned if I will!"

He envied people their capacity for serenity.

"Mental serenity is not for me," he wrote. "I must follow to the end my 'pattern,' chemical mixture, or whatever it is that I was born with. And it's not so bad. I am as free from mental pain as anyone could reasonably hope to be. I may not be happy. That is too much to expect. If I were, I should suspect myself, in view of all the misery and suffering that is daily revealed to me in letters and telephone calls."

His letters at this time held the shadows of this deepening mood:

"I am getting so damned old that I can't work up much interest in anything, except getting through with the day's work and heading down the Peninsula for the porch and the bed. It seems as though I had plunged suddenly into the depths of old age. The enemy crept up on me so stealthily that I hardly noticed him."

To a stranger who wrote in despair, Older dictated the following:

"I am quite sure these moods of depression at times assail everyone. I am sure the one that has you in its grip will pass away.

"I woke up this morning in the very depths of one of them. But I managed to shake it off, and proceed with the day's routine. What else is there to do? We have within us the will to live, which is difficult to overcome. I don't know why we are here, or whether or not there is any design in it. The mystery is too deep, apparently, for human penetration. At least, I think it is.

"But millions of people are perfectly sure we are here for a purpose, and that is why the will to live is so deeply implanted in us all. It may be so. I cannot disprove it. No one can. So why not drift along with life and complete the adventure? That is what I have decided to do.

"I sincerely hope that by the time this letter reaches you, the mood will have passed away."

Despite these troubled moods Older lived more or less serenely through 1934 and celebrated his seventy-eighth birthday.

This year there was no gathering under the trees. Only

three guests were at the dinner-table that evening. They had driven down to the ranch ahead of the train, to greet him at his own door. He sat up late that night—until nine o'clock. Everything pleased him—the cake with many candles, the clustered scarlet roses he loved on the table, the long talk that followed. Never for an instant faded that rare and beautiful smile.

"Now aren't you glad you stuck it out?" someone asked, seeing his happiness.

"Yes," he answered simply.

This was capitulation for the pessimist Older. Not for many years had he admitted that life, violent and heart-rending and terrible, could be worth while.

And he said this had been the nicest of all his birthdays—his seventy-eighth.

The men of both sides of his family who were not destroyed by war were powerful and lived long. To many of the host who leaned on Older, he seemed immortal.

People began saying with surprise, "Older's getting old!" Few knew how terribly old he seemed to himself.

Yet he found much to interest him and make him happy. His step was alert when he swung into his office mornings, the worn brief-case dangling from his long arm. As he talked, read, advised, he was dynamic. To the staff, to the city, he was still the great editor of whom Bruce Bliven wrote:

"To understand Fremont Older is to understand San Francisco."

If he had his hours of tragedy, he had also his joyous hours. Seldom did a day pass for Older without some tremendous discovery.

He met an old well-digger of eighty who lived in great content on four dollars a week.

"Absolutely the greatest philosopher I've ever met!"

exulted Older, preparing to write an article on his latest find.

There was always an interesting letter in the mail, a new book to be read, an adventure to meet in the day's routine. Life might sadden, but it never grew dull for Fremont Older.

His mind was tentacled; it clutched and retained.

He continued to read with passion and devoured Dickens as he had for sixty years. *David Copperfield* was his favorite, and the character Steerforth he considered the greatest in literature.

Mrs. Older was curious to see how many characters he could name from the various books of his idol. She sat beside him one evening and checked them off as he named them.

"He gave me forty from *Pickwick*," she said. "Forty-seven from *David Copperfield*. Thirty-five from *Our Mutual Friend*. Twenty-two from *Bleak House*. Thirty-one from *Martin Chuzzlewit*. Thirty-one from *Dombey and Son*."

At this point her spouse grew tired of the game and refused to play any longer. He stamped off to bed and his nightly chapter of Dickens.

"I think he knew more about Dickens than anyone living," Cora Older said. "He read every book about him that was ever written."

Often he judged people by their love for Dickens. His life-long friendship with Northcliffe was based on their adoration of the great novelist. Older shared this passion for Dickens with Hearst.

Christmas of that year found Fremont Older with a new grip on life. Once, in impatient moods, he had been known to sweep his entire crop of Christmas greetings from his desk. Now the depression seemed lifting from the world and from Older. He wrote an article in defense of Christmas, regretting Russia's wiping out of the noël spirit. He carried home his Yule messages on Christmas Eve. Among them was a card from the janitor.

The Editor-in-Chief left a letter on his desk in reply:

"My dear Janitor:

"Thank you ever so much for your kind Christmas greeting that I found on my desk this morning. I appreciate it more than any card I have received because in its simplicity it expresses a genuine feeling of good will.

"May I, in return, wish you a very Merry Christmas and a Happy New Year.

Cordially,
Fremont Older"

And this holiday season, too, he said had been the happiest of all his seventy-eight years.

Mellowness and gentleness and understanding deepened, and that growing blackness wherein he was utterly alone, wherein no hand could reach out and touch his.

Walking along the street, he saw a man stagger with illness. Older was on his way to the doctor's office, feeling strangely weak, but he hurried forward to help the stranger—the only man out of that noonday crowd on Montgomery Street that went forward to help.

His editorials did not flag. He was still months ahead in his work, so greatly did he love writing. And he was able to say, "My fourteen years as a Hearst editor have been the happiest of the forty-eight I have spent as a newspaper man."

March of 1935 found Older reading with avid enthusiasm Marvin Lowenthal's *Autobiography of Montaigne*. He was greatly excited over the book. He wrote a letter of praise to its author. He drew strong lines beside paragraphs he liked best. He read extracts to everyone he met.

As always with his latest literary enthusiasm, he carried the book to and from the office. He took it with him when he drove to the Camellia Show in Sacramento.

This was on Sunday, March 3, 1935.

Mrs. Older and Mary d'Antonio sat in the back of the car. Older drove, and the chauffeur sat beside him. It was like Fremont Older to take a driver along and then do all the driving himself. A car seemed part of him, and he always loved to drive.

He was as eager as a boy for all they were setting out to see.

But when they came to Sacramento, he let the others go into the show, while he remained in the car with his book of Montaigne. He took yellow paper from his worn, old-fashioned grip. He was writing a series of three articles on the book. This was to be the last.

He sat in the Sacramento sunshine and wrote of death and Montaigne. He wrote in his large, dramatic handwriting, in pencil on the yellow copy-paper:

### "MONTAIGNE MODERNIZED
### *by Fremont Older*

"I have been unable to find a gloomy note in Lowenthal's autobiography of Montaigne, one of the world's greatest philosophers.

"He refused to be depressed by death, which is the inevitable end of us all.

"When he passed fifty he made up his mind that he could run no longer.

"He thought it was enough that he crawled.

"No complaint of the natural decay which slowed up his pace, nor regret that his life was not as sound nor as long as an oak. . . ."

Older wrote clearly and logically as he always wrote,

thinking his way through to the words. He was interrupted by Mrs. Older and Mary and one of the patronesses of the flower show. They brought out a tray of camellias for him to judge.

"If you had waited fifteen more minutes, I would have finished my article," he said good-humoredly, as he folded and put it away.

From the tray he selected three camellias of white and red, his favorite colors. Years before, in the season of camellias in this very city of Sacramento, he had met for the first time the woman now his wife. The first flowers he gave her were camellias. Now they smiled at one another over the flower-burdened tray.

When they left, Cora Older was carrying the camellias.

He smiled again, and joked, as he drove the car away. He had never looked better or more handsome. He was wearing a new green suit for the first time. Older loved green.

"It's nature's color," he explained.

He drove rather slowly down the highway, looking with interest at the signs of spring in the lovely valley.

The chauffeur noted that the speedometer stood at thirty. Thirty—the sign left by printers at the end of a story that is finished.

Those with him saw the splendid head droop suddenly and the slender, eloquent hands drop from the wheel. And that was all. It was ended, and Fremont Older had driven out of life, without pain or sign of weakness, but with interest and beauty around him, as he had wished to die.

His funeral was simple, strangely like many of the gatherings he had presided over at "Woodhills." Flowers bloomed around his house, and within flowers banked the walls with color and life. He lay there in such calm, such dignity, like a tower fallen. He wore the new green suit, with a spray of the daphne he had loved and carried each spring in great masses to distribute among the office girls at the *Call.*

The guests, too, were like "Woodhills," were like Fremont Older. They represented all his interests and devotions, all his multitudinous lives. The Mayor of San Francisco and District Attorney and Police Chief, editors and publishers, country neighbors, judges, men and women he had helped. Abe Ruef, the man he had once sent to prison, wept. The Kid, one-time "King of the Pickpockets," brought a crucifix for the grave. There were flowers from Tom Mooney, who had wept in prison upon hearing of the death of the man who had tried for eighteen years to free him.

Friends carrying flowers followed the body down the hill, to the glade under the live-oaks where his dogs lay buried, where he had long wished to lie. It was like Fremont Older that a Catholic priest should speak over his grave and a Protestant minister as well; and that, in the hushed woods, instead of song, a clear voice should read his favorite poem, Emerson's "Good-bye."

Probably everyone present, at one time or another, had heard Fremont Older read that poem. It was like his voice speaking:

> *Good-bye, proud world! I'm going home;*
> *Thou'rt not my friend, and I'm not thine.*
> *Long through thy weary crowds I roam;*
> *A river-ark on the ocean brine,*
> *Long I've been tossed like the driven foam;*
> *But now, proud world! I'm going home.*
>
> *Good-bye to Flattery's fawning face;*
> *To Grandeur with his wise grimace;*
> *To upstart Wealth's averted eye;*
> *To supple Office, low and high;*
> *To crowded halls, to court and street;*
> *To frozen hearts and hasting feet;*

*To those who go, and those who come;*
*Good-bye, proud world! I'm going home.*

*I'm going to my own hearth-stone,*
*Bosomed in yon green hills alone, . . .*

*O, when I am safe in my sylvan home,*
*I tread on the pride of Greece and Rome;*
*And when I am stretched beneath the pines,*
*Where the evening star so holy shines,*
*I laugh at the lore and the pride of man,*
*At the sophist schools, and the learned clan;*
*For what are they all, in their high conceit,*
*When man in the bush with God may meet?*

As we listened, it was easy to imagine Fremont Older one with his guests, glad for their presence, loving each for the secret good he saw in him that the world perhaps could not see, forgiving them all their trespasses, welcoming them to his beloved hills.

He had lived many lives, forgiven many things.

Only a few nights before his death Fremont Older attended a dinner. A man present had maligned him cruelly.

"I must go over and speak to him," he said.

"After all he has done to you?" protested his wife, who sometimes had difficulty in forgiving her husband's enemies.

His smile was beautiful.

"Cora, I hold no ill-will against any human being," he said tenderly.

It was his farewell to mankind that he had loved, that had wounded his trust in many ways.

There was left only a mound in the whispering forest and a cairn of stones brought by friends, but his passing left eddies in the surface of the world's life.

Thousands of telegrams and letters came to Cora Older.

Thousands of news articles carried the story of the death of one of the last great editors.

Now he was gone, many who had been unjust could be kind, could admit he had been fair and righteous.

"When the fury of battle had passed and time had added its mellowing influence, it was determined that Older was usually right." "A great leader has passed." "There is no one alive who can replace Fremont Older. He has taken his place with the legendary great of the Press." "Full to the end of unconquerable youth." "Foremost champion of social justice." "What made him great was his love for his fellow-men." "A great editor—a greater man." "His guiding influence among the fledglings who served under him will find its way into public print for many years to come."

William Randolph Hearst wrote in farewell:

"There can never be another Fremont Older, but his career, his example, may serve as a stimulus to many young men, coming forward in the profession of journalism, to follow in his footsteps, and to consecrate their lives to disinterested devotion to the common good."

Annie Laurie (Mrs. W. B. Bonfils), the famous woman journalist who has since followed him, wrote that the passing of Fremont Older was like the crash of a great sequoia falling in the forest. These two friends had been born within twelve miles of one another, on the Fox River in Wisconsin.

Arthur Brisbane wrote that were there no heaven, one must needs be created for such a man.

On that day of his burial the California Legislature adjourned in honor of the memory of Fremont Older, and a memorial was prepared and adopted in Assembly and Senate:

"*Whereas,* one of the most beloved, public-spirited, respected and revered citizens of the State of California has passed to the Great Beyond. He was for nigh unto half a century a leader of our thought and a champion of good government and of the cause of the under dog. He had no superior in American journalism. He will be missed most by those who knew him best. We refer to our friend and champion, the late-lamented citizen, Fremont Older of San Francisco. . . ."

The San Francisco Board of Supervisors likewise adjourned to honor the memory of Fremont Older, and Mayor Angelo Rossi signed the resolution, stamped with the city's seal, that said in part:

"In days when San Francisco was in the depths of political infamy, Older was chief crusader in the movement to purge the municipality of official corruption. He relentlessly pursued the bribe-givers as well as prosecuting the bribe-taker.

"In accomplishing these things he served a great purpose for moral uplift of the city, and once the fight was won for decency, he evinced a great tolerance for the victims of the malfeasances. In the latter years of his life his philosophy was that every man and every woman, though they make mistakes, were not to be blamed for all the evils that were forced upon them by so-called society. His motto became, 'Tolerance for the Intolerant.'

"He died with a host of friends, with the affection of many whom he had helped anonymously, and the gratitude and reverence of hundreds to whom he had extended a helping hand when they most needed it.

"Truly San Francisco has lost a noble Christian man whose forthright preachments will surely lead many people to better thoughts and lives."

He would have grinned, that warm and lovable grin, reading such tributes from the political world. He would have said, "If they think that much of me, why don't they set Mooney free?"

But he would have liked reading these things, because he had known so much of misunderstanding and abuse, and so much of the loneliness that comes with misunderstanding. And he would have liked a poem written by Edith Daley, which ended:

> *Hail and farewell! Upon your sunlit height*
> *Sleep well, O brave Crusader for the Right!*

He would have liked all these things because he loved all moments wherein men speak out truthfully and without calculation; because he had tasted so long and so fully of human loneliness; because he was Fremont Older and had loved deeply and lived profoundly through much of fighting and many changes and many lives.

# INDEX

Abbott, Joe, 231, 232, 233
Addams, Jane, 304
Anderson, Maxwell, 218, 320, 341
Appleton (Wis.) *Post*, Older employed on, 45
Appleton, Wisconsin, 9, 10; childhood home of Fremont Older, 19
Astor, Mrs. John Jacob, 109
Atherton, Gertrude, quoted on Ambrose Bierce, 75; quoted on Mr. and Mrs. Fremont Older, 121
Augur, Allan, uncle of Fremont Older, 11, 15; death of, 19
Augur, Duane, uncle of Fremont Older, 11, 15; death of, 17
Augur, Squire Lewis, grandfather of Fremont Older, 4; as Abolitionist, 5, 11; curses God, 15; gives Fremont Older a Christmas gift, 27; hires Fremont Older out to a farmer, 28; moves to Illinois, 39; goes to California, 46; death of, 150
Augur, Maria Kimball, grandmother of Fremont Older, 7, 10; attitude toward religion, 16, 23, 27
Augur, Mary, aunt of Fremont Older, 42
Augur, May, cousin of Fremont Older, 376
*Autobiography of Montaigne*, 390

Baggerly, Cora, description of, 84; marriage to Fremont Older, 85. *See also* Older, Cora Baggerly
Baggerly, Hiland, sports editor on San Francisco *Evening Bulletin*, 92; reports Durant murder case, 105; develops *Bulletin* sports pages, 220
Barbary Coast, 133
Barry, John D., 218, 243, 257, 349

Bart, Black, 284
Bashford, Herbert, 271
Bassity, Jerome, "King of the Maquereans," 133, 232
Beatty, Bessie, 218, 219, 271, 303, 320, 341
Benhayon, Henry, 77
Berkman, Alexander, 293
Berlin (Wis.) *Courant*, Older employed on, 31
Bern, Paul, 334
Bernhardt, Sara, interviewed by Mrs. Fremont Older, 121
Bierce, Ambrose, 75
"Big Six," the, rulers of San Francisco, 228
Billings, Warren K., 296; found guilty of Preparedness Day bombing, 298
Black, Jack, 2; reformed by Older, 276 ff.; writes *You Can't Win*, 281; Older's faith in, 377 ff.
"Black Friday," 163 ff.
Bliven, Bruce, 218, 388
Bombing, on Preparedness Day, 294
Bonfils, Mrs. W. B., 395
Bowen, Nettie, aunt of Fremont Older, 43
Bowers, Dr. Milton, 77
Bowers murder case, 76
Bowes, Ed, 136
Brastow, Virginia, city editor of San Francisco *Evening Bulletin*, 118
Braunan, Sam, 51
Brennan, Charles, 323
Brisbane, Arthur, 314; meets Fremont Older, 348; writes of Older's death, 395
Brooke, Henry L., 107
Brooke, Mrs. Henry L., 219
Brown, Luther, 191
Brown, Warren, 342

## INDEX

Bryan, William Jennings, 106
Bull Run, news of, reaches frontier, 12
Burns, William J., 149; investigates graft in San Francisco, 155, 161, 177
Byrne, John, 283

Calhoun, Patrick, 159, 160, 169, 171; indicted for bribery, 186; trial of, 196, 204; case against dismissed, 205
*California Star*, first San Francisco newspaper, 51
Capital punishment, Older campaigns against, 241 ff., 358
Capone, Al, 184
Carruth, Herbert, 264
Caruso, Enrico, entertained by the Olders, 150
Casey, James, 90
Central Pacific Railroad, 80, 111
Cheung, Chan, 135
*Chicago American*, 342
*Chicago Times*, Older employed on, 46
Chinatown, Older crusades against vice in, 229
"Church Scandal, The," 99
Civil War, beginning of, 12; effect of, upon frontier, 17, 19
Claudianos, John, 180
Claudianos, Peter, 180
Clifford, Edwin, actor, Older's first hero, 33, 34
Cobb, Charles, 190
Coghlan, John P., 218
Contract and Finance Company, 79
Cooper, J. Fenimore, 27
"Crime of the Century," 106
Crothers, R. A. publisher of San Francisco *Evening Bulletin*, 89, 108, 113, 123, 125, 128, 226, 308
Cullinan, Eustace, 218, 252

Daley, Edith, 397
Dalziel, Davison, publisher of San Francisco *Daily Mail*, employs Fremont Older, 56
d'Antonio, Mary, ward of the Olders, 253
Darrow, Clarence, 25, 208, 373; influence on Older, 250
Densmore, J. B., 326
Densmore Report, 325, 326; published by Older, 327
de Quille, Dan (William Wright), 52
Dewey, John, 369
de Young, Charles, 89
de Young, M. H., 89
Dickens, Charles, 59, 119; Older's admiration for, 370, 389
Dorgan, "Tad," 92, 220
Dorsey, Charles, 284
Duffus, Robert L., 218, 295, 320, 341
Durant, Theodore, 101 ff.
Durant murder case, 101 ff.

Emerson, Ralph Waldo, 370

Fair, James G., 328
*Fanchon the Cricket*, 33
Farley, James, 159
Felker, John B., Fremont Older's first friend, 24, 25
Fickert, Charles, 196, 205, 325; prosecutes Mooney case, 299
Finger, Emma, marriage to and divorce from Fremont Older, 69
Fitch, George K., 316
Flannery, Harry P., President of San Francisco Police Commission, 228; Older forces removal of, 234
Ford, General Tirey L., 170
Fort Sumter, 12
France, Anatole, 370
Fremont, General John Charles, 7, 47, 51
Furuseth, Andrew, 300

Gallagher, James L., 162, 179, 196
Gambling in San Francisco, exposed by Older, 134

# INDEX

General strike of 1934, in San Francisco, 383
George, Henry, 74, 316
Gillis, Steve, 52
Gleeson, Edgar T., 216, 218, 221, 294, 305, 323, 342
Goff, Charles, 325
Goldberg, "Rube," 92, 220
Goldman, Emma, visits the Olders, 286
Goodman, Joseph T., editor of Virginia City *Territorial Enterprise*, 52; establishes the *San Franciscan*, 74
Graft, in San Francisco, 146
Graham, Judge Thomas, 162, 166
Greeley, Horace, 11, 47, 54; Older's admiration for, 30, 31, 41, 56
Griffin, Judge Franklin, 300

Hall, Joe, publisher of Oconto (Wis.) *Free Press*, employs Fremont Older, 45
Hand, Draper, 330
Harley, Emily Kimball, great-aunt of Fremont Older, 10
Harley, Henry, cousin of Fremont Older, 10
Harmsworth, Alfred, meets Fremont Older, 119
Havenner, Franck, 218
Hayman, Jessie, 247
Headlines, Older's use of, 115
Healey, Timothy, 218
Hearst, Millicent (Mrs. William Randolph Hearst), 118
Hearst, William Randolph, 58, 115, 335, 354; crusade against Southern Pacific Railroad, 79, 111; Older's respect for, 111; meets Fremont Older, 118; Older opposes, 224; compared with Fremont Older, 310; employs Older on San Francisco *Evening Call*, 315; buys San Francisco *Evening Bulletin*, 353; influence on newspaper salaries, 366; writes of Older's death, 395
Heney, Francis J., 148, 154, 161, 177; appointed deputy district attorney in San Francisco, 162; removed from office, 162; begins graft prosecution, 168 ff.; shot in court-room during graft prosecution, 198
Henry, O., 343
Hill, Edwin C., 222
Hoffman, Carl, 218, 274, 295, 341, 342
Hopkins, Ernest J., 217, 218, 259, 294, 305
Hudson (Wis.) *Democrat*, Older employed on, 35

International Policy-Holder's Commission, Older member of, 182

Jacobson, Pauline, 218, 220, 222, 232
Jennings, Al, 343
Johnson, Hiram W., 200, 235; joins graft prosecution, 201; Governor of California, 208; fights railroads, 236
Jordan, David Starr, 304

Kearney, Dennis, 80
Kellogg, F. W., 317
"Kid, the—King of the Pickpockets," 130, 177, 254
King, James, founder of San Francisco *Evening Bulletin*, 90, 101, 316
Kipling, Rudyard, 223
Krueger, Howard, 278

Lamont, Blanche, 101 ff.
Lane, Franklin K., 138, 185, 194, 195, 210, 307
Lane, Rose Wilder, 218, 271, 320, 341; as serial-writer on San Francisco *Evening Bulletin*, 272
Langdon, William H., District Attorney of San Francisco, 156, 161, 162, 166, 200
Lawrence, W. H., 69
Lawrence College, 11

"League of Justice," 202
Leno, Dan, 92
Lewis, Sinclair, 218
*Life of Horace Greeley, The*, 29, 38
*Life of Schuyler Colfax, The*, 29
Lincoln, Abraham, political rally for, 4; inaugurated President, 8; call for volunteers, 13; assassination of, 21
Livernash, Edward J., 175
Llanuza, Peter, 92
London *Times*, 182
Lowenthal, Marvin, 390
Lowrie, Donald, paroled to Fremont Older, 244; writes "My Life in Prison," 245

Maestretti, Frank, 168
Markham, Edwin, 223
Maslin, Marshall, 255, 342, 345
McAtee, Sylvester J., 218
McCarthy, P. H., mayor of San Francisco, 196, 227; Older attacks, 230
McDonald, John, 330
McEwen, Arthur, 57, 138, 143; Older's friendship with, 58; establishes the *San Franciscan*, 74; influence upon Older, 75; employed on *Bulletin* by Older, 110; employed on New York *Journal*, 116
McGeehan, William O., 174, 218, 269, 348
McGowan, Ned, 51
McKinley, William, 149
McNevin, William, 332
McNutt, Maxwell, heads Mooney's defense, 297
Medbury, John, 342
Meherin, Elenore, 343, 347
*Men of Our Times*, 29
Michelson, Miriam, 218
Michelson, Peter, 216
Miller, Joaquin, 210
Miller, John, 80
Montaigne, 370
Montez, Lola, 54
Mooney, Rena, 296

Mooney, Thomas J., 1; listed as dangerous agitator, 293; arrested for Preparedness Day bombing, 295; trial of, 298; sentenced to hang for Preparedness Day bombing, 300, 324; wins reprieve, 325; sentenced to life imprisonment, 328
Mundell, Dr. William A., 134
"Municipal Crib," 137, 173
Murphy, Frank, 262
"My Own Story," Older's autobiography, 348

Nesbit, Evelyn, 183
New York *American*, Older offered managing editorship of, 310
New York *Journal*, 111
New York *Tribune*. See *Tribune* (Greeley's)
New York *World*, 111
Neylan, John Francis, 218, 236, 342
Nicol, Frank, 139
Nockels, "Big Ed," 302
Nolan, Edward I., 296
Norris, Kathleen, 218
Northcliffe, Lord, 119, 286, 315
Norton, Emperor, 51

Oakland *Herald*, 152
Oakland *Post-Enquirer*, 342
O'Connor, Kate, 266
Oconto (Wis.) *Free Press*, Older employed on, 45
Older, Celia Augur, mother of Fremont Older, 7; aids the family's fortunes, 29; goes to California, 32; remarries, 32; death of, 150
Older, Cora Baggerly (Mrs. Fremont Older), ancestry of, 85; courage and loyalty of, 85-88; aids husband on San Francisco *Evening Bulletin*, 92; loyalty to *Bulletin*, 121; at "Woodhills," the Older ranch, 253; reports West Virginia coal strike for *Bulletin*, 274; campaigns for reëlection of President Wilson, 291; writes life of Vasquez the bandit, 346; writes *George*

Hearst, *California Pioneer* with Fremont Older, 374; writes *William Randolph Hearst, American*, 374, 382

Older, Emma Finger. *See* Finger, Emma.

Older, Emory, father of Fremont Older, 5; marriage of, 7; enlistment of, in Civil War, 14; returns from the war, 18; death of, 18

Older, Fremont, personal characteristics of, 1-3, 215 *ff*., 337 *ff*.; first memory of, 4-6; ancestry of, 6-8; hatred of injustice, 6, 73; birth of, 7; naming of, 7; childhood of, 8 *ff*.; pioneer experiences of, 8 *ff*.; first day of school, 13; sensitiveness of, 16, 21, 44, 73, 367; goes to grammar-school, 19; removal to Appleton, Wisconsin, 19; becomes school janitor, 20; his first crusade, 21; his first job, 22; goes to live with grandparents, 23; doubts a Bible story, 24; learns about Thomas Paine, 24; his first friend, 25; is fascinated by a saloon-keeper, 25; sees his first play, 26; introduction to adventure, 27; is hired out to a farmer, 28; enters Ripon College, 29; first ambition to be an editor, 29; reads *Life of Horace Greeley*, 29; chooses a trade, 30; end of his schooling, 30; his first love, 30; printer's devil on Berlin (Wis.) *Courant*, 31; first experience of wholesome family life, 32; influence of drama upon, 33; cabin-boy on Fox River steamer, 34; joins his brother Herbert in printing trade, 35; roustabout on Mississippi River boat, 35; type-setter on Hudson (Wis.) *Democrat*, 35; goes to St. Paul, 36; becomes a wanderer, 38 *ff*.; employed on St. Paul *Morning Press*, 38; parts with his *Life of Horace Greeley*, 38; visits his grandfather in Illinois, 41; attitude toward religion, 42; returns to Wisconsin, 42; employed on Appleton (Wis.) *Post*, 45; employed on Oconto (Wis.) *Free Press*, 45; his first editorial job, 45; employed on Chicago *Times*, 46; goes to California, 47; employed on Sacramento *Union*, 49; type-setter on San Francisco *Morning Call*, 50; explores San Francisco, 51; employed on Virginia City *Territorial Enterprise*, 52; first gambling experience, 53; becomes a tramp printer, 54; employed on San Francisco *Daily Mail*, 56; reads the classics, 59; becomes a landowner, 61; becomes a job printer, 63; employed on Redwood City *Weekly Journal*, 65; betrayed by Redwood City bosses, 67; business manager of Redwood City *Times-Gazette*, 69; youthful marriage and divorce, 69; editor of Redwood City *Times-Gazette*, 70; his first big news story, 70; San Mateo County correspondent for San Francisco papers, 71; his first police story, 72; reporter on San Francisco *Alta California*, 72; reporter on San Francisco *Morning Call*, 73; meets Ambrose Bierce, 75; star reporter on San Francisco *Morning Call*, 76; works on Bowers murder case, 77; desire for justice, 79, 82, 321; reports Southern Pacific Railroad investigation, 80; marriage to Cora Baggerly, 85; improvement in personal appearance, 88; city editor on San Francisco *Post*, 89; city editor on San Francisco *Morning Call*, 89; managing editor on San Francisco *Evening Bulletin*, 90; increases *Bulletin* circulation, 95, 107, 108; as cigar smoker, 98; first private office, 98; the sensationalist, 101 *ff*.; and Durant murder case, 103, 106-8; *Bulletin* editorials of, 110; employs Arthur McEwen on *Bulletin*, 110; admiration for William Randolph Hearst, 111; supports James D. Phelan for mayor of

Older, Fremont (cont.)
San Francisco, 114; his use of headlines, 115; salary increased, 115; employs women on the *Bulletin*, 117-18; goes to Europe, 118; meets William Randolph Hearst, 118; member of Special Health Commission, 118; meets Alfred Harmsworth, 119; crusade against political grafters under Mayor Schmitz and Abraham Ruef, 123 ff.; is arrested, 128; breaks news-boys' strike, 130 ff.; exposes gambling and prostitution, 133 ff.; summoned before Grand Jury, 135; exposes bribery in State Capitol, 138; fights reëlection of Mayor Schmitz, 139 ff.; reverence for honesty, 139, 146; supports John Partridge for mayor of San Francisco, 141; mayoral campaign defeated, 143; continues crusade against graft, 146 ff.; determines to "get" Abraham Ruef, 146 ff.; seeks aid in Washington, 149; and earthquake and fire, 151 ff.; is rude to Caruso, 151; renews crusade against graft, 154 ff.; and street-car strike, 160; aided in graft fight by Francis J. Heney, 162 ff.; calls mass meeting of citizens on "Black Friday," 164; gets evidence against Abraham Ruef, 168; attacked by public, 172, 187, 332; murder plots against, 177; receives threats of dynamiting, 179; chooses a mayor to succeed Schmitz, 185; goes after Patrick Calhoun, 186 ff.; traps laid for, 189; is kidnapped, 191 ff.; his victory over Abraham Ruef, 202; visits Ruef in San Quentin, 206; fights to free Ruef from prison, 208 ff.; friendship with Abraham Ruef, 214; as man and journalist, 215 ff.; increasing success of, 216; reporters under, 218; as a creative editor, 219; as a voracious reader, 222; opposes Hearst, 224; his capacity for friendship, 225, 285, 362; crusade against the "Big Six," 228 ff.; attacks Mayor McCarthy, 230; breaks power of the "Big Six," 234; supports Hiram W. Johnson for Governor, 236; assists in breaking power of railroads, 238; interest in prison reform, 240 ff.; interest in prisoners, 240, 271 ff.; campaigns against capital punishment, 241 ff., 358; interest in Donald Lowrie, 244 ff.; buys a ranch, 251; his interest in dogs, 254; his daily routine, 256; publishes "A Voice from the Underworld," 259; exposes prostitution in San Francisco, 260 ff.; aids prostitutes, 261; develops serial-writers, 271 ff., 344 ff.; as man and journalist, 274 ff.; reforms Jack Black, 276 ff.; editorial policies interfered with, 289; advocates peace, 292; receives a warning, 292; suspects Mooney of Preparedness Day bombing, 295; crusades for Mooney, 301 ff.; is convinced of Mooney's innocence, 302; branded as a "red," 303; publishes Oxman letters, 303; as pacifist, 304; prohibited from continuing his fight for Mooney, 305; compared with William Randolph Hearst, 310; resigns from *Bulletin*, 311; becomes editor of San Francisco *Evening Call*, 315; editorial policy on *Call*, 318; continues his crusade for Mooney, 321 ff.; publishes Densmore Report of Mooney Case, 327; fights to free Mooney, 329; friendship for Hearst, 335; meets Arthur Brisbane, 348; writes "My Own Story," 348; becomes a pessimist, 351; editor-in-chief of San Francisco *Call-Bulletin*, 354; writes a daily newspaper column, 356; writes "Growing Up," 357; and the depression, 366 ff.; favorite authors of, 370; health of, 371; loses interest in politics, 372; honorary member of Sigma Delta Chi, 374;

## INDEX

president of Hearst's Fiction Board, 374; writes foreword for *William Randolph Hearst, American*, 374; writes *George Hearst, California Pioneer* with Cora Older, 374; addresses American Civil Liberties Union, 375; revisits scenes of his childhood in Wisconsin, 375 ff.; his belief in Christ, 380; in old age, 382 ff.; loses faith in man, 385; writes of death, 391; death of, 392
Older, Herbert, brother of Fremont Older, 7; enters Ripon College, 29; becomes a printer, 35; employed on San Francisco *Evening Bulletin*, 98
Older, Thomas, great-grandfather of Fremont Older, 6
Older, William, grandfather of Fremont Older, 6, 7
"Older's Traveling Circus," 27
Oliver Grand Jury, 167
O'Neil, Nance, 225
Osborne, Thomas Mott, 246
"Outcast at the Christian Door, An," sensational *Bulletin* serial, 270
Oxman, Frank, 297, 323; testifies against Mooney, 300

Padeauvaris, Felix, 180, 181
Paine, Thomas, 24
Parson, George, 326
Parton, Lemuel F., 218, 222
Partridge, John, 141
Pennsylvania Transportation Company, 10
Phelan, James D., 112, 113, 123, 149, 150, 161, 177, 200; elected mayor of San Francisco, 114
Pickering, Loring, interferes with Older's editorial policy, 289
Pico, Pio, 51
Political graft, in San Francisco, 228 ff.
Pratt, John, city editor of San Francisco *Morning Call*, employs Older, 73, 76

Preparedness Day bombing, 294
Preparedness Day parade, 291
Prince of Wales, 11
Prison reform, Older's interest in, 240 ff.
*Progress and Poverty*, 74
Prostitution, in San Francisco, exposed by Older, 133, 173, 259 ff.

Rader, Reverend William, 200
Ralston, William C., 56
Ramaly, David, printer, employs Fremont Older, 37
Red Light Abatement Act, 269
Redwood City *Times-Gazette*, 66; Older employed on, 68
Redwood City *Weekly Journal*, Older employed on, 65
Reese, Lowell Otus, 120, 218
Renaud, Ralph E., 218, 221
Rigall, Ed, 301
Ripley, Robert, 92; artist on *Bulletin*, 220
Rolph, James, mayor of San Francisco, 284
Roosevelt, Theodore, 161, 199, 208, 209; promises aid to Older, 149; encourages Older, 187
Rossi, Angelo, mayor of San Francisco, 396
Roth, Herb, 92, 221
*Roughing It*, 52
Rowell, Chester, 182
Rowley, R. G., attorney and publisher, employs Older, 65
Ruef, Abraham, political boss of San Francisco, 123; fought by Fremont Older, 123 ff.; attempts to stop publication of *Bulletin*, 129; celebrates reëlection of Mayor Schmitz, 144; fought by Fremont Older, 146 ff.; appoints himself district attorney, 162; removes Deputy District Attorney Heney, 162; removes District Attorney Langdon, 162; indicted by Grand Jury, 169; confesses to bribery, 170; pleads guilty to extortion, 171; trial of, 183; retrial of, 197;

Ruef, Abraham (cont.)
  mob threatens life of, 200; found guilty in graft prosecution, 202; sentenced to San Quentin, 203; friendship with Fremont Older, 214
Russell, Charles Edward, 111, 349
Russo-Japanese War, 120

Sacramento *Union*, Older employed on, 49
"Sage-Brush School," Nevada writing group, 52
St. Paul *Morning Press*, 36; Older employed on, 38
San Francisco, political graft in, 124, 146, 228 ff.; prostitution and gambling in, 133-34, 173, 259 ff.; streetcar strike in, 159 ff.; general strike of 1934 in, 383
San Francisco *Alta California*, 90; Older correspondent for, 71; Older reporter on, 72
San Francisco *California*, 90
San Francisco *Chronicle*, Older correspondent for, 71, 89
San Francisco *Daily Mail*, brilliant staff of, 56; Older employed on, 56; collapse of, 60
San Francisco earthquake, 151
San Francisco *Evening Bulletin*, 90; history of, 90; Older managing editor on, 90; becomes sensational under Older, 94; increase in circulation under Older, 95, 107, 108; moves to new quarters, 96; art work in, 97, 117; woman's page in, 97, 109; serials in, 109, 271 ff.; editorials in, 110; political news in, 110; makes a profit under Older, 115; publishes a Sunday Magazine, 115; becomes a crusading paper, 125; news-boys' strike on, 129; boycotted by trades unions, 137; plant destroyed by earthquake and fire, 152; reëstablished after fire, 153; announces graft prosecution, 161; becomes respectable, 214; increasing success of, 215; brilliance of staff of, 218; poetry in, 223; boycotted by politicians, 231; circulation of, 317; merged with San Francisco *Evening Call*, 353
San Francisco *Evening Call-Bulletin*, Older editor of, 354
San Francisco *Evening Call-Post*, Older managing editor of, 315; history of, 316; circulation of, 317; editorial policy under Older, 318
San Francisco *Evening Report*, 90
San Francisco *Morning Call*, 90; Older employed on, 50; Older correspondent for, 71; Older reporter on, 73; Older city editor on, 89
San Francisco *Morning Examiner*, 90, 111, 184, 224; crusade against Southern Pacific Railroad, 79, 111; Older reporter on, 118
San Francisco newspapers, in 1895, 89-90
San Francisco *Post*, founded by Henry George, 75, 90; Older city editor on, 89
San Francisco *Star*, 90
Schmitz, Eugene E., mayor of San Francisco, 123; fought by Fremont Older, 125 ff.; reëlection fought by Older, 139; flees from San Francisco, 162; indicted by Grand Jury, 169; returns to California, 173; trial of, 183; conviction reversed by Supreme Court, 186
Scott, Sir Walter, 59
Scripps, Edward W., 310
*Sea of Ice, The*, 33
Serials, in San Francisco *Evening Bulletin*, 271 ff.
Sheehan, General John F., 50
Sigma Delta Chi, honorary journalism fraternity, 374
Smith, Alice, writes "A Voice from the Underworld," 259
Smith, Reverend Paul, his church invaded by prostitutes, 267
Sonora *Herald*, Older employed on, 54

# INDEX

Southern Pacific Railroad, Congressional investigation of, 79; fought by Hearst's San Francisco *Examiner*, 79, 111; California controlled by, 79, 112
Spanish-American War, effect upon San Francisco *Evening Bulletin*, 1, 6
Sparks, Will, 97
Spreckels, Rudolph, 150, 177, 200
Stallings, Lawrence, 341
Standard Oil Company, 10
Stanford, Leland, 81
Steffens, Lincoln, 207, 208, 210
*Stories of the Great Railroads*, 112
Stork, Thomas, 195
"Story of a Reformer's Wife, The," 155
Street-car strike, in San Francisco, 159 ff.
Sullivan, John L., interviewed by Mrs. Fremont Older, 121
Sullivan, Matt I., 201
Sullivan, Pat, 85, 240
Swanson, Martin, 294, 298
Symes, Lillian, 350
*System, The,* 169

Tarbell, Ida, 10
Taylor, Dr. Edward Robeson, mayor of San Francisco, 185, 200
"Teachers' Popularity Contest," 95
*Ten Nights in a Bar-Room,* 26
Thackeray, William Makepeace, 59
Thaw, Harry K., 182
Thomas, Fanny, Fremont Older's first love, 30
Thoreau, Henry David, 370
Tobin, Joseph S., 123
Trades unions, boycott *Bulletin,* 137
Treadwell Sophie, 218, 269; writes "An Outcast at the Christian Door," 270

*Tribune* (Greeley's), influence of, on frontier, 11, 17, 18
Twain, Mark, 47, 50, 52, 74, 370

*Uncle Tom's Cabin,* 26

Valentine, John J., 99
Van Loan, Charles, 92
Vieller, Bayard, 218
Vigilance Committee, 90
Virginia City *Territorial Enterprise,* Older employed on, 52
"Voice from the Underworld, A," sensational *Bulletin* serial, 270

Waldorf, John Taylor, 218
Wallace, Grant, 120
Washington, George, 6
Watterson, Henry, 314
Watts, Amelia, actress, 34
Waymire, Judge James A., 149
Weinberg, Israel, 296
*Weir of Hermiston,* serialized in *Bulletin,* 109
West, George P., 218, 315, 337
White, Stanford, 182
Wide-Awakes, political rally of, 4
Williams, Minnie, 102 ff.
Wilson, William B., 324
Wilson, Woodrow, 291; appoints Mediation Committee to investigate Mooney Case, 324
Wisconsin, birth place of Fremont Older, 7
"Woodhills," the Older ranch, 251
Wright, William (Dan de Quille), 52

*You Can't Win,* novel by Jack Black, 281

**53758**

John Willard Brister
Library
Memphis State University
Memphis, Tennessee